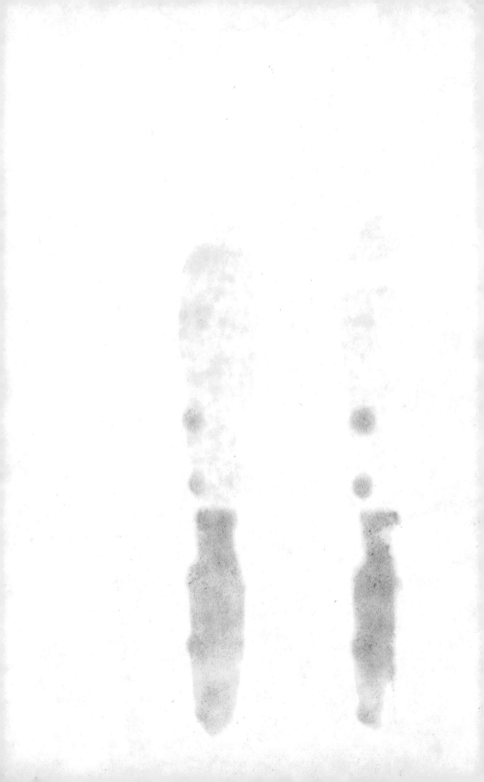

GONE CRAZY AND BACK AGAIN

GONE CRAZY AND BACK AGAIN

THE RISE AND FALL OF THE *Rolling Stone* GENERATION

Robert Sam Anson

1981
DOUBLEDAY & COMPANY, INC.
Garden City, New York

Permission to quote from the following sources is gratefully acknowledged:

Clive: Inside the Record Business by Clive Davis, copyright © 1975 by William Morrow and Company, New York, New York, used by permission; "Aquarius" by James Rado, Gerome Ragni, Galt MacDermot, Nat Shapiro, copyright © 1966, 1967, 1968 by United Artists Music Company, Inc., all rights administered by United Artists Music Company, Inc.; "Like a Rolling Stone," copyright © 1965 by Warner Brothers, Inc., All Rights Reserved, used by permission; *Howl* by Allen Ginsberg, reprinted by permission of City Lights Books; excerpts from *U.S. News & World Report* copyright © 1967, used by permission; excerpts from *Time* magazine, copyright © 1967, 1973 by Time, Incorporated, All Rights Reserved, used by permission; "All Things Must Pass" by George Harrison, copyright © 1969 by Harrisongs, Limited, used by permission; "Cover of the Rolling Stone" words and music by Shel Silverstein, copyright © 1972, 1973 by Evil Eye Music, Inc., New York, New York, used by permission; "For What It's Worth" by Stephen Stills, copyright © 1966 by Cotillion Music, Ten East Music and Springalo Toones, All Rights Reserved, used by permission; excerpts from *Playboy* magazine, copyright © 1966, used by permission; excerpts from *Esquire* magazine, copyright © 1974, used by permission.

Portions of the book have appeared in *New Times* magazine, copyright © 1976 by New Times Publishing Company, Inc.

For Sam, who came next.

Girl: "What are you rebelling against?"
Brando: "Whaddya got?"

                from *The Wild Ones*

ACKNOWLEDGMENTS

This book owes its creation to an extraordinary number of people. I would like to thank some of them, however inadequately.

My greatest appreciation goes to Ellen Pollock and Arnon Mishkin, my research associates on the project, without whose dogged assistance this book would not have been possible.

Jon Larsen, the former editor of *New Times* magazine, provided the initial resources for my reporting. For his continuing encouragement and support, I owe him a special debt. I would also like to thank George Hirsch, the former publisher of *New Times,* for his kind permission to incorporate in this book material that originally appeared in *New Times.*

To Sandy Richardson, my publisher, Reid Boates and Michael Ossias, my editors, and Peter Shepherd, my agent, goes my gratitude for ignoring missed deadlines.

In reconstructing *Rolling Stone*'s history and that of the youth culture it served, I have relied on a number of published accounts. I would particularly like, though, to acknowledge my debt to Chet Flippo, who graciously allowed me access to his unpublished master's thesis on *Rolling*

Stone and rock journalism, and to Mel Ziegler, of the San
Francisco *Chronicle,* for sharing the unpublished notes of
his interviews with Jann Wenner and other members of the
Rolling Stone staff.

I would also like to thank the following people for
giving of their time and their memories during the reporting
of this book: Michael Aaron, Renata Adler, Muriel Appen-
seller, Joe G. Armstrong, Peter Arnett, Maxwell Arnold,
Ken Auletta, Tom Baker, Lester Bangs, Banjo, Melinda
Bergman, Porter Bibb, Ben Bryant, Sandy Bull, Judy
Bunce, John Burks, Bo Burlingham, Carol Bussey, Pat Ca-
dell, Tim Cahill, Bill Cardozo, Jon Carroll, George Carrol-
ton, Luria Castel, Margaret Lee Chadwick, Bob Christgau,
John Clancy, Alexander Cockburn, Page Cole, Peter Col-
lier, Stan Cornyn, Timothy Crouse, Cameron Crowe, Dale
Curtis, Richard Daugherty, Clive Davis, Larry Dietz,
Christine Doudna, Judy Dunce, Larry Durocher, Cindy
Ehrlich, Ken Emerson, Joe Eszterhas, David Felton, Mi-
chael Ferguson, Timothy Ferris, Danny Fields, Harriett
Fier, Lacey Fosburgh, Stephanie Franklin, Judy Freed, Ben
Gerson, Michael Glazer, Jeanie Gleason, Richard Gold-
stein, John Goodchild, Doris Kearns Goodwin, Michael
Goodwin, Richard N. Goodwin, Bill Graham, William
Greider, Cloyd Hall, David Hamilton, Ellen Harmon, Wil-
liam Randolph Hearst III, Amie Hill, Warren Hinckle,
George Hirsch, Madeleine Hirseiger, Jan Hodenfeld, John
Holum, Gretchen Horton, Richard Irvine, Ken Kelley, Rob-
ert Kingsbury, Joe Klein, Douglas Kneeland, Peter Knobler,
Howard Kohn, Valerie Kosorek, Jim Kuntsler, Jon Landau,
Tony Lane, Chandler Laughlon, Sarah Lazin, Chuck Lea-
vell, Richard Levine, Michael Levitt, Grover Lewis, John
Lombardi, Chris Lydon, Michael Lydon, Susan Lydon,
Peter McCabe, Paul Major, Frank Mankiewicz, Greil

Marcus, Dave Marsh, Janet Maslin, Pat Matlock, Jim Miller, Stephanie Mills, John Morthlund, James Naughton, Martin Nolan, David Obst, Linda Obst, Max Palevsky, Dan Parker, Marianne Partridge, Abe Peck, Charlie Perry, Tom Petit, Jody Powell, Nick Profitt, Richard Reeves, Suzy Rice, Allen Rinzler, Travis Rivers, John Rockwell, Valentine Rose, William Roth, Roy Rowan, Jerry Rubin, Joan Russ, Phil Russ, Mike Salisbury, Paul Scanlon, Robert Scheer, Joel Selvin, Robert Shrum, Jim Silberman, Bob Simmons, Paul Solman, Sheila Paul Sonenshine, Erica Spellman, Dugald Stermer, Sol Stern, Geoffrey Stokes, Jean Theiss, Hunter Thompson, Sandy Thompson, Hank Torgramson, Bruce Train, Lucian K. Truscott IV, Carl Wagner, Phil Walden, Adam Walinsky, John Walsh, Ed Ward, John Warneke, John Wasserman, Gordon Weil, Don Weineke, David Weir, Jann Wenner, Sim Wenner, Ann Wexler, Tim White, John Williams, Paul Williams, Baron Wolman, and Alice Yarish.

Finally, there is Maggie, who stood by.

CONTENTS

INTRODUCTION

On November 18, 1967, a few minutes past 5:30 in the afternoon, in a rundown print shop in San Francisco, California, a new magazine was born. It was called *Rolling Stone*, after the words of a Bob Dylan song:

> *How does it feel*
> *To be without a home*
> *A complete unknown*
> *Like a rolling stone?*

This is the story of that magazine, the culture it served, and what became of both of them.

There is no way of separating the two. To have come of age in the Sixties was to be aware of the presence of *Rolling Stone*—if not by reading it, then by sharing in the events it uniquely covered and, by its coverage, helped create. It was a magazine of and for those times, addressed to the generation that made them: the young men and women who grew up on Dr. Spock, puzzled their parents, saw their heroes murdered, dropped out, turned on, protested, made love, went to war, and, in the space of a decade, changed America as it has seldom been changed before.

These were the people of the Sixties, and *Rolling Stone* was their magazine. The writers and editors who filled its pages, the journalistic superstars like Hunter Thompson, Timothy Crouse, Jon Landau, and Joe Eszterhas, and scores of less-well-known others, wrote from a special vantage point: not as detached observers, attempting to estimate the events they were witnessing, but as the people who were living them. They were young, as the times were young, and they wrote as the young will—with enthusiasm and hope, anger and passion, feeling and heart. Their reporting was high voltage, personal, charged with intensity, not always the most accurate or finely crafted, at times crude, outrageous, meanly biased, but always real, human, impossible to ignore. Out of it a magazine emerged—not so much a journal as a running statement of what it was like to be alive in the Sixties.

The man who made it so was Jann Wenner. It was he who, at the age of twenty-one, a year after dropping out of Berkeley, created it with $7,500 in borrowed capital, nurtured it, shaped it, and, for better or worse, made it what it is today—a $16 million publishing enterprise, with two million readers around the world and an equal number of dollars in the bank.

Jann Wenner's rise to power and prominence is the prototype Sixties fable. A young man, cut off from his past, uncertain of his future, begins searching. He samples everything—drugs, sex, protest, all the currents that run through the decade—and finally settles on rock. Success follows, plus fame and riches. And, at the fade, he is still searching.

There are scores of such stories out of the Sixties—many of which are recounted in these pages—but none embodies quite so much as that of Jann Wenner. He did it all. And the result was a life like that of the generation's—

brilliant, troubled, contradictory, rushed, ever looking after something, never sure what it was, only that it was important to have all of it, and now.

This, then, is his story, too: the people he encountered, the adventures he had, the trips he took, the end to which he came.

His life continues today, as *Rolling Stone* does. But the adolescence is over, the generation older. Rock and roll has lost its meaning. And *Rolling Stone,* now fatter and more prosperous, has moved to a different city, to another time. It is no longer the magazine that it was, and neither are the people who read it what they were.

Something has happened. Something larger and more profound than the passing of time or the ending of an era. Something no less than the failure of a dream.

Every generation grows up believing it is special, and looks back later, in wonder and regret, at why it has not turned out so. There are always reasons. A war intervenes, someone gets sick, an unexpected baby is born, an economy suddenly turns sour. People give up, settle, start worrying about their own lives. No one escapes.

But for the young men and women who came of age in the Sixties, for Jann Wenner and his readers, it was supposed to be different. The times in which they lived were different. The things they did were different. *They* were different, better than their parents had been, more open, more loving, more in touch with themselves—to use a phrase with special Sixties meaning—unlike any generation who had ever come before, or would ever come again. They were so full of themselves, so confident of their abilities. Fate was with them, magic was on their side. "We want the world," went one of their chants, "and we want it now . . . now . . . *now!*" And if the world was too slow in coming, they would build a world of their own, paint it over in bright colors, restore it to its natural state, fill it with strange music, give it a new mood, a different sense of the possibilities of life.

Time made them "Man of the Year," said they were "not just a new generation, but a new kind of generation," predicted they would "land on the moon, lay out blight-proof, smog-free cities, enrich the underdeveloped world, and, no doubt, write finis to poverty and war." They did not doubt it. No other generation had been bred in such comfort, a culture so rich—"the go-go years," they called them on Wall Street, where corporate profits were at an all-time high and the brokers cheered the rallies every day—they could, if they chose, afford to reject it all. Allen Ginsberg told them to burn their money in the wastebasket, and some of them did. There was no need to worry. They could live on the leavings alone. Life was there for the taking. They could have and be whatever they wanted. And they wanted it all.

And, for a time, they had it, every license imaginable, all the pleasure life could offer, and in complete protection, because they had the Pill—so many pills. Pills for making love, for getting high and coming down, pills to forget about the world entirely. They consumed them, as they did life, voraciously, crowding in every sensation possible, as if each day would be their last.

They called the way they lived a revolution and, for the country that hated them and envied them, it was. An upheaval not of politics nor of form—though those were changed, too—but of feeling and mood. The first mass cultural revolution in history. Anyone could take part. Class and education did not matter. They were not the bored young men who got out of Princeton in the Twenties and wanted to kick up their heels a few years before settling down in Father's firm. Many of them did not go to college at all; the universities, they decided, were irrelevant. They had no need to go to Paris, or mount the barricades in Spain, as the rebels of other generations had done. Their revolt was at home, now. If you sat in at Cal, went South with the Freedom Riders, took a bus and headed West, let your hair grow down or listened to the music, you were part of it, a brother, a sister.

They had their war, as others had their wars, but it was not one of which they could be proud, as their fathers had been proud of theirs. They had their heroes, as every generation has its heroes, but they were murdered, so many of them, with such regularity, that they came to expect that anyone they looked up to would have to be killed, as if there were some curse on them. They asked the world for justice, and it gave them Mississippi and Vietnam. As deeply as anyone, they wanted to believe in the things that hold families and countries together. When they couldn't, because of who they were—brighter, more questioning and demanding, the people, in short, their parents had reared them to be—they tried to change it as few have tried before.

They grew up on their own, without guides or models, convinced that law—any kind of law—was a code word for repression. And so they broke all the laws. Everything they did was extreme, *had* to be extreme, continually testing the limits of the possible, lest the natural order of things reassert itself. Because, in the back of their minds, they knew the end was coming. Something so good could not possibly last. Death was all around. They wanted to be crazy— "freaks," they proudly called themselves—because the world was crazy.

They were different in those ways, and in so many others,

and they knew it. It was that sense of being apart from everyone else—children with no pasts, no predetermined futures, and no special need to worry about either—that lent a special quality to everything they did: the war they protested, the music they made, the drugs they took, the culture they tried to make for themselves as a womb that would protect them, keep the world at bay, help them to stay younger, longer.

And then their time ran out. They changed, they grew up. They became like everyone else. No one escaped.

Looking back, it all seems so unreal, like a picture book from childhood, filled with fantasies and fairies, myths in which a child believes, as only children can. It is so different now. America has cooled. Haight-Ashbury is a slum. And the people who were going to make the new world have changed to simply making it. "Good news for American business," the *Playboy* ads proclaimed. "Those young men who wouldn't sell out in 1967 are buying in 1977 . . . They've traded in the SDS for IBM and ITT and DDB . . . They're selfish about their success."

And so time passes, and a generation changes. But something is missing—an explanation. What happened? Why?

Rolling Stone was never a magazine that answered questions; like the generation, it only posed them. But there is, in the story of Jann Wenner and his magazine and the changes that overtook them, a moral and a metaphor for the fate of a whole generation, a people who grew up believing in myths, and none so strong as rock: "the magic that will set you free."

To the millions who listened and believed in it, rock and roll was never just music. At its purest, rock and roll defined a way of looking at life, seeing all its beauty and possibility, all its horror and desolation, and, in their mix, the attempt to make something better and new. For a time when nothing was holding, no rules applying, rock was the perfect accompaniment—jarring, discordant, rebellious, raucous, vulgar, violent, electric, emotional—a music out of control, at once terrifying and soothing, a million three-minute symphonies for a world gone inexplicably mad. No other voice spoke with such power or held such mystic meaning for so many. No other movement commanded such adulation, so willing a suspension of disbelief. From protest at Cal to confrontation at Chicago, from the Summer of Love to the apocalypse at Altamont, rock was the common link, the single unifying element pulling the young together, making them, helter-skelter, a culture apart.

But, for all its mythic power, rock, like the generation that believed in and worshiped it, proved vulnerable—to exploitation, commercialization, overdose, and, ultimately, the lure of its own success. What happened in the end was something the counterculture never counted on: Dad came into the bedroom, not, as one commentator put it, to turn off the music, but to dance along with it. For a culture that took its meaning from opposition, acceptance was a death sentence.

Rolling Stone was there then, as it was from the beginning. It was a magazine that existed because of change; change was its beat and reason for being, and change—the evolution of a culture—brought it to what it is today, no less a reflection of the cooled-out Seventies than it was a mirror of the frenzied Sixties. To leaf through the faded pages of its early years is to be carried back to a simpler time, a moment when choices seemed clearer, when it was US against THEM. The lines are not so well drawn today. The very success of the culture has blurred the distinction between enemy and friend. Rock and roll is in the White House, and

Rolling Stone helped put it there. The feeling that was the Sixties is but a memory, sad and bittersweet. And nothing reflects the mood better, or more symbolically, than *Rolling Stone,* grown from shaggy adolescent to razor-cut middle age.

"And now, I, too, am over 30," Jann Wenner wrote in the tenth anniversary issue of his magazine. It was a statement of fact and, for a generation that grew up believing it would never grow old, a confession of failure. They did as they had to. Because, in the end, living free was not enough. Magic was no protection. Rock and roll could not save the world, and it could not save itself. And so their moment ended. "All things must pass," goes a song by George Harrison.

> *All things must pass someday*
> *All dreams must fade away*
> *I must be on my way*

Moving, never stopping, like a rolling stone.

R.S.A.
New York City
1980

1

Two Summers

A summer night in New York, hot, sticky, oppressive. It is July 1976. The war in Vietnam has been over now for more than a year, and Richard Nixon is about to mark the second anniversary of his exiling to San Clemente. Rennie Davis, one of the leaders of the Chicago Seven, has just gone into the insurance business. Tom Hayden, one of his co-defendants, and a co-founder of Students for a Democratic Society, has married a movie star and is running for United States Senator from California. A recent survey of college students has found that their chief priority is finding a well-paying job; law and medicine are two of the favored professions. Religion is enjoying a revival, particularly the fundamentalist denominations. One of the latest converts is Eldridge Cleaver, the former Black Panther Party leader, who, in Paris, has told of forsaking Mao and revolution and being born again in the Lord Jesus Christ. One of Cleaver's friends, Jerry Rubin, the former leader of the Yippies, has just written a book describing the peace he has found by attending est, a quasi-psychological series of seminars, which centers on the acceptance of selfishness as a virtue. Est itself is locked in a fierce competition with the Unification

Church of the Reverend Sun Myung Moon, a Korean evangelist who has proclaimed himself the Messiah, for the allegiance of young people.

Elsewhere, the country is quiet. Twenty-four hours from now, the Democratic Party, meeting in national convention, will name a born-again Georgia peanut farmer its candidate for President of the United States. He has said that he listens to Bob Dylan frequently. Now, past midnight, in a townhouse on New York's fashionable East Side, a rock magazine publisher is hosting a party for his staff. The mood is turning ugly.

Too many people have shown up. The guest list had been confined to a select four hundred, but at least twice that number have arrived. The house has been crammed to capacity, and the overflow has spilled into the street. Police have just ordered everyone back from the door and into the street. No one is budging. People are being crushed and women are screaming. One of the cops raises his nightstick threateningly and repeats the order to move back. There are more shrieks, cries of "police brutality," and oaths about "Chicago." A few in the crowd wave their invitations in the air, the ecru notecards with blue engraving that spells out "Rolling Stone magazine invites you to a supper with the Jimmy Carter campaign staff." They have a right to be there, they are shouting. The cops ignore them. Reinforcements are summoned. A riot seems to be in the offing.

Then, suddenly, calm. It is as if, at the last moment, everyone has finally realized who they are. How would it look for *them* to be carted off to jail, like common rabble? How would Walter Cronkite explain it? Or Hamilton Jordan or Dolly Schiff or Stewart Udall? Jane Fonda and Shirley MacLaine may be used to having their noses bloodied, but for the rest of them there—the Kay Grahams and Frank

Churches and Steve Smiths, the Felkers, Bernsteins and Bradlees, the Harts, Van den Heuvels and Beattys, not to mention Cyrus Vance—no, it wouldn't do. It just wouldn't do, at all.

Lauren Bacall is disgusted. "This is a fuck-up," she huffs, and departs for P. J. Clarke's. Theodore White and a few others tag along. Many more arrive. The pushing and shoving resumes. Ron Kovic, a paralyzed Vietnam veteran, is being rocked back and forth in his wheelchair by the surging crowd around him. He mentions the war, about being spat on when he got home, and now, not even being able to get in to a party. "That's tough, kid," a tuxedoed figure tells him. Bella Abzug appears and tries to restore order. No one listens to her. Paul Newman peers out a window, as if to bait them. They hurl obscenities. Just then, Harrison Salisbury staggers out the door, gasping for breath. The crowd demands to know what is going on inside. Salisbury is too exhausted to tell them. Finally, Seymour Hersh has a report. "The mood is very high-powered and tense," he announces solemnly. "It's a collection of the remainder of the New Left. The last fling of the New Left." Off to one side, lips pursed, arms akimbo, pollster Pat Cadell surveys the scene: a most unusual representative sample. Sally Quinn is asking questions. What are they doing here? Why have they come? How, in God's name, did it happen? No one answers her. They are chanting now—"We Want Wenner! We Want Wenner! We Want Wenner!"—trying to get the attention of the short, rather pudgy young man who, drink in hand, surveys the scene from two floors above them.

Their host of the evening gazes down in amusement, a wide, self-satisfied smile tracing his lips. He spots a familiar face in the crowd and, with a point of the finger, beckons the person inside. The chanting resumes: "We Want

Wenner! We Want Wenner! We Want Wenner!" He salutes
them with champagne, half bows, and turns inside, giggling.

Jann Wenner has a right to laugh. The world he cares
about has literally come to his doorstep, begging him to
take it in. Even now, he can't quite believe it. Ten years
ago, who could have guessed that he would be where he is
this evening? He was a no one, an unemployed college
dropout, apparently with no brighter prospects than becoming a mailman for the United States Post Office. And now,
this. "The young publishing genius," *Fortune* calls him;
"The boy wonder of American journalism," the Los Angeles *Times* says; "One of the most influential young men in
the country," *Time* chimes in. Mansions on both coasts,
good art, a matched set of Mercedes, millions at his disposal
—all the requisite accoutrements of status, class, position.
And out there in the streets is the final acknowledgment.
Those are the heavies down there: the people who count,
whose opinions matter, who snap their fingers—*click*—and
make things happen, chanting for him.

"Jann gave Carter a constituency." It is one of Wenner's editors, talking to Sally Quinn, who, by now, has pushed her
way into the house, still wondering why everyone is there.
The editor explains: "With that one Hunter Thompson
piece, he delivered the youth." The Gonzo Prince does not
hear what is being said about him, which is fortunate. He
already feels taken by that particular piece of work. Hunter
Thompson, the battler of fear and loathing, does not en-
dorse politicians; that is something Jann Wenner does.
Thompson has no interest in explaining now. The hour is
late, and it is a very long story; besides, he is doing his best
to get drunk. Standing off in a corner, trademark shades in
place, stoned as usual, he looks oddly depressed. This is not

his kind of crowd. Everyone appears to be over thirty. They are wearing suits and ties. None of them is stoned. And they are all so calm. That is the real problem: none of them is crazy. They wouldn't understand the demons that live in his head. He drains his glass in a gulp and orders another drink. And then another. By the end of the evening, he will have had many drinks, and will still be sober. It is his special curse: to be able to fill his body with alcohol and drugs, and always have it function; never to be able to blot out what he has seen, what he knows. And looking around, he knows that it is over: the revolution, the fighting, the chance to be different. The counterculture has become The Culture, and out there in the streets is the proof. Believe in the magic, the Sixties line went, and it will set you free. Believe in the magic, and you will never grow old. Only here they were on East Sixty-eighth Street, drinking champagne and acting like the Establishment. Who were they kidding? They *were* the Establishment.

Jann approaches and feints a mock punch, trying to loosen him up. It is a kind of game between them, the two young studs, one nearly a foot taller than the other, trying to tough it out, like kids. But tonight it isn't working. Jann does not have time to pursue the game further. Over there is Chevy Chase, and behind him is Jean Kennedy Smith, the late President's sister. There's Jody Powell, and next to him Billy Carter, looking for a beer. So many people, all come for him. Leaving Hunter, Wenner drapes his arm around a guest, kisses her on the cheek, whispers a joke, then moves on to the next guest, and then the next, always in motion, eyes alert for the next attraction. His tie knot is pulled down toward his vest, and sweat is pouring off him. When he laughs, it is a little too loud, perhaps a trifle nervous. But there is no mistaking his pleasure. He is fairly bubbling

with enthusiasm. Rarely has he been more pleased. This is
his night, the affirmation and climax of everything he has
been working toward for the last ten years.

We Want Wenner!
We Want Wenner!
We Want Wenner!

They are calling his name again. And, once again, he
giggles. Jann Wenner has to laugh. Better than Hunter, better than anyone, he remembers . . .

It is 1967. Chicago, Altamont, and Kent State are still light
years away. In New York, a new play called "Hair" is taking Broadway by storm. The "tribal love-rock musical," as
its promoters bill it, features four-letter words, draft-card
burning, frontal nudity and an anthem that tells of the day
"when peace shall rule the planets and love will steer the
stars." It is the dawning, the song says, "of the Age of
Aquarius." Washington apparently has not gotten the message. The Vietnam War is now in its sixth year, and President Lyndon Johnson has just committed an additional
50,000 combat troops to the battle, bringing the total number of Americans fighting in South Vietnam to 530,000.
Casualties have passed the 100,000 mark and resistance is
increasing. Already, several thousand young men have been
charged for refusing to enter the Armed Forces, and the
number of others fleeing to Canada and Sweden has topped
10,000. The protests are heating up. In New York, 100,000
march; in San Francisco, 60,000, while in Washington a
"peace army" of 250,000 advances on the Pentagon. When
army troops appear, young people put flowers in the rifle
barrels.

The country unravels. Black rioters have devastated Newark and Detroit; in the latter city, the violence is put down only with the dispatch of federal troops and the slaying of forty-three persons. The Justice Department is reported to be drawing up contingency plans for the imposition of martial law in the event of future disturbances. In California, the Black Panthers are openly toting rifles and shotguns in the streets. There are calls in Congress for suspension of certain provisions of the Bill of Rights. Even as the statements are issued, the polls report that confidence in established institutions has dropped to an all-time low. The churches are in decline, and families are disintegrating. The number of marriages ending in divorce is now one in four, and the figure is headed toward one in two. Parental authority is breaking down. The FBI puts the number of runaways in the past year at 90,000, with unreported tens of thousands still at large. *Time* frets:

> Never have the young been left more completely to their own devices. No adult can or will tell them what previous generations were told: this is God, this is Good, this is Art, that is Not Done. Today's young man accepts none of the start-on-the-bottom-rung formula that directed his father's career, and he is not even sure that he wants to be A Success. He is one already.

University enrollment is at an all-time high, but so, too, are the numbers dropping out. *Fortune* is worried that a consumer revolution may be in the offing, that the coming generation will not buy as much as their predecessors did, not because they can't afford to—per capita income has never been higher—but because they won't want to.

The news is apparently too much for many Americans.

The international edition of the New York *Herald Tribune* reports that during the year, the country will consume some 800,000 pounds of barbiturates, along with some 10 billion amphetamine pills to counteract the effect of the barbiturates. One out of four Americans is said to be using tranquilizers of some sort. In Berkeley, an underground newspaper prints a hoax letter warning of "narcs lurking in the fresh produce section" of a local supermarket, and claiming that there are highs to be had from smoking banana peels. There is an instant run on bananas, driving up the price of the fruit several cents per pound. The United Fruit Company, fearful and eager, hires an associate of Dr. Timothy Leary, the high priest of LSD, to investigate the psychedelic properties of bananas. Leary himself is arrested in Texas on charges of possession of half an ounce of marijuana and is sentenced to thirty years in prison. Undaunted, the former Harvard professor predicts America "will be an LSD country within fifteen years. Our Supreme Court will be smoking marijuana within fifteen years. It's inevitable."

In Florida, a Baptist minister attributes the rise in drug use, especially among the young, to the burgeoning influence of rock and roll. "The same coarse bodily motions which lead African dancers into a state of uncontrolled frenzy are present in modern dances," he warns. "It is only logical, then, that there must also be a correlation in the potentiality of demons gaining possessive control of a person through the medium of the beat." The admonition has no effect; record sales for the year top the $1 billion mark. At Monterey, California, a three-day rock festival draws 50,000 fans, and turns 35,000 more away. The star of the show is a Texas blues singer named Janis Joplin. Columbia Records, under its new president, Clive Davis, a Harvard-educated corporation lawyer, begins negotiating with her. She is said to be demanding a $250,000 advance. As the talks continue, the Beatles release their *Sgt. Pepper's* album. Within two weeks the record sells 1.2 million copies, and one respected music critic writes that the album's debut is "the closest Western Civilization has come to unity since the Congress of Vienna in 1815." The Beatles themselves depart for India and the spiritual guidance of the Maharishi Mahesh Yogi. Before departing, Beatle Paul McCartney reveals that the group has used LSD; fellow Beatle John Lennon calls the group "more popular than Jesus." Their manager, a multimillionaire named Brian Epstein, commits suicide, motive unknown. "Something's happening here," a rock group called Buffalo Springfield sings. "What it is ain't exactly clear." That is the trouble: nothing is clear anymore.

Especially in San Francisco. Everything pales before what is happening in San Francisco.

They are calling it "The Summer of Love," and there has never been a time quite like it. What is happening, so unexpectedly, so utterly detached from sense or sensibility, is hard to characterize except by saying that the young are invading.

By the hundreds they come, then by the thousands, finally by the tens of thousands—driving in, hitchhiking, riding in buses, some walking barefoot as if approaching a holy shrine. From all over America they are arriving, the Billy Vellons of New York and Shelley Nolans of Bellingham, Washington, and Stuart Wrights of Lagunitas, California, drawn by something they cannot fully explain, hoping, simply by being here—"Ready for anything, hanging out, watching," as Peter Webster of Ashland, Oregon, puts it—they will find whatever they are after. Everyone is here:

Kesey and Ginsberg, Graham and Helms, Kantner and Slick, Leary, Hinckle and Savio. And everything: Sproul Hall and Telegraph Avenue, the Fillmore and Mount Tam, Sausalito and the Haight. All the sights and sounds, freaks and visionaries that give the Sixties their special feel and shape. For a brief moment, San Francisco is the center of the storm.

It has never been an ordinary place, even in the best of times. Something there is about the city that makes it different, a little lonelier, a little lovelier, a little more bizarre. It shouldn't have existed in the first place; the Great Earthquake of 1906 had proved that. Everyone knew another one was coming, was, in fact, long overdue, and that when it came, there would be no saving any of them. And yet they stayed, built skyscrapers on the faultline—hideous structures that blocked the view, and somehow added to the city's charm—and trusted that St. Francis would protect them. Maybe it is that sense of living on borrowed time, of every day spent in the shadow of death—but, oh, such lovely death: the fog, the Bay, the Golden Gate—that accounts for San Francisco. The city never pauses to wonder. Events move faster here. "The first time you do anything in San Francisco," observes one of the city's leading newspapermen, "it is a great pioneering effort; the second time, it becomes a great San Francisco tradition." What is merely experienced anywhere else has a way of intensifying once it crosses the Golden Gate. The city's suicide rate (highest anywhere in the Western Hemisphere) is nearly triple the national average, the incidence of alcoholism nearly double. Elsewhere, homosexuals account for only a tiny fraction of the population; in San Francisco, one in three registered voters is gay, and the annual transvestite ball is one of the highlights of the social season.

The city takes it all in stride. Anywhere else the mad eccentric who dubbed himself Norton I, Emperor of the United States and Protector of Mexico, might be locked up; here he is accorded the perquisites of royalty. "People come and do things here they wouldn't do back home," shrugs a pollster. "They don't want to answer to neighbors. They want to be who they are and what they are when they want to. It's sort of a Paradise situation." And so they come—"the outcasts, the misfits, the fortune-seekers, all the people who couldn't make it at home," as Herb Caen, the town's leading columnist, puts it—knowing that San Francisco will take them in. It is here—where, according to the Gallup Poll, the majority of Americans would most like to live—where the Beats made their headquarters and Carol Doda first exhibited the wonders of mammarial silicone, and the Hell's Angels gave the motorcycle a bad name. It is here that wonders happen.

But even San Francisco is unprepared for what is happening now.

Across the Bay in Berkeley, the University of California has just been brought to its knees for the second time in three years by young protesters. The issue this time is not the right to organize on a few square yards of blacktop outside Sather Gate, the cause that had galvanized the Free Speech Movement in 1964, but the administration's right to run the university itself. Would military recruiters be admitted to campus? That is a question students will decide, as they will decide the relevance of their courses, in which companies the university will be permitted to invest, their hours and standards of conduct, even whether the university itself—"a collection of buildings connected by plumbing," Clark Kerr used to call it, before encountering a young philosophy student named Mario Savio—makes any sense at all. As the students rally, they sing the Beatles' "Yellow Submarine"—nonsense verse for a nonsense world.

A world so absurd that thousands of other young people are building a new one of their own in a former slum centered at the cross streets of Haight and Ashbury. They live communally, sometimes as many as fifty to an apartment, in extended families or "tribes," changing partners at will, and pass their days body-painting, making trinkets, listening to music, taking drugs, or, often as not, simply doing nothing. Here strangers call each other "brother" and "sister," share what little they have, and pay no worry to what the morrow will bring. In Haight-Ashbury, there is no need to. Everything is free. Free concerts in the park, free food from the Diggers, free shelter for the runaways, free medicine from the clinic, free love on every block. And, when bodily pleasures dull, for a few dollars—the price of a tab of the very best Owsley "White Lightning" acid—a trip is available to the technicolor pit of the human soul. There, you can dream dreams, see visions, and, if you survive, become a new person. Haight-Ashbury is filled with them, strange new creatures with names like "Morningstar" and "Blackbird," or, as the former Alan Noonan, proprietor of the Here and Now Coffee Shop, fancies himself, "World Messiah," and "Supreme Officer of the Galactic Command."

By the spring of 1967, there are an estimated 30,000 Alan Noonans living in the city, and 700 more arriving each week. They are not like the last cultural outcasts to come to the city, the Beats who had camped in North Beach a decade before. The Beats were older, fewer, and darker. By contrast, the young who come to San Francisco today are, for the most part, well adjusted and charmingly ingenuous. "We need to shed hypocrisy, dishonesty and phoniness and get back to the purity of childhood values.

That's where God is at," a twenty-three-year-old who calls herself Joyce Francisco tells an interviewer. Material things mean little to her, as they do for most of the San Francisco young. What can't be clipped on a belt or tucked in a knapsack is not worth having. "I live from meal to meal," she says. "I have no money, no possessions. Money is beautiful when it is flowing. When it piles up, it's a hang-up. We take care of each other. There's always something to buy rice and beans for the group." Does she ever pray? the interviewer asks her. "Oh yes," Joyce Francisco smiles. "I pray to the morning sun. It nourishes me with its energy so I can spread my love and beauty and nourish others. I never pray *for* anything; I don't need anything. Whatever turns me on is a sacrament: LSD, sex, my bells, my colors . . . that is the holy communion, you dig?"

The country is beginning to. There are other places where young people are gathering in the Sixties—the East Village in New York, the Strip in Los Angeles, across the Bay in Berkeley and Marin—but none concentrates more energy in less space with more bizarre results than this forty-block neighborhood in San Francisco. The Haight is the testing place, the human laboratory, the prototype Nirvana. If the young are to succeed as a separate culture, it will be decided here.

You can be what you want to be in the Haight. Buffalo Bill? His sartorial representation can be found every day in front of the "Drog Store" chatting with people who appear to be Count Dracula, Captain Video, and the Dalai Lama. Listening in is a conventionally attired young man who insists he is the 16th Reincarnation of the Emperor Hadrian. No one disputes him. In the Haight, the past has no meaning, tomorrow only slight significance. The motto of the Diggers, the free food collective patterned on the seventeenth-century English agrarian radicals of the same name, says it all: "Today is the first day of the rest of your life." "Do your own thing," advises their leader, a freckle-faced, redheaded Irishman named Emmet Grogan. "Be what you are and nothing will ever bother you."

The Haight already supports its own newspaper (*The San Francisco Oracle,* which claims a circulation of 100,000), its own medical and legal services (both of them free), its own transportation system (a gaily painted 1930 Fugol School bus, complete with bathtub, which, as a point of principle, operates on no set schedule with no fixed destination), even its own merchants association, the Haight Independent Proprietors—HIP, for short. What isn't free is bought and shared collectively. It is possible for an entire extended household to exist on the part-time labors of one underground newspaper salesman.

Living is cramped, and the city's health commissioner, unfortunately named Ellis D. Sox, is forever warning of all manner of nefarious plagues about to break out. Few people worry. The whole point of the Haight is not to worry much about anything, not to ask too many questions, and certainly not to be judgmental. There is only one rule: "Don't lay your trip on anyone else." Roughly translated: If someone who thinks he is General Custer meets someone who says he is Sitting Bull, they are to be cool about it. Life is to be experienced, not defined. There is too much definition in the straight world already: to be a success, go to college; to be in love, get married; to be happy, acquire possessions; on and on through a whole litany of rules, designed to put lives into neat little boxes and render them meaningless. In the Haight, order is synonymous with death. Vietnam, Mississippi, the universities, the lives their parents lead—all of them are very orderly, and all of them are deadly. The

Haight thrives on chaos, on the unpredictable, on living life from moment to moment, never knowing—or wanting to know—what is coming next.

Life is a trip. Behind every doorway and around every corner a new adventure awaits. "It was like this," says a writer of the time. "If you heard a rock dance named for a magician in Marvel Comics who could travel between dimensions by mind power, it might just be what you always wanted, but had never realized it until then."

But the secret of the Haight is out. Some days the streets are so clogged it takes twenty minutes to drive down a single block. In desperation, some of the residents hold mirrors to the faces of the Bermuda-shorted gawkers. Still others put nickels in parking meters and take half-hour sunbaths in the street. But still the tourists come. Many blame a Los Angeles musician named Keith Mitchell. "If you're goin' to San Francisco," his song goes, "be sure to wear some flowers in your hair, there's lots of gentle people there." The success of the record, which quickly climbs to the top ten on sales charts, further panics San Francisco city fathers, who are bracing for an onslaught of 100,000 more young people. Already, 20,000 native hippies have gathered in Golden Gate Park for the first "Human Be-In." They listen to rock music, chant mantras with Allen Ginsberg, and get thoroughly stoned on acid-dosed turkey sandwiches distributed free by a food collective. State assemblyman John Burton, whose district includes the Haight-Ashbury, warns: "Hippies are potentially the greatest threat to the nation's social structure." The San Francisco Board of Supervisors, acting at the recommendation of Mayor John Shelley, officially resolves that hippies are unwelcome in the city.

It is a vain gesture. The hippies come as expected. To accommodate the sightseers, who have arrived in even greater

numbers, the Gray Line Tour Bus Company inaugurates
"The Hippie Hop: the only foreign bus tour within the con-
tinental United States." *"We are now entering the largest
hippie colony in the world and the very heart and foun-
tainhead of the hippie subculture,"* the Gray Line guides tell
the tourists. *"We are now passing through the 'Bearded
Curtain' and will journey down Haight Street, the very
nerve center of a city within a city . . . Marijuana, of
course, is a household staple here, enjoyed by the natives to
stimulate their senses . . . Among the favorite pastimes of
the hippies, besides taking drugs, are parading and demon-
strating; seminars and group discussions about what's
wrong with the status quo; malingering, plus the ever-
present preoccupation with the soul, reality, and self-expres-
sion, such as strumming guitars, piping flutes and banging
on bongos."*

George Harrison of the Beatles visits. Margot Fonteyn
and Rudolf Nureyev are busted with sixteen others at a
Haight pot party. Arnold Toynbee flies in to probe the
meaning of it all, and goes away describing what he has
seen as "a red warning light for the American way of life."
Frank Marinello, the chief of police of Monterey, California, tells a reporter, "I feel the hippies are my friends. I am
asking one of them to take me to the Haight-Ashbury."
Episcopal Bishop James Pike, who has made the trip already, enthuses, "There is something about the temper and
quality of these people, a gentleness, a quietness, an interest
—something good."

Others have different descriptions. Marshall McLuhan
says they are the inheritors of "the outlawed and furtive social ideal known as the 'land of Cockaigne,'" the fairyland
where all desires can be instantly gratified. Robert Kennedy,
who, according to a recent survey in the Haight, is running

second in presidential popularity to Snoopy, says approvingly, "They want to be recognized as individuals." *U.S. News & World Report,* alarmed at the rise of the hippie nation, quotes Confucius: "With long hair unkempt and bodies unwashed, they would lay down the philosophy of their times and persuade all others with their constant denigrations and mournful fears. They are sick, and would inflict their sickness on all who ignore or deride them." The definitive word comes from *Time,* which examines the scene and concludes: "Whatever the meaning and wherever they may be headed, the hippies have . . . given . . . American society . . . something to think about."

Finally, in October, exhausted by the continual poking, probing and editorializing, the Summer of Love comes to an end with a mock funeral procession to mourn the "death of Hippie," victim of media hype. As a cardboard casket filled with charms, peacock feathers, orange peels, money and a marijuana-flavored cookie is borne through the streets to the strains of "Hare Krishna" and "God Bless America," a cry goes up: "Hippies are dead. Now the Free Man will come through!" Half a dozen television cameras on hand capture the ceremony in loving detail.

Thirty blocks away, in a second-floor loft of a squat green building on the wrong side of Market Street, a few young people pound intently at their typewriters. These are the offices of Garrett Press, publishers of, among other items, *The Hillsdale Merchandiser,* the *Irish Herald,* and, if all goes well, a new magazine to be called *Rolling Stone.* In the cluttered loft space, which Garrett has provided rent-free in exchange for the magazine's printing business, the first issue is now in progress. The air is heavy with the smell of molten lead wafting up from the presses that rumble

noisily on the floor below. In the center of the room an FM
radio is blaring out the sounds of the Rolling Stones. When
the song finishes, a smooth-sounding female voice quotes
the day's drug prices: "In La Honda, LSD is $60 a gram.
In Mountain View, mescaline $40 a gram. In Mill Valley, a
lid of grass is going for $25, but be careful, it may be cut."
The music resumes and the typing continues. They are only
days from deadline, and there is a special urgency to their
labors. With all the clattering and rumbling and music, the
din is deafening, yet the work proceeds, and nowhere more
determinedly than at the desk in a corner of the room
where, seemingly oblivious to the commotion around him, a
short, straggly-haired figure in denims gnaws on his thumbs,
runs his fingers through his hair, and drags deeply on a cigarette. He glances at the page in his typewriter and begins
working anew. ". . . It would appear that vocalist Jim
Morrison is making a direct appeal to the pubescent market," Jann Wenner taps out, "but upon closer inspection, it
is revealed he is not."

Suddenly, the phone on his desk rings. Wenner keeps on
typing. At the next desk, a short, dark-haired girl named
Susan Lydon, pregnant with her first child, pauses from her
own work, a cribbing of items from a British music magazine, wheels around and picks up the receiver. Wenner likes
that. "A chick's voice on the line sounds like class," he has
told her. Class is important to him. His car out in the street,
the old Porsche, that is class. The filing cabinets in the
office, the $40 models they really can't afford, they are
class, too. Even his girlfriend, the dark-eyed New York
beauty who sits a few desks away, processing subscription
forms—one look at her establishes that she is class as well.
And class is what Wenner's magazine will be.

Jann Wenner is young, but he is no hippie. The jeans he

wears are always freshly pressed. He would like very much
to be a success. At twenty-one, he has experienced it all: the
alienation from his parents, the revolt at Berkeley, the dropping out and turning on, and, more than anything, the
magic that is the music. It has been his passion now for the
past three years, almost his only passion. From everything
else, he is slightly detached, watching events, sampling
them, but never giving himself over to them. Only rock—listening to it, playing it, thinking and talking about little else
—fully engages him. The adults to whom he has tried to explain its power have never understood. Rock is more than
just music, he tells them; it is the energy core of the entire
culture, the one means whereby the young can express their
rebellion creatively. His elders smile indulgently and then
ignore him. They don't get it, any more than they get what
is happening around them, how, all at once, the world has
been turned upside down.

If only they would listen, Jann Wenner has been saying.
Then they would know. Then they would understand how it
is all linked, the drugs, the protest, the music, organically,
like parts of the same breathing being. He has a way of
showing them now. It is not an underground sheet he is putting together, but a publication of quality, of class. Wait until they see the look that John Williams, the art director he
has borrowed from *Ramparts*, is giving it: the column rules
and Times Roman type and neat ordered headlines—the almost dignified appearance. They will think it is the London
Sunday Times. Wait until they see the talent he has assembled, the writers like Ralph Gleason, the old friend and
mentor who has been covering music for the San Francisco
Chronicle for the last twenty years; Jon Landau, the Brandeis graduate whom many regard as the premier rock critic
in the nation; and Michael Lydon, Susan's husband, a

twenty-four-year-old correspondent for *Newsweek*—a news-magazine reporter, a heavy from the Establishment itself. And wait until they read it, all twenty-four pages of it, the record reviews he has written, the essay on John Lennon's first dramatic film role, the interview with Donovan, the British pop star, the investigative report on the embezzlement of some of the proceeds of the Monterey Pop Festival, the "Random Notes" on various musical happenings (a drug bust for Electric Flag; the formation of a new band called Blood, Sweat and Tears); grown-up quality on every page. Even the name of the magazine is striking: *Rolling Stone*—heavy sounding, symbolic. They will have to notice.

That somehow he will succeed, he and this handful of volunteers and friends, operating out of a littered loft with a few thousand borrowed dollars and their own enthusiasm, Jann Wenner has no doubt. The times do not allow for pessimism. The moment belongs to the young. Half the country is now under thirty, the lowest median age in the nation's history. The time between generations has shrunk from twenty years to five, about the run of a successful television series. Believe, and anything can happen. "Imagine a tree whose hole swells up to fill a room, when joined with others forms a cluster of rooms," a resident of the Haight has written in the newspaper on Wenner's desk. "Plants will do this for us, if only we learn their language, their genetic code." Why not? The same newspaper is already reporting the imminent arrival of flying saucers. Unlikelier things have already occurred this year. If flying saucers and talking plants are possible, why not a magazine called *Rolling Stone?*

At a moment like this, why not indeed. It was only a second ago that everyone liked Ike and read Herman Wouk, hardly a blink since Lawrence Welk and Howdy

Doody and "The Man in the Gray Flannel Suit." How
many years has it been since the "end of ideology" was supposed to be at hand, and the signs on the campus bulletin
boards read "Conform or Die"? Damn few. It hasn't taken
much to change it: a President being assassinated, a foot-
weary domestic named Rosa Parks refusing to give up her
seat on an Alabama bus, a few thousand college kids going
South to meet the clubs and dogs and firehoses, a college
president like Clark Kerr, a group called the Beatles, and,
all at once, everything is different.

So much of it seems chance. If Kennedy hadn't been
wearing a back brace in Dallas and had slid down in the car
before the fatal shot . . . if the postwar baby boom hadn't
exploded at that exact moment . . . if Dr. Spock had
specialized in gerontology . . . if Mario Savio had stayed at
Queens College . . . if Dylan hadn't brought an electric
guitar to Newport in 1965 . . . if Leary hadn't eaten the
handful of strange mushrooms that sunny day beside a
swimming pool in Cuernavaca . . . if one vote had
changed on the Board of Supervisors and the freeway had
been built through the Haight . . . if the *Turner Joy*'s sonar
had been working properly that dark night in the Tonkin
Gulf . . . if, if, if. So many freakish occurrences coming
together all at once, creating something wholly unexpected,
and yet, given everything, inevitable.

The social scientists and journalists are still puzzling over
the answers. Is it too much affluence or too much comfort?
Too much adolescence or too much leisure time? Too much
despair or too much education? Too much freedom or too
much Dr. Spock? Is Allen Ginsberg to blame, or Chairman
Mao? Does C. Wright Mills have the answer, or Norman O.
Brown? Is it something in the drugs they take, or the music

they listen to? Can rock and roll have started it all? Or is it simply that the world has gone insane?

Jann Wenner doesn't care. He and his generation have ceased listening to measured explanations for the grotesque. They have read *Catch-22*, and they know, as Yossarian did, that the people in charge are trying to kill them. They have heard the evening news and, if the village had to be destroyed in order to save it, then the world is a madhouse. Kesey has spoken the truth: the free men like McMurphy must be lobotomized, lest they threaten the insane order of things. Sooner or later, it will happen to them. Now is the time to organize, to sit in a tree naked, to hold a sign that says "Fuck," to follow Leary and escape from the planet altogether, to take every pleasure imaginable, without delay, because time is running out.

"We are blind and live out our blind lives in darkness," William Carlos Williams writes in the introduction to *Howl*. "Poets are damned but they are not blind, they see with the eyes of angels . . . He avoids nothing, but experiences it to the hilt. He contains it—and, we believe, laughs at it . . . Hold back the edges of your gowns, Ladies, we are going through hell."

Hell in stereophonic, multi-track, woofered and tweetered sounds, because that is the medium in which the poets of the young speak. Gut-busting rock and roll. Rock—because adults hate it. Rock—because it is the one thing they cannot control. Rock—because the young make it. It is their music. It is "their one means of protest," Wenner says, "their only outlet for creative expression; their rebellion." And San Francisco, because of what it is, shakes to it, trembles and resounds beneath it, as if the ultimate earthquake, the one that will finally end it all, has come at last.

By the fall of 1967, there are more than five hundred regularly performing rock bands in San Francisco, a city of 750,000, and double that number forming, breaking up, or playing for their own enjoyment. No other city comes close to this total, or matches what San Francisco produces in sheer noise. There are major concerts being staged every night of the week—some massive and elaborate, like those at Bill Graham's Fillmore Auditorium, mixing music with multimedia light shows, two and three bands sometimes performing at the same time; others simple affairs on street corners and in the parks.

Every night the halls are packed, dark, sweaty, and odorous with the press of a thousand bodies come together in ritual communion. Suddenly lights, bolts of color streaking across the room, and, from a dozen shrieking loudspeakers, the incredible roar, electric, powerful, overwhelming in its intensity. These are not musicians, but gods. This their church, and these their believers. Myth and metaphor, fantasy and magic, and, all at once, the world is beginning to shake.

Now they will begin to notice; they will have to. Because, somehow, it has worked. All the articles have come together. The deadlines none of them believed could possibly be met have been met, and the presses are running. Jann Wenner and the few friends that are his staff have gathered in the press room to watch the first fruits of their labor become reality. As the finished copies begin to appear, Wenner reaches out and pulls one from the loading table, the paper still warm from the friction of the presses. He leafs through it excitedly, pausing only to read the words he has written on page two:

You're probably wondering what we are trying to do. It's hard to say: sort of a magazine and sort of a news-

paper. The name of it is *Rolling Stone,* which comes from
an old saying: "A Rolling Stone gathers no moss." Muddy
Waters used the name for a song he wrote; The Rolling
Stones took their name from Muddy's song, and "Like a
Rolling Stone" was the title of Bob Dylan's first rock and
roll record.

We have begun a new publication reflecting what we see
are the changes in rock and roll and the changes related to
rock and roll. Because the trade papers have become so
inaccurate and irrelevant, and because the fan magazines
are an anachronism, fashioned in the mold of myth and
nonsense, we hope we have something here for the artists
and the industry, and every person who "believes in the
magic that can set you free."

Rolling Stone is not just about music, but also about the
things and attitudes that the music embraces. We've been
working quite hard on it and we hope you can dig it. To
describe it any further would be difficult without sounding
like bullshit, and bullshit is like gathering moss.

Just then, there is a sharp, popping sound. Startled,
Wenner turns to see Michael Lydon licking the roiling foam
from a bottle of champagne. A look of irritation flickers
across his face—they cannot afford such extravagance—but
it quickly dissolves in a smile. This is an occasion, a birth to
be celebrated. They lift the plastic glasses Susan has bought
from the dime store and toast their success, laughing and
hugging each other. They have done it. The magazine is
theirs. Off to one side, Jann Wenner stands alone. He holds
a glass of champagne, but there are tears brimming in his
eyes. "It's just so good," he chokes out to his friends. "It can
never be better."

2

Nowhere Man

It was not the most auspicious of beginnings. Of the 40,000 copies in the first press run, all but 6,000 were returned unsold. For the next few months, the magazine struggled from issue to issue. More than once, an issue was skipped or delayed until Wenner could scrape together enough money to put it out. "He'd sit there at that corner desk of his," Michael Lydon recounted, "get some record guy on the phone and not ask him for an ad—Jann would demand it. 'You've just *gotta* give us a page,' he would say. 'We need that page. You just *gotta* put it in.' You couldn't believe his balls, but the incredible thing was, it worked. They put in the ads." He cut corners where he could—many of the musical items in the first issues were lifted whole out of other music magazines. He scrimped and saved—Lydon was instructed to continue working at *Newsweek,* where he would have access to "free phones." When all else failed, as with the issue that came to deadline with no cover photograph, and no funds to buy one, he relied on brazen ingenuity—in that instance by dressing up Juliana Wolman, the wife of Baron Wolman, the magazine's photographer, as a rock star, shooting her picture, and slapping it on the cover with no further explanation.

What Wenner lacked in resources, he made up for in panache. As a promotional gimmick, he offered a free roach clip with every new subscription. The accompanying coupon contained two boxes for checking—one to begin a new subscription, another which read: "Gentlemen: *Rolling Stone* sucks." The new subscriptions poured in by the hundreds, until the office was fairly awash in unopened mail. Many of the letters contained suggestions for stories *Rolling Stone* should be covering; others included words of encouragement with the check, even "love gifts" of marijuana. "Rolling Stone is a high," said one note. "Keep it up."

In the bedlam of the office, the screaming and tension, nervousness and paranoia born of continual dosings of speed, the wonder was they published anything at all. And yet they did. Each issue was getting better, the writing more crafted, the ideas more imaginative, the tone more professional. But with Wenner, it was never enough. He drove his staff mercilessly, continually lashing them to greater and greater efforts. Always he wanted more. That was the one certainty about him; everything else was unpredictable. He could be charming and lovable one moment, tyrannical and demanding the next. Frequently, he contradicted decisions he himself had made only hours before, switched covers, changed headlines, altered copy, until the last possible moment, and sometimes beyond, eating into *Rolling Stone*'s slender treasury by holding the magazine past deadline with yet another change of mind. "He'd do something one day," said one of his editors, "sleep on it, then awake to realize that the Jann Wenner he was today didn't at all approve of what the Jann Wenner he was yesterday had done."

He drove himself hardest of all. Most days, he did not leave the office until well after midnight, and when deadline neared, he worked straight through until dawn, sustaining himself with doses of speed and his own nervous energy. "He never seemed to sleep," Susan Lydon remembered. "Whatever time of day or night you'd go in there, you'd always find him, pounding away at his typewriter." The relentlessness with which he worked was almost frightening; one editor likened it to "a nuclear reactor always coming to the point of critical mass." They kept waiting for the explosion—"Sometimes," said Susan Lydon, "he'd be so worried, he'd literally be tearing his hair out." Instead, the reactor only grew hotter. He seemed to live on his very nerve endings. Everything was a crisis; nothing could wait; all of it had to happen now.

It showed, even in the way he moved around the office; not a walk, but a sort of bustling dogtrot, small body bent forward, as if heading into an invisible wind. He was constantly fidgeting, getting up, sitting down, then getting up again, running both his hands through his hair, scratching himself, tapping his pencil, playing with the letter opener on his desk, drumming his fingers, and, in those moments when nervousness threatened to overwhelm him entirely, gnawing on the lower part of his thumb, as if consuming himself. His ideas gushed forth like his speech, in short, not always comprehensible bursts, punctuated by jerks, grunts, repeated "ya knows" ("There's this group, ya know, and, ya know, they're really hot, which is why, ya know, we just gotta do them"), and, when speech left him altogether, strings of "blah, blah, blahs." Somehow, though, he managed to communicate, if not in words, then in sheer enthusiasm, not sure of where he was going, or why, only that it was important to get there, and in a hurry. "Wow!" he'd exclaim, when anything was brought to his attention. "Wow, what a trip!"

Jann Wenner's life had been like that: a trip.

He had grown up in the mellow nowhereland of subur-

ban Marin County, across the Golden Gate, in the San
Rafael hills overlooking San Francisco Bay. People didn't
simply live in Marin, they liked to boast, they *mellowed*
there. Marin had it all: green hills and golden meadows,
stands of virgin redwoods, swimming pools in the yards,
Mercedes in the driveways, steaks sizzling on the grills—and
the highest divorce rate in the nation. They joked about
Marin across the Bay, told stories about the orgies and wife-
swapping that went on there, laughed about its bourgeois
decadence, but Marin paid them no mind. It was a little island separate in time and space from the world around it,
the land literally at the end of the rainbow. There were no
troubles here, only momentary unpleasantries, the sort of
"interpersonal crises" that could be *dealt with* at the weekly
rap session, in the hot tub, with the shrink—and, if they
didn't work, in the class at the community college in "creative divorce." The important thing was to stay loose and, at
all costs, remain mellow.

The Wenners, Ed and Sim, had moved to Marin from
New York in 1947. Jann, their first child, was still an infant
when the Wenners packed up their belongings in a battered
Dodge coupe and headed West. "Like pioneers," his mother
put it. "You had the feeling of being in a wagon train." To
the Wenners, both recently discharged from the military, a
couple just beginning their life together, California was, in
Sim's words, "the Great Golden Mecca," a mysterious place
of opportunity and enchantment. They knew nothing about
the state. Sim chose San Francisco "because it sounded like
a classier place to live than L.A." All the rest was unknown,
new, different. It was reason enough to come.

Sim Wenner longed for new experience. She was a bright,
independent woman; impatient, ambitious, self-involved,
determined, as one of her girlhood friends put it, "to try

every trip." Estranged from her businesswoman mother, adoring of her father, a New York reform politician, she had grown up intent on leaving her mark, anxious that everything she did be noticed and different. When World War II broke out, she enlisted in the Navy, attended Officer Candidate School at Radcliffe, and was commissioned a lieutenant j.g. It was not something most women did. But then, Sim Wenner was not an ordinary woman. "She was not like the rest of us," said a New York friend. "She always had a sense of time running out, of getting older. She wanted to taste it all before it was too late."

Her husband, on the other hand, was an easygoing, settled sort; sweeter, gentler—some said weaker—than his highly driven wife. Ed's open-faced, gee-whiz appearance— "He has the keen, sincere look of a college freshman, ruthlessly searching for life's answers," his wife wrote of him —could be deceptive, however. An engineer by training, and a tinkerer by inclination, Ed Wenner possessed a first-class, if linear, mind. After discharge from the Army Air Corps, he considered starting a feeder airline between New York and suburban Nassau County, New York. He was still figuring out how to gather the necessary capital when Jann was born and, with him, Sim's own idea of a business—marketing baby food formula to new mothers.

They began working in earnest after arriving in California. The business thrived. The Wenner family, which soon grew to five with the births of two girls, Kate and Martha, did less well. Ed traveled often and worked late. When he was at home, he relaxed by designing new baby formula machines and working out crossword puzzles against a stopwatch. He was brusque with his children, almost cold. Sim, by contrast, lavished attention on Jann. "He was her latest project," a family friend explained. "When something was

new, she gave herself over to it entirely. Whatever she was
doing just then was the most important thing in the world.
She was that way with Jann. But Sim always gets bored.
There are new things to try. And then she drops what she
had been doing. It was that way with Jann, too." As the
business grew in size and complexity, Sim devoted more
and more time to it. Finally she made a decision. "With an
exhausted sigh, I quit everything and concentrated on making enough money so that when my kids grew up, we could
have them psychoanalyzed," she recounted in a book about
her experiences. "I missed a great deal of my children's
childhood, and they missed a great deal of me."

The immediate result was that, of necessity, Jann became
uncommonly self-sufficient. By the age of three, he was
scrambling eggs and putting on the coffee. What help he
needed came, his mother said, "from a steady parade of
housekeepers, each one funnier than the last." His parents
bragged about their son's precociousness, how bright-eyed
and gifted he was, so unlike his playmates. He had few of
them, but he did not seem to mind being left alone. Growing up with Ed and Sim, he had no choice.

Jann was not unaware of what was happening around
him, the neighbors constantly moving in, taking lovers, having fights, splitting up. His own parents were in the midst of
it. "We were into social groups," Sim told a reporter years
later. "You know, four couples fall in love, everyone in love
with everyone else." With so much going on, it would have
been hard for anyone to keep track of who was with whom.
Not Jann. He was obsessively curious about Marin's unique
sociology and, in third grade, he rounded up all the tidbits
of local gossip, published them in a crudely typed newspaper—"The Bugle," he called it—and circulated his
findings through the neighborhood. The Wenners' friends

were not amused. Young Jann's first publishing venture was quickly put out of business.

In eighth grade, his parents packed him off to boarding school. They chose Chadwick, an exclusive co-ed academy outside Los Angeles, run with iron-fisted discipline by a retired naval officer. Shortly after his arrival, the inevitable Marin happening befell Jann's parents. Ed broke the news of the divorce to his son in the San Francisco airport coffee shop. Years afterward, Wenner could recall every detail of the scene vividly: his father's matter-of-fact, apologetic voice, the cheeseburger growing cold on the plate in front of him, the tears it seemed would never stop.

Ed moved to Los Angeles and eventually remarried. For a time, Sim remained behind, running the business and dabbling in local politics. Then, at the age of thirty-nine, with her children still in boarding schools, everything changed. She moved to a small town in Hawaii, let her hair grow down to her hips, dyed it blond, began riding a motorcycle, and embarked on a new career as a writer. "I wanted some action and suburbia was not the place to find it," she explained. "I became me. I was no longer my mother's daughter, or my husband's wife, or my children's mother. I went into the career of being Sim Wenner. I lived for me."

She seldom saw her son anymore. Too many other adventures occupied her time. At one point, she became a devotee and patron of Victor Boronko, a Berkeley-based used-car salesman turned sexual guru, and the guiding light behind "More House," an experimental community whose members claimed to be able to sustain orgasms for three hours at a time, and to increase penis size two to three inches in length and an inch in diameter. She also became increasingly involved in the women's movement.

Jann never quite forgave her. Years later, when Sim

needed money and came to him for a loan, he turned her
down. Later still, when he was running a book company
and she asked him to publish one of her works—a collection of hip aphorisms entitled *Ass on the Line*—he turned
her down again, even after she threatened to write his
biography, revealing what she claimed would be portions
of his life he wanted no one to know. She was, he said
repeatedly, "a goddam hippie."

Yet in many ways, Wenner and his mother were remarkably alike. He possessed the same curiosity, that wanting
to sample everything life offered, mingled with the same de-
tachment and aggressive insecurity—sometimes to the point
of callousness—the same self-absorption, and, over-arching
all, coloring every impression, the same desperate need to
be noticed, if not always loved.

It showed even at Chadwick. What was happening to his
parents was hardly unique at the school; many of Wenner's
classmates were from broken homes. Jann, however,
took the break-up of his parents' marriage extremely hard.

That he needed inordinate recognition was obvious.
He seemed to be anywhere and everywhere, all at once
—writing for the school newspaper, editing the yearbook,
running for office, launching a political party, managing the
athletic teams, singing in the glee club, starring in the
school plays (he played Faustus in *Dr. Faust*) and finally,
as if there were not enough to keep him occupied, starting his own newspaper, *The Sardine*. He was, in addition
to everything else, one of the brightest students in the
school, a light he did not attempt to hide under a bushel.
He had a curious attitude toward his own intelligence. For
friends, he usually sought out classmates less gifted than he
—then proceeded to belittle their abilities. It did not make
him Chadwick's most popular boarder. He was almost de-

terminedly different, challenging the rules, arguing with teachers, publishing articles that landed him in trouble, wearing his hair long and unkempt years before it was fashionable. He owned a letter sweater, but, unlike everyone else who did, never wore it. "While we listened to the Beach Boys," as one of his friends put it, "he went to see Fellini." His difference was not without its cost: several times he was on the verge of expulsion (at one point, Chadwick's frustrated administrators blamed him for the academy's "lack of school spirit") or getting punched. It didn't bother him. He relished the attention. For the first time in his life, people were beginning to notice.

He graduated in 1964, and that fall entered the University of California at Berkeley. He took an apartment off campus, and busied himself in his spare time writing punning traffic reports for the local NBC radio affiliate. Soon he moved over to the news department, and worked as a campus stringer for the network's television correspondents. There was no lack of news to report. He had arrived at Berkeley just as student politics were about to turn to protest, and from protest to revolution.

At a distance, Berkeley seemed a most unlikely setting for an uprising of any sort. It was a quiet, somnambulant campus, a place where jocks were heroes, frats filled to overflowing, and the only question of any consequence was when, if ever, the football team would beat U.S.C. As late as 1956, a poll of the university's undergraduates had found that 80 per cent of them had supported Dwight Eisenhower's reelection while, across the Bay, San Francisco was going overwhelmingly for Stevenson. "The employers will love this generation," Clark Kerr, the university's president, said three years later. "They aren't going to press many grievances. They are going to be easy to handle. There aren't going to be any riots."

Clark Kerr liked it that way. He was a man of reason and order, balding, bespectacled, unprepossessing, as quiet and dignified as the white shirts, muted ties and blue suits he wore to work each day. Nothing ruffled him. It was that self-assured calm, even in the midst of crisis, that had brought him to the position he held. In the early Fifties, as a labor negotiator, Kerr had mediated a dispute between the faculty and the state legislature, which, caught up in McCarthyite wrath of the day, was insisting that Cal's professors sign a loyalty oath. Kerr had successfully steered a middle course, managing to appease one and all. In gratitude, the university's regents named him Berkeley's chancellor. A few years later, they elevated him to the presidency of the entire state university system. Their confidence was well rewarded. Under Kerr's leadership, Berkeley moved to the forefront of American universities, and the system became a model for other state institutions. He studded the faculty with Nobel laureates, improved facilities, attracted millions in research grants, and, in the space of less than five years, nearly doubled student enrollment.

But with Cal's growth came problems. The undergraduates like Jann Wenner who jammed Berkeley's classrooms seldom saw the prize-winning professors. Instead, their education was left to a small army of ill-prepared graduate teaching assistants. Individual attention was increasingly infrequent. A computer system Kerr installed to cope with the crush transformed Berkeley's students into code numbers. One Cal student got his picture in the paper by holding a sign that read: "I am a U.C. student; please do not fold, spindle or mutilate me."

Kerr recognized the hazards of the "multiversity"; it was,

after all, his invention. From all over the country the experts came to listen to him, to sit with him in the backyard of his hilltop, landscaped home in El Cerrito, swimming pool glistening in the sun, velvety lawns rolling down to a cliff overlooking the Bay, while he waxed philosophical about the alienation of students—a new class, Kerr called them, a "privileged lumpenproletariat"—and about how, somehow, a way had to be found to provide diversity within huge institutions. "If you invest all of yourself in an institution," Clark Kerr was fond of saying, "you become a slave. It becomes a prison, not an agency of liberation."

By 1964, Wenner's freshman year, Berkeley's students needed no instruction in alienation. They had already lived through the Cuban missile crisis, the Civil Rights revolution, the assassination of John Kennedy, and the beginnings of the war in Vietnam. The more political of them were already beginning to organize. A tension hung over Berkeley like a mist of gasoline. All it needed was a spark to set it off.

It was one of those mindless, apparently insignificant spasms of bureaucracy that at first seem harmless, and only later mean everything. In mid-September 1964, as Wenner and the rest of the student body were preparing to return to classes, the Dean of Students, without warning or prior consultation, banned political activity on "Bancroft Strip," a 22-by-60-foot brick-topped area just outside Sather Gate, the main entrance to the university, and long a headquarters for organizers of various stripes.

At first, the students simply ignored the ban and continued organizing as usual. Then, on October 1st, a police car arrived to enforce the order. A nonstudent named Jack Weinberg immediately lay down in front of it, and was just as promptly arrested. A crowd of students thereupon surrounded the car and refused to let it move. For the next thirty-two hours, the students held the police prisoner, rocked the car back and forth, used its roof as a platform from which to deliver speeches, and beat off a band of fraternity boys who arrived to throw eggs. Meanwhile, the university administration, fearful of the image that the spectacle would present for the visitors who were coming on "Parents Day" forty-eight hours later, debated what to do. Ultimately, they decided to capitulate, and promised not to press charges against Weinberg. But the next day, Kerr ordered the suspension of eight protest leaders, including a twenty-one-year-old philosophy student recently transferred from New York named Mario Savio. With that, the Free Speech Movement was born.

Savio was its leader. He had the look of a revolutionary: gaunt, six-foot frame; intense, deep-set eyes; wiry, Brillo-like hair; tattered, casual clothes—an appearance so perfect, so close to media specifications, it was as if Central Casting had sent him for the part. The truth, which seldom surfaced in press accounts, was more banal. He was, in fact, a painfully shy young man, burdened by the attention that swirled around him, contemplative, good humored, and—the quality that diverged most radically from the image—adoring of his parents. They were working-class Sicilian immigrants and, when they moved to California from New York in 1962, their son Robert Mario came with them. He planned, when his studies at Berkeley were completed, to become a philosophy professor. If the times had been different, he probably would have made a good one. Certainly he possessed all the requisite intellectual talents. As a high school student, he had won twenty-seven medals and awards for scholarly achievement, and had never received a grade lower than A, a record unequaled in the 134-year history of his school. There was only one problem, and it was an especially griev-

ous one for a would-be professor, as well as for a putative
organizer: in moments of tension, he stuttered badly.

The first two years of Savio's college career had been er-
ratic. He transferred out of two schools, and switched his
major from physics ("too easy," he pronounced it) to philosophy. When he arrived at Cal, he was more unsettled
than ever. "I'm tired of reading about history," he complained to a friend in the fall of 1963. "I want to make it."

A few months later, when students started sitting in to
protest discrimination, Savio joined them. The demon-
strations were his first taste of action, and he liked it. When
classes were dismissed for the year, Savio went to Mississippi to organize. He chose McComb, a particularly volatile
racial tinderbox, and already the scene of a number of
bloody encounters. Less than a month after arriving, Savio
and two companions were set upon by a group of club-
wielding whites and severely beaten. "The beating didn't
bother him so much," said one of his friends, "as the fact
that the people who beat him could do it in broad daylight
in the middle of a street and get away with it."

At that, Savio was lucky. One of his close friends in Mississippi was Andrew Goodman, the Brooklyn College student who, with two other young organizers, was murdered
and mutilated outside Meridian in June 1964. Goodman's
murder devastated Savio. "What can you say?" he asked a
friend, weeping. "What can you do? What can any of us
do?"

He returned to Cal tougher and far more radical than the
young sophomore who had left the spring before. When the
ban on Bancroft Strip was announced, Savio was one of the
few who protested immediately, by sitting in in front of
Sproul Hall, the university administration building. The police soon arrived, and one of them pushed Savio and stuck

his foot in his face. "Please either remove your foot from my face," Savio said with all the humor the situation would allow, "or at least remove your shoe." Instead, the cop hit him, only to have Savio bite him in the leg. Savio was still facing disciplinary charges for that incident when the confrontation occurred at Bancroft Strip. His chance for making history had arrived.

Savio and others who were suspended after the police car incident were soon reinstated by order of a special faculty committee, and the ban on political organizing on Bancroft Strip was lifted. Briefly, the campus returned to normal. It required the talents of Clark Kerr to rekindle the trouble.

The events at Berkeley had unhinged Kerr. The orderly processes by which the university was supposed to run were in ruins. All around him was chaos, violence, obscenity, the things Clark Kerr had fought against all his life. "Anarchy," he called it, a university held hostage by "students who take their inspiration from Fidel Castro and Mao Tse-tung." Clark Kerr would not have it. Within weeks of Savio's reinstatement, he again threatened him with disciplinary action, this time over the Sproul Hall episode. The FSM responded by presenting the university with an ultimatum, warning that if charges against Savio and the others were not dropped within twenty-four hours, the students would resort to massive civil disobedience.

At noon the next day, when the deadline expired, Savio addressed a crowd of a thousand students and nonstudents. The old fear was missing, the stuttering gone. In its place was raging oratory. "There is a time," he rasped into the microphone, "when the operation of the machine becomes so odious, makes you so sick at heart, that you can't even tacitly take part, and you've got to put your bodies upon all the levers, upon all the apparatus, and you've got to make it stop. And you've got to indicate to the people who run it, to the people who own it, that unless you're free, the machine will be prevented from running at all."

Then, as Joan Baez sang "We Shall Overcome," the crowd rose as one and marched into the building. For the next fifteen hours they remained there, listening to Baez play the guitar, auditing courses of their own devising ("The Nature of God and the Logarithmic Spiral," "Wild Spanish," "Arts and Crafts"), plotting strategy, and waiting for the cops. They showed up more than six hundred strong, decked out in full riot regalia, badge numbers covered up to prevent identification, and none-too-gently—some of the students were pulled by their hair; others had their heads bounced down flights of stairs—hauled more than eight hundred nonresisting students off to jail. It was the largest mass arrest in the United States since the internment of the Nisei in World War II. "This is wonderful," Savio yelled as the police dragged him away. "Don't you know what you've done? You've given us life!" The next day, the FSM called the student body out on strike. Berkeley was seething.

There was never any question about which side Jann Wenner would enlist on. Since coming to Berkeley, he had acquainted himself with the various FSM leaders, including Savio, who had become a casual friend and news source. As the months wore on and the siege at Berkeley continued, Wenner drifted closer to student politics, eventually joining SLATE, an umbrella organization for the campus's various left factions. One of SLATE's activities was the publishing of a "Counter-Catalog" evaluating the university's course offerings. Politically active professors invariably got good marks in the SLATE catalog; the less politically inclined received lower ratings. Wenner had little use for most of FSM's politics, which he found hopelessly ob-

tuse, but the SLATE catalog spoke to him in a language
he understood; it was not unlike what he had been saying at
Chadwick. After the appearance of the first SLATE catalog,
Wenner phoned Phil Russ, a radical sociologist who was
compiling the evaluations, and volunteered his services.
Russ, taken with Wenner's enthusiasm, invited him over.
Soon Wenner became a regular houseguest.

Phil Russ and his wife, Joan, were the sort of faculty couple who would have appealed to any undergraduate. Bright,
understanding, generous almost to a fault, they were everything Wenner's own parents were not. Jann spent frequent evenings at their house, joking to Joan that she was
his "real mother." Late into the evening, he regaled them
with the latest campus gossip, the bullheadedness of the correspondents he was working for (the story they ought to be
covering, he kept insisting, was not at Berkeley, but in the
Haight, the scene of the "real revolution"), and accounts of
his own exploits, which, as time went by, increasingly re-
volved around drugs and rock and roll.

Rock was a recent enthusiasm of Wenner's. He had come
to it later than most of his contemporaries. While they were
grooving on Elvis, he was still going to the opera. It was not
until 1964, and seeing the Beatles' first film, *A Hard Day's
Night,* that he became a convert. The Beatles were unlike
anything he had ever witnessed, not merely the music they
played—the first truly "white" rock and roll—or the easy
self-assurance with which they carried themselves, so cool,
so casual, so utterly certain, but the mood they created.
After the events of the last few years, they were like a
breath of desperately needed fresh air. "You can have fun
again," they seemed to be saying. "Laugh, dance, make love
. . . everything'll be all right . . . yeah, yeah, yeah."
Watching their flickering image on the screen in front of

him, Wenner said later, "was the moment that changed my life." There was only one way to cope: he got a guitar.

As a singer-musician, Wenner proved to have only modest abilities. They were sufficient, though, once he gathered a band around him—the Helping Hand-Out, they called themselves—to be booked into North Beach topless joints, where artistry was less important than a raucous, boom-boom beat. The more Wenner played, and listened to records, the more immersed he became in the music. Nights found him prowling the Haight-Ashbury in search of jam sessions, music clubs, ballrooms, anywhere he could indulge his newfound love.

It was during one such excursion that Wenner met the man who would have more impact on his life than any other: Ralph J. Gleason. The date was August 9, 1965. The place, the Longshoreman's Hall, a modernistic, domed structure near Fisherman's Wharf. The occasion, the first Family Dog Dance, an event which marked the beginning of San Francisco's rock history.

Gleason had helped put the evening together. A few weeks before, a group of young people had come to him, asking his aid in arranging a series of rock dances they wanted to organize. They called themselves the Family Dog, in memory of a member's Rhodesian Ridgeback, recently crushed beneath the wheels of a truck. They were an eclectic group—a few artists, a couple of amateur musicians, a dealer or two, a woman who had lived for a year in a tree, and a resident "wizard" who dressed in magician's robes and claimed to be in direct contact with King Arthur's court. Some of them had recently returned from Nevada, where, in Virginia City, at an establishment called "The Red Dog Saloon," a rock group known as the Charlatans was winning a small but fanatic following. Although the Charlatans

never achieved commercial success, their music was the prototype for what would later be called "the San Francisco
Sound." It was that music that the Family Dog wanted to
promote. They had already held a number of informal rock
dances in a loft where they lived, and, encouraged by their
success, wanted to mount them on a larger scale. There was
money to be made, they figured, and just then they needed
cash badly to finance the purchase of a large tract of land in
Arizona, where they planned to open a "mail-order pet cemetery." But they needed Gleason's help. Did he know of a
place where they could get started?

Anyone else probably would have thrown them out of his
office . . . Martoon the Magician . . . living in a tree . . .
mail-order pet cemetery . . . but not Ralph Gleason. Instead, he thoughtfully sucked on his ever-present pipe, considered the enterprise for a moment, and finally answered:
indeed, he did.

Ralph Gleason was like that—loose. Young people were
always showing up at his house, a mile from the Berkeley
campus, asking his advice, borrowing money, looking for
encouragement, seeking a bed for the night when they were
strung out on drugs or there was trouble at home. Gleason
never denied them. He could be gruff at times, crusty and
irascible, especially when he suspected that he was being
conned. But his prickliness was a pose, and all of San
Francisco knew it. When he was forty-eight, the joke
around town was that Gleason couldn't make up his mind
whether he was two twenty-four-year-olds, three sixteen-
year-olds, or four twelve-year-olds. Gleason, typically, took
the gibe as a compliment. He had an almost childlike excitement about whatever was young and fresh, whether it was
rebellion at Cal, or rock at Monterey, a festival he helped to
create. "It has been a contest and a confrontation in styles

all along," he wrote after the Sproul Hall busts, "a struggle between the C. Wright Mills/Paul Goodman/*Catch-22* generation for whom the bomb dropped before they were born and a generation where cleanliness is next to godliness, and you don't make waves, just ride on them." He was no less enthusiastic about their music. "With the inspiration of the Beatles and Dylan," he declared in print, "we have more poetry being produced, and poets being made than ever before in the history of the world . . . For the reality of what's happening today, we must go to rock and roll, to popular music." The lines were pure Gleason: gushy, naïve, hyperbolic, full of enthusiasm and hope.

He was deceptive on first meeting. Tweedy, pipe-smoking, graying at the temples, Gleason had the look and demeanor of a mild-mannered professor of English at a small Midwestern college. That, in fact, is what he might have become had it not been for the student friend at Columbia University three decades before who insisted on taking him to a Bunny Berrigan concert at the Apollo Theater in Harlem. It was the beginning of Gleason's love affair with jazz. After the war, Gleason came to California and went to work for the *Chronicle,* writing what at the time was the only regular music column in the country. But it was Gleason's heart that most distinguished him. There was no group, however mediocre their talent, that he could not find something kind to write about. They had tried, at least. For Gleason, that was the important thing. "Don't define it," he was always saying, "dig it." Help the Family Dog and their bizarre scheme? Gleason could not resist.

So it was that they came to be there that night in San Francisco—Gleason, Martoon the Magician, the woman who lived in a tree, Allen Ginsberg (togged out in hospital whites), a smattering of Hell's Angels, Berkeley rads (the

Vietnam Day Committee had marched that afternoon
25,000 strong), and, jerking back and forth in the weird
half-light of a dozen strobes, kids by the hundreds, most of
them stoned, some of them dressed up like cowboys and
spacemen, all of them going out of their heads to the music
of the Jefferson Airplane.

Wenner had heard of the dance through Gleason's column, and he came determined to meet him. For the last
year, he had been reading Gleason's column religiously, and
Gleason had become one of his personal heroes. When he
met him, he was not disappointed. By the end of "A Tribute to Dr. Strange," as the dance was appropriately christened, their friendship was well on its way. Gleason, always
receptive to young people, found in Wenner a young man
more eager than most, bubbling with excitement, nearly
babbling with the wonder of what was happening. "A roly-
poly rock and roll kid," Gleason described him. Wenner,
who saw Gleason frequently in the succeeding months, was
almost reverential in his regard for the older man. "Ralph,"
he told his friends, "is my father."

With all his new interests, Jann seldom found time to attend classes any longer. A whole universe was opening up
for him that his professors could not comprehend. Music,
the Haight, his writing—they were what mattered now. They
and the new reality that came in tabs and sugar pills—lysergic acid diethylamide: LSD.

Wenner began experimenting with drugs about the time
he began listening to music. It was a common coincidence.
The experiences were synergistic, like parts of the same
breathing being, each enhancing and enlarging the other. If
listening to music produced uncontrolled euphoria, a dropping of all defenses, and a giving in to the senses, so did
drugs, especially acid. There was no control with acid. You

took it, and rode with it, Wenner told his friends, as if on a
cosmic roller coaster, until, hours later, it decided to let you
go, excited, exhausted, sometimes out of your mind. When
it was especially good, it was that way with the music—long,
spiraling riffs that spun through the curves and chasms of
the mind, fluttered, peaked, then spun on again, always at
top speed and full volume, hitting notes and making sounds
that had never been heard before. "Acid rock," they called
it, a uniquely San Francisco sound that, of its very being,
had to break all the rules. Jann Wenner couldn't get enough
of it.

He was not the first to have that taste. During the Fifties,
the Beats had mainlined smack to the accompaniment of
jazz. But heroin was a "body" drug, dangerous and addic-
tive. Wenner, who hated needles, steered clear of it. What
turned him on were the drugs of the mind—the hallucino-
gens. The Beats had also experimented with them, notably
peyote, a cactus bud derivative used by some Indian tribes
in religious ceremonies, and mescaline, a chemical relative
of LSD. But mescaline was difficult to produce, and peyote,
if readily available, had a noxious taste. LSD, on the other
hand, was odorless and tasteless, and easily manufactured;
with the right materials, a high school chemistry student
could synthesize it. And nothing could compare with LSD's
power, a hundred times more intense than psilocybin, another drug favored by the Beats. One *ounce* of LSD was
enough for more than 285,000 trips. Most improbable of
all, LSD was, for the moment, perfectly legal. There was, as
Jann Wenner and thousands of other young people were
discovering, nothing remotely like it.

The drug was first synthesized in 1938 by Dr. Albert Hofmann, a chemist for Sandoz Ltd., a Swiss pharmaceutical

firm. Hofmann was looking for a cure for migraine headaches, and had produced LSD from the spores of rye mold.
The chemical did not seem to hold much promise, however,
and Hofmann put it aside. But five years later he acciden-
tally inhaled a tiny amount of the whitish powder. Within
minutes, the room started spinning. "Objects as well as the
shape of my associates in the laboratory appeared to un-
dergo optical changes," he recorded in his notebook. "Fantastic pictures of extraordinary plasticity and intensive color
seemed to surge toward me."

LSD did nothing for headaches, but some psychiatrists
saw its effect on the nervous system as a possible treatment
for mental illness, particularly schizophrenia. Eventually,
LSD made its way into the psychiatric wards of a number of
hospitals, including the veterans hospital in Menlo Park,
California, not far from Stanford University. There, in the
late Fifties, researchers were using it in combination with
other drugs to produce temporary states of schizophrenia.
Volunteers who agreed to submit to the experiments were
being paid $75 a day.

The promise of so much money for seemingly so little
was a heady inducement for a recent University of Oregon
graduate and former collegiate wrestling champion who had
come to Stanford to study creative writing. His name was
Ken Kesey.

To look at Kesey, so blue-eyed, so blond, so utterly
wholesome and all-American, it was difficult to imagine him
having anything to do with anything the least bit sordid, especially drugs. Everything about this tanned, muscular
young man called up images of clean living: fresh air and
open skies, deep woods and rushing streams, the kind of
world, in short, where Ken Kesey had grown up, a hard-
working, God-fearing place like Springfield, Oregon. They

thought a lot of Ken back in Springfield. His high school class had voted him "most likely to succeed," and the people in town still recalled their favorite son, the quickness of his mind, the alertness of his eyes, how the stories he told—if usually too loudly—were always pointed and funny. There was no doubt about it: Ken Kesey was going places. Only at the moment there was a problem: Kesey was broke.

Life had not gone as well as expected since leaving Oregon. An attempt at becoming an actor had gone awry; a first novel had been rejected by every publisher who had seen it and, for the better part of the last year, Kesey had been living like a beatnik, drinking wine, smoking pot, and telling anyone who would listen to him of the great novel he would write one day, how, when the moment was right, his genius would change the world. No one disputed him. There was something about Kesey—an undefinable Karma, an almost hypnotic charm—that took the edge off his arrogance, and made the preposterous things he said seem altogether possible. All the same, Kesey had a family to support and no money to do it. When a friend mentioned that the veterans hospital was paying cash to try a few weird drugs, Kesey signed up.

The doctors gave Kesey three pills: a placebo, a drug called Ditran, which produced terrifying visions, and, finally, LSD. Kesey took the acid and waited for something to happen. Then, all at once, it did. The ceiling above him began moving, then breaking into planes of multicolored swirling light; an acorn dropping to the ground outside his window sounded like a bomb exploding; his eyes became like X-ray machines; an approaching doctor dissolved before him. One pill, and he had become a seer, a man of visions, a teller of truth. And he owed it all to LSD.

Things changed quickly after that. Kesey's next book,

One Flew Over the Cuckoo's Nest—the story of a prankish roustabout who, to beat a six-month sentence at a county work farm, fakes insanity, is committed, attempts to joke the inmates out of their madness, and is finally lobotomized so the insane order can be restored—was a critical and commercial sensation, hailed as one of the most influential books of the decade. A second novel, *Sometimes a Great Notion,* did less well at the cash register, but the estimation of the critics was, if anything, increased. Kesey was plotting new ground, they said, charting worlds with his novels that had never been dreamed of before. He was, the more enthusiastic of them proclaimed, the most important writer to emerge in the last twenty years. And then, even as the hosannas were ringing in his ears, Kesey gave it all up. "Rather than write," he announced, "I will ride buses, study the inside of jails and see what goes on."

He moved to La Honda, bought a small ranch, gathered a coterie of fellow freaks and sensation seekers around him (including the redoubtable Neal Cassady, model for Dean Moriarity, the hero of Jack Kerouac's *On the Road*), acquired a 1930s vintage school bus, painted it in psychedelics, crammed it with elaborate electronic gear, stocked the ice box with acid-laced orange juice, and made ready to begin life anew. Ken Kesey, the writer, was about to become Kesey, "The Chief," the Johnny Appleseed of LSD. From La Honda, the Chief and his "Merry Pranksters" ranged through the countryside like an overage, stoned Boy Scout troop run amok. The purpose of their aggressive merriment was to shock whomever they encountered—gas station attendants, Highway Patrolmen, straight, law-abiding folks—record their reactions on film, and edit it all as "The Movie" of their adventures. It was not difficult. "Furthur," as the Pranksters' bus was dubbed, was a motorized riot.

The Pranksters themselves dressed in a variety of ever-changing costumes—Indians one day, spacemen the next, storm troopers the third—and, to heighten the effect, painted their faces in iridescent Day-Glo colors. Strangest of all, though, was Kesey, who customarily rode in the place of honor in a perch on the roof of the bus. For reasons known only to himself, Kesey always seemed to be laughing.

Something was happening in Kesey's head. Out of the psychedelic phantasmagoria, a plan was being plotted, a scheme to impart the knowledge he had gained to the masses, to push them to the limit, to put them to the test—yes, the Acid Test.

The idea was fiendishly simple: bombard the mind with every possible sensation—acid; full-volume, endless rock music; strobe lights; amplified shrieks, hisses, howls, and explosions; projections of color—every device technology, chemistry and imagination could provide. Lay it on as many people as possible at a single time, and those who survived, who didn't go crazy, would pass. Thus, Kesey's slogan: "Can you pass the Acid Test?" Now and again, Kesey would add a twist or two. Sometimes he would pass out punch spiked with acid, without telling the people who drank it. Other times, he would do just the opposite: say there was acid in something, when there really wasn't.

There were certain risks, of course. Not everyone handled acid as well as Kesey and the Pranksters. Two of the Pranksters themselves had ended up in mental hospitals, and the number of victims of "bad trips"—temporary psychotic delusions—being admitted to area emergency rooms was growing every week. In Los Angeles, one young man who checked into the UCLA Neuropsychiatric Center after taking acid refused to let anyone come near him, claiming that he was an orange, and that if anyone touched him, he would squirt juice. In San Francisco, another tripper, convinced that he could fly, announced, "As long as I'm taking a trip, I might as well go to Europe," and, with that, stepped through a window and plunged ten stories to his death. As the catalog of suicides, deaths and commitments mounted, researchers, once so enamored of LSD's curative powers, started sounding the alarm. Prolonged acid use, they cautioned, could well result in brain damage or genetic mutations.

Kesey was not about to be stopped by such mundane considerations. Each succeeding acid test was bigger and, by his standards, more successful than the last—freakier, farther out, more outrageous. The authorities did not share his enthusiasm. Twice Kesey had been arrested for possession of inconvenient amounts of marijuana, and his lawyer had warned him to trim his sails. Kesey got the message. His next project, he promised, would be his most ambitious yet: a three-day "Trips Festival" filled with rock music, multimedia slide shows, guerrilla theater, mime exhibitions, films, videotape replays and light displays, climaxed by the inevitable Acid Test. "The general tone of things has moved on from self-conscious happening to more JUBILANT occasions where the audience PARTICIPATES because it is more fun to do so than not," he advertised. "Maybe this is the beginning of the ROCK REVOLUTION. Audience dancing is an assumed part of all shows & the audience is invited to wear ECSTATIC DRESS & bring their own gadgets (a.c. outlets will be provided)." Only one thing would be missing: this time there would be no acid.

Acid or not, the festival more than lived up to its advance billing. For three days and nights—from January 21 through 23, 1966, 72 hours of nonstop ecstasy—the Longshoreman's Hall shook with the most amazing assemblage of humanity:

hippies, students, beats, freaks, crazies and Holy Men—even
a few sociologists, come to probe the meaning of it all. They
danced, they freaked, they shouted, they moaned, a few
even tore off their clothes. Some sat stoned and silent waiting for the messages Kesey, dressed up in a silver spacesuit,
flashed from the light projector. ANYBODY WHO
KNOWS HE IS GOD, he ordered, GO UP ON STAGE.
There was a pause, an expectant moment, and then they
danced some more, hours on end, until finally, overcome
with delirium and exhaustion, they collapsed in heaps. It
was the beginning, it was said later, of acid rock. Whatever
it was, those who had been there came away knowing that
some turning had been made, a line had been crossed, and,
from now on, there would be no heading back.

One of them was Jann Wenner.
    Since early 1965, he had been a semi-regular at the La
Honda ranch. Kesey himself had given him acid, and he
had passed the Acid Test. He had hung out, listened,
tripped, survived. And, after taking everything in, he began
to write. The accounts of his exploits started appearing in
the pages of Berkeley's student newspaper, *The Daily Cali-
fornian,* in 1965, under the pen name "Mr. Jones," a pseu-
donym taken from Dylan's "Ballad of a Thin Man." To
complete his disguise, Wenner was pictured wearing dark
glasses, with a fake goatee and moustache pasted to his
face. It was an ironic cover, since, to read his columns, one
would gather that, unlike the "Mr. Jones" of Dylan's song,
Wenner most definitely knew what was happening, at least
with drugs and music. He was critical of the mind games
Kesey and the Pranksters were playing, likening them to
"experiments with rats in a maze." "As a whole it doesn't
work," he reported after one session at La Honda. "The real

act of getting people loose, person-to-person contact and
mass community is the work of rock and roll. The Acid
Test is at its best as a dance but once the music stops, it becomes very dull. The primary mood change is one into
boredom." But for acid itself, Wenner had only praise.
Nearly every column brought the latest update on Wenner's
acid weekends, recounted just as he had lived them. One
passage is typical:

> To the silver judges and the golden jury, it was not a ques-
> tion of Sitting Bull or Standing Up, but of Ringworm's
> sudden materialization as Blue Ned. No one had whistled,
> but there was a dog ready for walking by another more
> benevolent trainer, this time P.J. It was Blue Ned who was
> in fact simultaneously a striking typical example of No-
> where Man and a bit of bored imagination; Both at once.
> Nowhere, Neverwas, Notnow, Notobe. World Without
> End. People without Names; Friends without Friendship.

Amid the gibberish profundities, there were also record
reviews, notices of upcoming concerts, and scattered odds
and ends of personal information: Wenner had finished
reading all of F. Scott Fitzgerald . . . in an acid fantasy, he
had seen a train wearing his mother's pajamas . . . next
weekend he would meet the Grateful Dead. The students
loved it. Wenner's column became one of the best-read features in the newspaper, and made "Mr. Jones" a notable, if
shadowy, figure on campus.

As it happened, the life Mr. Jones was leading was not as
carefree as the one he was writing about. Wenner did not
handle psychedelics well, and his trips were often terrifying
experiences. After one acid weekend, he wrote: "Does Mrs.
R care that her son would soon be thin air? Did she know
that he was darkly fair, and that he had lost the where?" He

was bored and depressed, and his encounters with drugs were getting him into trouble. Once, the police had raided his apartment, arrested one of his roommates on drug charges, and briefly detained him for questioning. The line about "friends without friendship" was all too true. Since coming to Berkeley, several of his friends, including James Pike, Jr., the son of the Episcopal bishop, had committed suicide, and their deaths had deeply shaken him. To a friend of Gleason's, an older, prominent Berkeley woman who often met him at Gleason's home, he was "this very bright, terribly insecure young man, always wanting people to notice him." "You couldn't help but be charmed by him," she said, "and feel sorry for him at the same time."

By the spring of his junior year, Wenner desperately wanted to do something different. Berkeley had become a sullen place. The excitement of the early days of the FSM had given way to a grim, often mindless state of siege, with no apparent end or purpose in sight. Wenner had a girl-friend, whom he thought he might marry, but he did not want to settle down just then. At nineteen, he longed for more experience. He found it finally, in a most unlikely spot: on the cover of *Time* magazine.

"Swinging London," *Time*'s April 15, 1966, cover story announced. "As never before in modern times, London is switched on . . . The city is alive with birds (girls) and beatles, buzzing with mini cars and telly stars . . . The Rolling Stones reign as a new breed of royalty . . . Everything new, uninhibited and kinky is blooming at the top of London life . . . It is the place to be." Three weeks later, Jann Wenner was on an airplane, headed for England.

At first, London was everything *Time* said it would be. Arriving with a suitcase, guitar and Olivetti typewriter, Wenner checked his belongings in a locker, popped two tabs of speed, and headed for Carnaby Street. He got there just in time to see a silver Rolls Phantom pull to the curb and Brian Jones, leader of the Rolling Stones, step out. All Wenner could say was "Wow." For a time, there were a lot of wows. He took a small flat, got a job playing guitar in a West End gambling club, and briefly considered taking up permanent residence. Then things started to turn sour. A call home established that his engagement was off. Next, he lost his job. Finally, he had to pawn his guitar and, scraping his last few dollars together, buy a ticket home.

For the next few months, Wenner lived at the upstate New York country estate of Andy Harmon, a classmate from Chadwick. The summer days passed easily. Wenner relaxed, roamed the woods, and debated what to do with the rest of his life. He was a college dropout with few skills and—even he had to concede—neither the talent nor the patience to succeed as a musician. There was still his writing, though. He decided to try a novel, a story about San Francisco, rock, acid and lost love. He was still struggling with it when a letter from Gleason arrived, informing him that *Ramparts* was starting a weekly newspaper and needed someone to edit the entertainment page. Gleason had already spoken to *Ramparts* editor Warren Hinckle and suggested him for the slot. Hinckle had agreed. So the job was his, if he wanted it. Wenner did indeed.

Professionally, Wenner's experience at *Ramparts* was not destined to go well. Personally, it was an altogether different story. For it was here that he met the woman he would marry.

The first day he walked into the office, he saw her sitting there, demure, stylish, lovely, a bit of Bloomingdale's set down by the Bay. "Jane," she said her name was. "Jane Schindelheim." "I took one look at her," he said later, "and *bam,* that was it." It was an understandable reaction. Jane Schindelheim was a woman who would have attracted anyone's attention. She was "a soft Bianca Jagger," in a friend's words: sleek, smooth-skinned, petite, a look that bespoke money, good background, careful finishing. They began talking and casually flirting, and the details of her background tumbled out. Home, New York; father, a prominent dentist; family, one sister, also in San Francisco; employment, circulation clerk, a temporary necessity brought on by an aversion to panhandling. She had come to San Francisco a few months before, after hearing all her friends talk about how exciting life there must be. The city had been fun, but already she was homesick. She was a New York person and she couldn't deny it. Wenner smiled knowingly. Well, he was New York, too. And so it began. Within weeks, they were lovers, then housemates. Before the year was out, in a quiet Jewish ceremony attended by a few close friends, they were married.

Meeting Jane was about all that went well for Wenner at *Ramparts.* The more political types around the magazine ignored or resented him, and none more studiously than Hinckle himself. One could never be sure about Warren Hinckle, whether his chief love was drinking, telling tales, or giving the United States government fits, since Hinckle did all three in such profusion. Rascal by temperament, swashbuckler by disposition (an image made all the more vivid by the black patch he wore over his sightless left eye), and genius by personal estimation, "the Mike Todd of the New Left," as Hinckle fancied himself, was, at that moment, if not the leading muckraker in the United States, certainly the noisiest. Expose the CIA, skewer the Pope (a particular labor of love, since the Jesuit-trained Hinckle had rejected Catholicism), uncover conspiracies real and imagined—they

were but a few of the notches on Hinckle's rapid-fire journalistic six-gun. And here was Jann Wenner, "a fat and
pudgy kid hanging around the office," as Hinckle later described him, insisting that the fate of Western civilization
hung on the next record by the Beatles. Hinckle's one good
eye glazed over. About hippies and music, and the reporting
thereof—a journalism Hinckle placed "on a par with Ben-
Gay ads"—Hinckle had his mind made up. Which is to say,
closed.

Wenner did not help matters. He seemed to go out of his
way to offend his superior's sensibilities, from smoking pot
in the office to parading his friendship with counterculture
icons like Joan Baez. But the worst offense, as far as
Hinckle was concerned, was his consorting with Dr. Timothy Leary, then in residence at a San Francisco night-
club, and a particular bête noir of Hinckle's.

In truth, Leary was not overly popular with anyone in
San Francisco just then. Stylistically, he was the complete
antithesis of Kesey and his Pranksters. Where Kesey and his
associates regarded acid as little more than a cosmic joke,
Leary took it nearly as seriously as he did himself, which
was most seriously indeed. Vain, pompous, continually
proclaiming his intellectual pretensions, Leary, then in his
mid-forties, regarded LSD as "a Holy Sacrament" and himself as its spokesman here on earth. With Tim Leary at the
controls and acid in the water supply, Leary promised,
"man will discover and make love to god," the wisdom of
the ages would be revealed (Leary himself claimed to have
witnessed his pre-Cambrian ancestors battling saber-toothed
tigers during one trip), the world would be at peace, homo-
sexuality would be "cured," and women would experience
"hundreds of orgasms," many of them at the hands of Dr.
Leary himself, who claimed that, thanks to acid, his sexual

potency had increased "a thousandfold." "Any charismatic person who is conscious of his own mythic potency awakens this basic hunger in women and pays reverence to it at a level which is harmonious and appropriate at the same time," he immodestly explained to *Playboy*.

But, then, with Timothy Leary, almost anything was plausible. Raised near Boston by devout Roman Catholics, Leary came to chemical mysticism by a roundabout route. At nineteen, he dropped out of Holy Cross ("The scholastic approach to religion didn't turn me on"), attended West Point for a time, dropped out of there ("My interests were philosophic, rather than militaristic"), and finally took a B.A. in psychology at the University of Alabama. After graduation in 1942, he enlisted in the Army, served as a psychologist at a Pennsylvania hospital, and, at war's end, once again resumed his studies, receiving his doctorate in psychology from Berkeley. He quit his first major job—the directorship of Oakland's progressive Kaiser Foundation Hospital—charging that traditional psychiatric methods were hurting as many patients as they were helping. Harvard took him in as a lecturer in clinical psychology, and Leary soon began drawing notice for his unconventional teaching methods. Abandoning usual techniques, he urged his students to go to the source of social problems, rather than relying on textbook theories and clinical experience. Leary himself started delving into drug literature, notably Aldous Huxley's *The Doors of Perception*. Huxley, who twenty years before had told of a drugged society in *Brave New World* ("A gram is better than a damn"), had experimented with mescaline, and wrote of seeing "what Adam had seen on the morning of creation—the miracle . . . of naked existence."

Thus inspired, Leary traveled to Cuernavaca, Mexico,

and there, one sunny afternoon beside a swimming pool in 1961, ate a handful of strange-looking mushrooms he had purchased that morning from a witch doctor in a nearby village. Within moments, Leary felt himself "being swept over the falls of a sensory Niagara into a maelstrom of transcendental visions and hallucinations." He later wrote, "The next five hours could be described in many extravagant metaphors, but it was above all and without question the deepest religious experience of my life."

On his return to Harvard, Leary abandoned his curriculum altogether, and with a colleague, Richard Alpert, the son of a Boston philanthropist and railroad magnate, devoted himself wholeheartedly to the wisdom he had discovered at Cuernavaca. In time, others, including such notables as Allen Ginsberg, came to partake of the truths Leary was dispensing; indeed, so many others that Leary's supply of "magic mushrooms" (they were actually psilocybin) was quickly exhausted. But by then Leary had discovered the even greater bliss of LSD, whose wonders he promoted with such missionary zeal that within a year it had begun showing up in large quantities in New York's Greenwich Village. Two years later it hit the West Coast, and the psychedelic revolution exploded into full bloom.

Harvard, meanwhile, was becoming increasingly uneasy with Leary's growing notoriety. It was one thing when Leary and Alpert kept their supposedly scholarly investigations to themselves. But when the dynamic duo began publishing—notably, a pseudo-scientific letter in the *Bulletin of the Atomic Scientists* warning that the Russians might try to undermine the United States by dumping a few pounds of acid in the water supplies of major cities, and that the country should brace itself for this possibility by dousing its own water first—the rumblings around the Yard grew louder.

They reached intolerable levels when the university discovered that Leary had violated a pledge not to turn his own students on. Finally, in 1963, Harvard fired Leary and Alpert with an official expression of regret. "You may want to turn the world into Buddhas," their dean informed them, "but that's not what *we're* trying to do."

Leary then proceeded to form a nonprofit foundation— The International Foundation for Internal Freedom (IF-IF) —and set up a psychedelic study center in Zihuatabejo, Mexico, only to have the Mexican government expel him from the country. To further complicate his life, he was arrested while trying to cross the border into Texas with what U.S. Customs officials claimed was a half ounce of marijuana. Leary was tried, convicted, and eventually sentenced to thirty years in prison for failing to pay the U.S. marijuana tax. While his appeal was still pending, he set up camp at the Millbrook estate turned over to him by a multimillionaire New Yorker and fellow tripper named William Hitchcock, who saw Leary's work as a holy mission—as, indeed, did Leary himself. He let his hair grow long, began wearing white cotton pajamas, and proclaimed himself "a prophet," leader of a new religion, the "League for Spiritual Discovery."

As Leary's fame spread, he regarded his "mythic potency" with increasing infatuation. He embarked on writing a four-part work which, he promised, would match the Old Testament in its revelatory power. Already he had a swell lead: "In the beginning was the turn-on." The authorities, unimpressed, continued to harass him. Leary protested that his drug use was part of sacred ritual, and thus protected by the first amendment. When that ploy failed, he commanded everyone in the country to stop taking acid for a year. In the interval, Leary conducted drug-free public seances, complete with films and light shows: interested parties could gain admittance to the master's presence for $4 a head. It was that enterprise that brought him to San Francisco and the attention of Jann Wenner.

Naturally curious about Leary, Wenner had gone to North Beach one evening to catch the doctor's act. He had been impressed, not by what Leary had to say—for Wenner was very much on Kesey's side of the great psychedelic divide—but by Leary's celebrity value. He was, Wenner decided, worthy of an extensive interview for *Sunday Ramparts*—a judgment in which Leary instantly concurred. The introduction Wenner subsequently wrote for the piece was glowing, a bit too glowing for his superior, senior editor Sol Stern, who, despite Wenner's vociferous objections, deleted the most laudatory material. Wenner was not about to be so easily put off. When business closed for the day, he stole into the printer's and personally replaced the offending paragraphs. His editors were livid.

Matters finally came to a head in early 1967, with the appearance on *Ramparts'* cover of a ferocious attack on hippies, written by Hinckle himself. Among other items, Hinckle pronounced Leary "Aimee Semple McPherson in drag," called Jack Kerouac "a fascist," and termed Kesey "a hippie has-been." "The hippies have shown that it can be pleasant to drop out of the arduous task of attempting to steer a difficult, unrewarding society," Hinckle concluded, "but, when that is done, you leave the driving to the Hell's Angels." When the article appeared, Gleason, whom Hinckle had quoted to unflattering effect, resigned in a fury. Wenner, who had done some of the reporting for Hinckle's story, left shortly thereafter, but for different reasons: *Sunday Ramparts* had folded.

Out of a job, with no other steady employment in sight,

Wenner tried free-lancing and, when that failed—his one
effort, a 2,000-word review for *High Fidelity* magazine of
the Beatles' *Sgt. Pepper's* album, was rejected as "too hyperbolic"—took the civil service examination, and prepared
to live out the next chapter of his life as a mailman for the
United States Post Office.

But bigger ideas were germinating. While at *Ramparts,*
he and Gleason had discussed the sorry state of the rock
press. Most of the writing divided into two categories: the
celebratory "fanzine" adulation of *Sixteen* magazine, the
wrong-headed, usually negative coverage of the established
press. The undergrounds, such as the *Oracle,* the Berkeley
Barb, and the Los Angeles *Free Press,* came closer to the
truth, but their ideological stridency was limiting, and
foreclosed the possibility of advertising. What was needed,
Gleason and Wenner reasoned, was a publication combining the professionalism of the straight press with the insights
of the undergrounds, a magazine with weight and substance. A voice, in short, that would be listened to. But
how?

Wenner was still considering the question when Chet
Helms, a wispy-thin former divinity student from Texas
who had assumed leadership of the Family Dog, came to
him with a proposal that they start a psychedelic magazine.
Helms was well connected in the San Francisco music
scene, but there was a visionary vagueness in his manner
that, as events would later demonstrate, made him something less than the complete businessman. After a few weeks
of talks the project died stillborn. But Wenner's appetite had
been whetted anew.

He resumed his conversations with Gleason, this time in
earnest. The more they talked, the more realistic the notion
seemed. Finally, as the Summer of Love drew to a close,

they decided to proceed. Gleason kicked in $1,500 to help get the magazine off the ground. The remaining capital came from friends, parents, and in-laws. Jane's mother contributed $2,000, Wenner's stepmother another $500. An additional $2,000 came from Sim, and a final $500 from Joan Russ, who asked for dancing lessons in return. Altogether, the original capitalization amounted to $7,500, enough, Wenner calculated, to let them operate until advertising and circulation monies started to flow in.

When word of what Wenner and Gleason were planning reached their former colleagues at *Ramparts,* there was general amusement around the office. Similar magazines had been tried, with far more backing and professional talent, and they had either been, or were quickly on their way to becoming, disastrous flops. *Esquire* had spun off *G.Q. Scene* ("The Magazine for Teen Men Only"); two Diners Club veterans had attempted *Cheetah;* and Hearst had pumped more than $2 million into *Eye,* not to mention the editorial talents of *Cosmopolitan* editor Helen Gurley Brown. ("Take my word for it," she told her staff, "when girls march, I know they dress up and look pretty to do it.") None of them had cracked the youth market. The editors of *Cheetah,* which debuted with a nude centerfold of Cass Elliott, the 200-pound lead singer of the Mamas and the Papas, and folded seven issues later, claimed that "kids' minds change so fast, it's hard to keep up with what they are thinking." Now came Jann Wenner, all of twenty-one, with no experience, barely any money, and none of the accepted prerequisites to launch a successful magazine, especially one centered around so ephemeral a subject as rock and roll. "Counterculture bullshit," Hinckle sniffed. "I give him two months."

The two months passed, and more months after that, and

Rolling Stone was still in business, not only running, but getting stronger. *Ramparts,* meanwhile, had begun the long dive toward extinction. There was no easy accounting for what was happening; Wenner seemed to violate every precept of publishing. He didn't follow formulas or take expert advice. His entire financial education consisted of what he had gleaned from a few books on business practice he bought from a secondhand shop. Words like "demographics," one of those grown-up terms always being tossed around Madison Avenue, meant nothing to him. "Seventy per cent are between 18 and 25," he tried to explain to a reporter not long after *Rolling Stone*'s founding, "and then . . . Good Lord, I don't know." He didn't know anything about running a magazine, in fact, except that, somehow, whatever he was doing was working.

That it was his doing, and his alone, there was no doubt. No article, no review, no word whatsoever appeared in *Rolling Stone* without his personal imprimatur. What he did not write, he edited; what he did not edit, he supervised—and often altered to suit his personal tastes. "There is no such thing as objectivity," he told an interviewer. "It does not exist. Nobody is objective. No perceived event is objective. It's patent bullshit." When his editors questioned his judgments, he snapped back, "It's my magazine." And so it was, with all his talents, flaws and contradictions. It could be maddening at times, even mindless; brash, vulgar, mean, distorted, all the things that he could be. And also shining, brilliant, beautiful and true, as he could be as well. Reading it, issue after issue, was like watching a life unfold. If, some weeks the view was not always steady or fully formed, then it was because Wenner himself was not complete, coherent, or always clear.

The *Cheetah*s and *Eye*s always had to guess what young

people were thinking. Wenner never did. He printed what interested him, trusting that his interests would be shared by his readers, never pausing to worry whether they would or not. His competitors tried to categorize the youth culture, breaking it into neat, easily identifiable boxes: this was rock, that was politics, those were drugs. Wenner served them all up in one grand helping, music mixed with politics mixed with drugs. He picked and chose, leaping from one enthusiasm to the next. He never talked down to his readers, as the slick hipsters at *Eye* did, describing their "underground bookshelf" as a guide to "what the 'real heads' are reading." When he used the argot of the culture, he did so naturally, with the ease of a man talking his own language. Occasionally, his language could be a bit too loose for the tastes of Garrett Press, as on the day when one of the printers picked up a slug of type with "fuck" printed on it and hurled it at him. Wenner could only laugh.

It was all such a grand adventure, such an improbable trip. The motto on *Rolling Stone*'s masthead said it best: "We believe in a Cosmic Giggle." If Wenner had less time for giggling than the rest of his staff, it was because *Rolling Stone* was more than a magazine to him. "It is my life," he said to Wolman. "It is the thing I value most in the world."

Everything else had gone so wrong for him. Parents, school, friends, his dreams of becoming a rock star, even acid—none of them had turned out well. Nor had they turned out well for most of the people who read his magazine. They were so alike, the editor and his readers—rootless, cut off from their pasts, contemptuous of the people who had spawned them, determined to build a culture of their own, a place where the world could not touch them. And all the while, they would make sure that adults—their parents—could not fail to notice. *Rolling Stone,* Wenner promised his editors, would be "another *Time*." The next few years was their chance, perhaps their only chance. To a generation still coping with the consequences of their rebellion, *Rolling Stone* was an assurance, a letter from home for those who had no homes. Jann Wenner was their guide. What would happen to him would, in a very real way, happen to them as well.

3

Some People

It was a strange time in San Francisco.

A year had passed since the Summer of Love, twelve months of very little love at all. Robert Kennedy and Martin Luther King were dead, cut down by assassins. Lyndon Johnson had been driven from office. The convention that had met to pick his successor had ended in chaos, hundreds of young demonstrators brutalized in what would later officially be described as a "police riot." The ghettos were burning more fiercely than ever. Columbia, following Berkeley's example, had gone out on strike, and more schools would soon follow. In Vietnam, where the effects of the Tet offensive were still rippling like so many aftershocks from an earthquake, the tonnage of bombs dropped had passed that of all those delivered during World War II. Back home, marijuana arrests had topped the 60,000 mark, double what they had been during 1966. Before the year was out, the Berrigans would be arrested and Dr. Spock indicted. And now, the newspaper on Jann Wenner's desk bore a stark headline: "Nixon Wins!"

Wenner felt only a fleeting distaste. Politics meant little to him. Like most of his friends, he had not bothered to vote. Still, there was something disquieting about everything that had happened leading up to this day. Wenner could not quite put his finger on it. There was only the gnawing sense that, somehow, for reasons he could not understand, events were not working out as he had thought they would a year before. Already, the Haight was slowly beginning to slide back to the oblivion from which it had sprung. It was a different place now; the fast-buck artists and plastic hippies were gobbling it up block by block. Berkeley was different, too. Savio had been unsuccessfully flirting with electoral politics, and the old FSM was being swept away by a new breed of student radicals, tougher and more ideological than their predecessors. All that hadn't changed in the last year, Wenner reflected, was the music and his magazine. He smiled at the thought. Of course, they had; they were both bigger and better than ever.

The picture in his office was the proof. He had had to finagle to get that picture, cajole and beg. But it had been worth it. In a few days, it would be on the cover of his magazine from coast to coast, and then people would notice. They could not help but notice a full-length rear-view shot of John Lennon and Yoko Ono, the superstar of rock and his woman—nude. He typed out the headline: "And they were naked, the man and his wife, and were not ashamed." Heavy. "Wait till they see this," he said to no one in particular. "They won't believe it."

They almost didn't. But there it was: the nude Beatle. The reaction was even bigger than Wenner had expected. In San Francisco, one of his vendors was arrested for distributing "obscene material," and the *Chronicle* bannered the story across four columns: "Nude Beatle Perils S.F." In Englewood, N.J., the postmaster refused to allow the issue to pass through the mail. In Boston, a distributor withheld the magazine from the newsstands. Bootleg copies quickly became collector's items. Soon Wenner's phone was ringing off the hook with press calls from around the country. Wenner was exultant. "The point is this," he wrote in the next issue. "Print a famous foreskin and the world will beat a path to your door."

Wenner had every reason to be happy. By the end of the year, the publicity, in combination with rock's burgeoning influence, was pushing *Rolling Stone*'s circulation toward the 100,000 mark.

The magazine, if still sometimes ragged in appearance, was no longer the fly-by-night operation it had been the year before. There was money in the bank, and fewer creditors pounding on the door. Wenner had even begun talking about spin-offs: foreign editions of *Rolling Stone,* regional versions, a radio network, television, on and on.

For some of the staff, *Rolling Stone* and its editor had become too successful. Michael Lydon had quit after two months. "Jann wanted a big, popular successful magazine," he explained. "He didn't want it to be an underground newspaper. He wanted to meet the Beatles. He wanted to do something that would put him on a par with the Beatles. I guess I had a more idealistic view. Anyway, I just split." Lydon joined *Ramparts,* free-lanced, and eventually dropped out of journalism altogether to become a singer and songwriter. Susan remained an additional six months. "Everything was going fine," she said, "and then one day, out of nowhere, I realized, 'Holy shit, the planet is dying while I'm writing about rock and roll stars. I might as well do nothing.' Which is exactly what I did." After her baby was born, she divorced Michael, moved to Berkeley, "became a hippie mother," and, for a time, lived on welfare.

By then, there were dozens of writers clamoring for their

jobs. They were, to put it mildly, a varied lot. Some, like
John Burks, a highly skilled former reporter for the Oakland *Tribune* who signed on as managing editor in early
1968, were relatively traditional. Others decidedly were
not. There was one secretary, a striking black woman
named Henri, whose previous employment had been as a
groupie. Wenner was less pleased by "Clarabelle," the so-
briquet for a new arrival in the business department who
had the habit of pulling open the blouses of women in the
office and pinching their breasts. Clarabelle's brief tenure
finally came to an end the day he announced to the staff
that, if they gazed into the parking lot precisely at noon
that day, they would behold something unusual. At
the appointed hour, the staff gathered to witness Clarabelle being orally ministered to by a secretary from a
neighboring office. Wenner, who partook of the apparition,
fired him on the spot. Ed Ward, a cheerfully slovenly New
Yorker who came aboard as a music critic, was a different
sort. Wenner found it hard to fault him as a writer; his
prose was clean and well ordered, everything, in short, that
Ward himself was not. The mess, however, had to go. The
two of them quarreled heatedly about it, but to no avail.
Then one day, Ward returned from lunch to find a broom
near his desk with a note attached to it: "Clean up this
pigsty, slob." Ward flew into a fury, snatched up the broom,
and issuing death threats at the top of his lungs, pursued
Wenner through the office. By the time Ward caught up
with him, he was too exhausted to do any damage. For his
part, Wenner could only utter a massive understatement:
"It doesn't look like the two of us are getting along." Ward
agreed, resigned, and, in his words, "promptly suffered a
nervous breakdown."

And then there was "Smokestack el Ropo."

"Smoke," alias Charlie Perry, who joined the magazine as copy editor in early 1968, was unusual even by San Francisco standards. Balding, thin, mild-mannered, his only distinguishing feature a pencil-thin Gilbert Roland moustache, he resembled nothing so much as a ladies' shoe salesman—that is, if ladies' shoe salesmen were given to wearing iridescent yellow-orange shirts and 1940-era ties. Charlie wore the same color shirt to work each day. It was the ties he kept switching. There was a revolving collection of more than two hundred of them, a hint that the mild-mannered little man was perhaps not so mild-mannered after all.

He had grown up on a walnut farm in the San Fernando Valley, outside Los Angeles. To relieve the tedium of rural existence, he decided at the age of thirteen to begin studying languages. By the time he was fifteen, Perry had mastered French, Italian, German, Spanish, Polish, Russian, Latin, ancient and modern Greek, and was beginning to work on south Indian dialects. On admission to Princeton, he had also picked up Sanskrit, Swahili, Gaelic, Welsh, Turkish, Persian, and, as he modestly put it, "just a smattering of Urdu." After two years, he transferred to Berkeley and settled down to serious Arabic scholarship.

Perry might have ended up an eccentric genius professor of obscure languages had it not been for the roommate he drew—Augustus Owsley Stanley III.

"Owsley," as he preferred to be known—dispensing with his last name for roughly the same reason Napoleon dispensed with his—was a bona fide youth culture legend. In certain circles, the mere mention of his name could produce a reverential hush. The Grateful Dead, with whom he was associated for years, wrote a song in tribute to him—"Alice D. Millionaire." When he appeared at the Fillmore, kids stopped dancing and gave him an ovation. One San Fran-

cisco writer compared him, favorably, to Pericles, Buddha
and Merlin the Magician. No less than *Time* likened him to
Henry Ford. The accolades were well deserved. Owsley was
the king, the undisputed maestro and mad magician, of
LSD.

If Kesey was the Johnny Appleseed of acid, and Leary its
high priest, Owsley was the Creator himself. During his
brief career, he turned out millions of hits of acid, with an
industry that would have put Du Pont to shame. So prolific
was his work that, virtually single-handedly, Owsley drove
the price of acid down from $7 a tab to $2, and in the process made acid available to the multitudes. And what right-
eous acid it was. "You could chip an Owsley," said one
satisfied customer. "I mean you could cut off a bit of the
tablet—and still get high. That means it was well mixed."
The Beatles took Owsley's acid, as did any band of consequence that could get their hands on it. "Simply to be in
possession of Owsley acid," wrote Tom Wolfe, "was the hip-
pest intelligence one could pass around." As *Newsweek* put
it: "Owsley became to LSD what Carter's is to Little Liver
Pills. His was the brand you could trust."

The worker of these wonders was a short, chipmunk-
cheeked young man of thirty years and longish hair—a
darker, stoned version of John Denver. His grandfather, the
first Augustus Owsley Stanley, had been a United States
Senator from Kentucky, and had distinguished himself during his congressional career by a regalness of bearing and a
continual railing over the federal government's interference
with free enterprise. Owsley inherited a lot from the old
man. His robber baron instincts were every bit as acute, and
it was said that he was the first hippie self-made millionaire.
There was some contention about Owsley's worth, but none
about his arrogance. He had a wise-cracking, smart-assed

aura about him, unusual for the Haight, which, in combination with his intelligence (his I.Q. was reputed to be 180)
and diverse talents (in addition to his demonstrated flair for
chemistry, he was also an accomplished poet, artist, ballet
dancer and Russian scholar), enlarged his legend all the
more. Owsley was not unaware of his notoriety, and not unwilling to exploit it. He preened himself like a hip peacock
(a colleague remembered he put his hair up in curlers before retiring for the night), walked with a self-confident
swagger, and, when meeting strangers, introduced himself
with two words, "I'm Owsley," as if that said it all. And in a
sense, it did.

The ultimate credit for Owsley's fame belonged to Perry.
Owsley had never tried acid before he moved into the old
rooming house Perry lived in at the edge of the Berkeley
campus. Perry, who had, regarded him suspiciously. Where
had he been all his life? Perry inquired. The answer was,
around: in and out of a series of Virginia prep schools; a
brief stint at the University of Virginia School of Engineering; then a tour of duty in the Air Force, which put his
tinkering abilities to work as a radar technician and brought
him to California. But in all that time, Owsley had never
tried acid. Everything else, yes; acid, no. Perry quickly
rectified the situation. With Perry's guiding hand, Owsley
delved deeper into the acid culture, and the deeper he
delved, the more incensed he became. The quality of acid
available in Berkeley, circa 1964, was wildly uneven, and it
infuriated Owsley. "The government isn't doing its job," he
complained to Perry. "Somebody ought to be setting standards." If the FDA wouldn't, Augustus Owsley Stanley III
would.

He got his opportunity a few months later, when a
girlfriend invited him to witness some experiments she was

conducting, *sub rosa,* in room 292 of the university's Biological Sciences Building. The "experiments" turned out to be synthesizing LSD. Owsley gazed at the bubbling flasks and was immediately intrigued. The formula seemed relatively uncomplicated; to a man of his scientific gifts, it was child's play. Yes, with the right materials . . . and then it came to him. Acid by the ounce. By the pound, even. Millions of hits. A stupendous enterprise. And all his: Owsley Acid.

He opened his first lab a few weeks later in the back of an old store not far from the university and, as it happened, directly across the street from a children's playground. The unfortuitous locale quickly brought the police down on him. Unfazed—at the time, acid was still legal in California—Owsley promptly sued the city for the return of his equipment. When the authorities proved uncooperative, he departed for Los Angeles and what he hoped would be more hospitable climes. Owsley was more imaginative this time. He set up shop as the "Baer Research Group," listed himself in the telephone directory, and had formal office stationery printed up. The ruse worked perfectly. Thinking they were dealing with the maker of Bayer Aspirin, reputable chemical companies began selling Owsley lysergic acid monohydrate, the basic ingredient of LSD. For an investment of less than $40,000 (his ill-gotten Berkeley profits), Owsley was able to purchase some 800 grams, enough for 2.5 million hits of acid with a wholesale value of nearly $5 million—a profit of roughly 12,500 per cent.

What became of all the money not even Perry knew. Owsley did not live pretentiously, and according to local folklore, he gave away as much acid as he ever sold. He further ate into his profits by consuming a good portion of his output. Much of the remaining cash was plowed back into the business, for as Perry put it, "Owsley was very quality minded." He was continually perfecting his craft, increasing purity, refining packaging, extending potency, experimenting with new blends, always advancing the state of his exotic art. "Descending the basement stairs was like entering a psychedelic spaceship," a visitor to one of his labs reported. "The walls were covered with machinery and bubbling flasks, coiled glass tubing dripping potential weirdness from container to container, floor to ceiling. Huge glass caldrons surrounded with dry ice covered the floor, oozing white clouds of spacey vapors into the room."

Owsley christened each new batch with a different name, and marked it with varying colors and symbols to designate its strength and potency. There were varieties like "Midnight Hour," "Purple Passion," "White Lightning," and, most famous of all, "Owsley Blues," which had a picture of Batman imprinted on the tab. "The heads," wrote Wolfe, "rapped over Owsley Blues like old juice heads drawling over that famous one-time brand from Owsley's home Virginia territory, Fairfax County Bourbon, bottled-in-bond . . . In the acid world, this was bottled-in-bond; certified, guaranteed and high status."

But an ominous cloud had appeared on the horizon. On October 6, 1966—three sixes, the mark of Satan, it was later noted in San Francisco—the California legislature made the possession, manufacture, sale and use of LSD a felony punishable by a large fine and a long jail term. All at once, Owsley's empire was in jeopardy. Indeed, the story was that the law had been written with Owsley specifically in mind.

Perry urged Owsley to be cautious; he already had more money than he needed, and all the fame anyone could want. But Owsley would hear none of it. "If you start off being afraid," he told Perry, "you destroy yourself." "Deep in his bones," Perry reflected, "Owsley believed that the police were really working for him."

Owsley was seen less around San Francisco now. He disappeared for long stretches at a time, and there were rumors that he was dead. In fact Owsley was still making acid, though now from a mobile lab which he moved from place to place, always one step ahead of the law. Without warning, the little man in the black cape with the bear claw hung around his neck would suddenly reappear, dispense some magic cubes from an embroidered leather pouch, then vanish as quickly as he had come. He seemed to take unnatural enjoyment from the chase, as if ducking the law were a new turn-on, undreamed of in any formula. His friends worried for his sanity. Owsley had given up eating fruits and vegetables, disdaining them as "rabbit food," and ate only beef, convinced that everything else was poisonous. One night, stoned on hash, Perry offered him a piece of apple pie. "What are you trying to do?" Owsley demanded. "Kill me?" Perry had trouble hearing him; the transistor radio Owsley always carried was playing full blast—to foil, Owsley said, the eavesdropping devices he knew were everywhere.

Poor old Owsley. He had to fall. Everyone in San Francisco—with the exception of Owsley—knew that now. He simply had become too visible a menace to public order to live free much longer.

They caught up with him, finally, just before Christmas 1967, in a nondescript house in the San Francisco suburb of Orinda, brewing up a special batch for the holidays. "They" were the thirteen federal and state narcotics agents who came bursting through his door. "How did you find me?" Owsley sputtered, his legendary aplomb slipping just a notch. "I want you to know," he coldly informed the raiders, "that even though you have a search warrant, I consider you uninvited guests in my home." As the law began hauling away the evidence—217 grams of acid, enough for 868,000 doses (Owsley reportedly protested that the acid was intended only for his personal use)—they also took 261 grams of STP, another of Owsley's creations, eight times more powerful than LSD, and so new that the legislature had not had time to make it illegal. "Please," Owsley implored, "only take the contraband."

The law was unmoved. Owsley got three years, the maximum, a sentence ameliorated only slightly by Wenner's award of a free, lifetime subscription to *Rolling Stone*.

Perry, meanwhile, had been caught in the throes of a career crisis. Since graduation, he had taken up Zen, oriental mysticism, gourmet cooking, oenophilia, Tibetan music, and, for a spell, publishing, notably a magazine printed on wallpaper ends. None of which paid very well. The trouble, Perry concluded, was that his Arabic education prepared him for a limited range of opportunities. "I could join the CIA," he mused, "enlist in the Marines, work for USIA or ARAMCO, or go back and teach other people Arabic to lead them down the same dead end." Pause for dramatic effect. "And so I became a dope dealer."

He had all the qualities for a successful future: iron nerve, innocent appearance, a taste for adventure, and utter unflappability. Smuggling marijuana in from Mexico, if high-risk, was relatively easy, and Perry found that he had copious spare time on his hands. It was looking for a way to fill up some of it that brought him, in February 1968, to Brannon Street and the offices of *Rolling Stone*. His intention was to stay a time, write a bit, do some editing, and continue dealing. He did not realize what awaited him. Charlie Perry had no time for dope any longer; no time for anything. *Rolling Stone* took it all.

Perry found what Michael Lydon had discovered earlier: *Rolling Stone* was not a hippie magazine. The hippies might like rock, take dope, even look like the *Rolling Stone* staff looked, but there any resemblance between the "do it" ethic and Jann Wenner's publication ended. With every issue, Wenner was demanding more of himself and the young men and women who worked for him: longer hours, greater effort, still more polish. A most unhippie-like regimen of twelve-hour days was now the routine and, as the issue moved toward closing, the hours got even longer, sometimes two or three sleepless days at a stretch, until they were giddy with exhaustion. Dosings of speed helped keep them going, but the primary fuel was their own enthusiasm. Wenner seldom had to demand of their time; they gave it willingly, as they would to no other boss on no other job. For most of them, *Rolling Stone* was not a job at all, but a grand adventure, the man who led them not a boss, but a brother, a father, the head of their family. Their attitudes were the same; their compensation identical. It was only in ambition that they diverged: Wenner, the young mogul-in-the-making; the Perrys and Wards and Henris, thinking only from issue to issue. What drew them together, what kept them there, was one over-arching obsession: rock and roll.

It was a different music now, a far more sophisticated sound than what they had been listening to even a year before. They knew that, because their own tastes had changed, grown with the music itself. Rock still moved the body and shook the senses, the way it always had. But now the head was involved as well—discerning, sampling, digesting, evaluating, in sum, judging. And that was because of Jon Landau.

His title was *"chief* rock critic." It was an odd appellation, since before Landau's coming there were almost no rock critics, chief or otherwise, at *Rolling Stone* or anywhere else. But then, Landau had always been outside the mold. His earliest exposure had been to classical music. In appearance, he still looked like an earnest student at Juilliard, all scrubbed and well turned out. But with Landau, it was not his looks that mattered, but his ear. And there was none better.

Born in New York to a musical family, Landau first became acquainted with rock at the age of five. His parents' radio was on, and inadvertently the dial had been tuned to WINS, at the time the city's leading rock station. The sound he heard was Old Jack Lacey, spinning through the Crickets' "That'll Be the Day." "Halfway through it," Landau recalled, "the love affair began. Two weeks later, I had my own radio next to my bed." From then on, he fell asleep each night listening to songs like "Sweet Little Sixteen," "Good Golly Miss Molly," "Great Balls of Fire," and "Johnny B. Goode," convinced that the sounds he was hearing would change his life as nothing else ever could or would. By the time he entered Brandeis in 1964, Landau was an accomplished player of both the guitar and banjo, a devotee of music whose tastes ranged from folk to bluegrass to blues. But it was rock that moved him most. Every chance he could, he slipped back to New York to attend Alan Freed's rock and roll spectaculars. There he watched, awestruck, as "Jackie Wilson ripped off his jacket and taught two thousand demented, screaming adolescents the meaning of soul"; Fats Domino "pushing the piano off the stage with his stomach while his band just kept on rocking"; groups like the Impalas "dancing holes through the stage floors." But the transcendent moment was the night he saw the Remains. "It was," he wrote later, "the first time I ever really *saw* rock and roll in all its grandeur, all its glory, and all of its greatness, and it did something to me that I haven't gotten over yet." Two weeks later, Landau traded his banjo for an electric guitar and formed a band.

One day in 1966, while rummaging through a Harvard Square book store, Landau met Paul Williams, the eighteen-year-old editor and publisher of *Crawdaddy!* Williams' publication neither looked nor read like a music magazine —at that moment, it consisted of a few stapled-together mimeographed pages—and Landau bluntly informed him that it was awful. What it needed, Landau immodestly added, was a rock reviewer of real taste and talent, namely himself. To his astonishment, Williams instantly accepted. At the time, Landau wrote, his "objectives were messianic, not literary. From the outset, I assumed the modest task of telling the world what it should and should not be listening to." Despite the awkward, overly formalized rhythms of his early prose style, Landau wrote with an insight and intensity that soon attracted considerable attention. *Eye* asked him to become one of its featured critics. Then, with no warning, a letter arrived from San Francisco in 1967. It was from Wenner, inviting him to contribute to a new music magazine he was planning to publish. Landau accepted. His first review appeared in *Rolling Stone*'s premier issue.

Landau gave the magazine immediate weight. He was a rarity in rock journalism: a critic who not only liked rock, but understood it, all its nuance and technical artistry. His perceptions did not stop when the music ended. Shy, quietly intense, Landau was very much a moralist, and worried when he saw immorality threatening the music he cared for so much. "We tell ourselves we are a counterculture," he wrote at one point. "And yet are we really so different than the counterculture against which we rebel? The truest expression of middle-class culture lies within the star system . . . It involves the selection of one person who is made to stand for all our fantasies and all our misplaced frustrations. It is the crudest and most primitive form of escape, in which we express our dissatisfaction with ourselves by endowing another with superhuman qualities. And it is a cornerstone of what is pretentiously called a counterculture." Against-the-grain sentiments such as those seldom if ever surfaced in the rock press, and when they did in *Rolling Stone,* Jann Wenner's reputation was enhanced.

Indeed, it had been precisely that kind of thoughtful criticism that had brought the magazine another of its early stars, Greil Marcus. A casual college acquaintance of Wenner's, Marcus was every bit as serious as Landau about the music and even more serious about himself and his intellectual powers, which, in Marcus' estimation, were considerable. On first meeting, Marcus left no doubt that he was a person to be reckoned with. Intense, deeply committed to left politics, with a breadth of knowledge that jarred with the usual image of a rock freak, Marcus sprinkled his conversation with references to Voltaire and Proust, and, lest there be any doubt about the extent of his learning (he was, after all, a doctoral candidate in political science), casually, if confidently, referred to himself as "an intellectual."

A native San Franciscan, Marcus had attended Berkeley and while there had become enmeshed in the Free Speech Movement. He had met Wenner when the two of them were freshmen, members of the same political club. But their interests at that moment were divergent, Wenner taken up with drugs and rock, Marcus just as heavily involved in various political intrigues. It was not until well after graduation that they became close. Marcus, then teaching American Studies at Cal, was moonlighting as the rock critic for the

San Francisco *Express,* one of the city's short-lived undergrounds. His reviews caught Wenner's eye, and Wenner invited him to write for *Rolling Stone.* Marcus quickly accepted.

His writing was not as musically detailed as Landau's. Instead, he focused on the relationship between rock and contemporary culture. "I am no more capable of mulling over
Elvis without thinking of Herman Melville," he wrote, "than
I am of reading Jonathan Edwards without putting on Robert Johnson's records as background music." To be sure,
few people, no doubt including the star himself, divined the
link between Elvis and Herman Melville, but what was
Marcus' conceit was also his genius. Wenner could only
fumblingly articulate that "rock and roll at once exists and
doesn't exist . . . it means nothing and thus everything."
Marcus translated the pseudo-existentialist vision into a coherent philosophy.

Marcus and the staff were an unlikely aggregation: sex
fiends and groupies, dope dealers and academics, writers
and poets, geniuses and pretenders, all of them come to a
single place for a single cause—the music that would make
them free. In the years to come, most of them would disap-
pear from *Rolling Stone,* go on to new interests and careers.
Just then, though, was a special moment in the lives of all of
them, a chance to build something better and new. What it
would become, what they would become because of it, none
of them knew. For all of them, the future was now. All except Wenner. "What do you think will happen with us?"
Charlie Perry asked him one day. "We'll all become rich
and famous," Jann answered. Perry laughed. Then he shot a
glance at his friend. Jann Wenner wasn't laughing.

4

Dance
to the Music

The voice over the phone was unmistakable. "I want you to know something, Mr. Wenner," it bellowed. "In all my life only three people have crossed me. *Three*. And you know what happened to them, Mr. Wenner?" Jann Wenner didn't bother to answer. Against this voice, he knew he couldn't. "They're dead, Mr. Wenner. I want you to understand that, Mr. Wenner. Dead!"

Click. The line went dead. Jann Wenner still held the phone three inches from his ear, as he had since he picked up the receiver. It was the only defense against the volume and hysteria. But then, that was the caller's way. It wasn't personal; everyone in San Francisco got the same abuse. In a perverse way, that was part of the voice's charm. But today was different. Wenner had never gotten a death threat before. Was it serious? Slowly he put the receiver back into place and reflected. He couldn't be sure. About Bill Graham, nothing was ever sure.

Except that there was no one quite like him. There were other concert promoters in San Francisco and the great space to the east, other dance hall proprietors, other talent managers, other record company owners, others who did all or part of what Bill Graham did; but none of them was Bill Graham, and, for rock and roll, the difference was everything. Because Bill Graham, as he would hasten to tell anyone, was the best: the best promoter, the best concert master, the best at everything he touched—and, in the music business, there was little that he did not. He managed the most popular groups (Jefferson Airplane, the Grateful Dead, Santana), promoted the biggest concerts, held the lease on the most cavernous halls (the Fillmores East and West). The presence of his name alone—a "Bill Graham Presents" atop one of his patented posters—was an all-but-certain guarantee of talent and success. Bill Graham was not merely a man, but a presence, "a character," as Michael Lydon put it, "right out of a Harold Robbins novel." "You'll never see the 'Four Freak-Outs' in my place," he boasted. "I'm the best."

Let someone question that judgment, as Jann Wenner and his magazine did from time to time, and the results were fearsome. "Let me tell you something about that slimy . . . little paper . . . and that little cunt you work for," he stormed at one of Wenner's reporters, after the magazine had characterized his countenance as "reptilian." ". . . You tell that cunt to meet me . . . on television . . . on the radio . . . in the park. I'll bury him verbally. I want people to know what kind of man is telling them about Bill Graham. You tell him I want him out in the street at sunset and I'll be on the other end with a gun." A telephoned death threat? For Bill Graham, that was mild indeed.

He was, to put it mildly, not an easy man. There was an intensity about him and everything he did, from the way he looked—like a rubber-faced Sicilian prize fighter—to the way he talked—tough, usually out of the side of his mouth—to the way he mounted his concerts—flat-out, foot-to-the-floor, balls-to-the-wall. With Bill Graham, even lighting a cigarette could seem a ferocious act. Blunt, brutally direct, naturally profane, he did not suffer fools gladly. The trouble was, with the business he was in, Bill Graham encountered more than his fair share. He dealt with them the way he did with everything else: head on. Let someone have the temerity to act up at the Fillmore (where the sign at the entrance read: "The law requires you to be an adult to enter. The management expects you to act like one to remain"), and he would feel the strong right hand of Bill Graham at the scruff of his neck, throwing him out of the place personally. His approach to labor negotiations was similar. When, during a strike of light-show operators, an organizer told Graham, "You've got our money so you can't have our love," and accused him of "fuck[ing] over our heads with your emotional trips," Graham had to be physically restrained. "I apologize, motherfucker, that I'm a human being," he screamed, as a crowd of a hundred artists, musicians, and reporters looked on. "Fuck you, you stupid prick! Do you know what emotions are? Get up and work. Get up and sing. Get up and act. You think I'm an actor? You're full of shit, man. I have more fucking balls than you'll ever see. You want to challenge me in any way about emotions? You slimy little man . . . YOU SLIMY . . . LITTLE . . . MAN. Fuck you! FUCK YOU! Don't get peaceful with me. Don't you touch me."

Such performances did not make Graham San Francisco's most beloved citizen. So relentlessly casual a place was aghast at Graham's two-fisted New York mien. Still, it might have forgiven him, were it not for Graham's cardinal sin: he liked making money. Not only liked making it, but did so without apology, almost pridefully, talking about his business acumen in terms consciously designed to paint him blacker than he was. "I will *never* share my profit," he roared. "As long as I control the show, no one will ever tell me how to run it or what to do with my money. I have a house in Pacific Heights and an $8,000 Mercedes-Benz and it's mine. I *earned* it."

There were endless stories about Graham in San Francisco, most circulated by Graham himself. He loved to recall incidents like the evening when, per usual habit, he was checking the line outside the Fillmore. A young man in his twenties approached and demanded to be let in for free. When Graham refused, explaining he had bills to pay and a payroll to meet, the youth began exhorting the crowd: "You are going into this capitalist pig's place, that motherfucker rip-off bitch bastard. Music should be free, power to the people, the musicians want it to be free. It should be in the park, but people like Graham won't let them play in the park for free! He stole the music from us!" Graham smilingly gestured him aside, as if he had relented after all. Then, safely out of sight, Graham grabbed him by the shirt and lifted him off the ground. "I *give* you, you love me," he screamed into his face. "I don't give you, you *hate* me! Get away from me! Just get away from me!" For the more sensitive souls who might be appalled by such tactics, Graham's answer was the life-size photograph of himself that hung on his office wall: fist clenched, middle finger upcast.

Bill Graham grew up tough. Born in Berlin in 1929, the sixth child and first son of middle-class Jewish parents, his real name was Wolfgang Grajanka. "Bill Graham" was a name he picked out of a phone book in the United States. "I wish I had never changed it," he said sadly. "Bill Graham is a nothing name." His father was killed in an accident two days after his birth, and Graham was placed in an orphanage so his mother could work. The orphanage had an exchange program with another orphanage in France and, by chance, Graham was in Paris when war broke out in 1939. "When the Germans invaded the Jewish kids were told it was flight or the labor camps," he told Lydon. "So 64 of us with a teacher started walking to Marseilles—with a million other people." From Marseilles, they walked on to Lisbon, then shuttled by boat to Casablanca, Dakar, Bermuda, and, finally, New York. Two years had passed by then; only eleven of the children who had started out remained. Graham himself never saw his family again: they had been gassed at Belsen.

He was placed in an orphanage and eventually adopted by a family in the Bronx, where the neighborhood children teased him about his accent. Graham wound up on the losing end of dozens of fights. In self-defense, he taught himself accentless English. He also became handy with his fists and adept at crapshooting, talents which were of particular use as a rock promoter. "It was eat or be eaten," he said to Lydon. "From the time I was a kid, I thought that a person who says 'hello' is saying 'How can I use you?'"

When war broke out in Korea, Graham was drafted and went into combat. His record at discharge included a Bronze Star for valor, and two court-martials for insubordination. Back home, he attended City College, majored in business administration, and decided to make piles of money.

The business world proved to be a disappointment. After his first job—paymaster with a San Francisco railroad—Graham struck out for Hollywood, determined to become an actor. He landed a few minor roles and put together

enough cash to finance several expeditions to Europe. It
was obvious, though, that his film career was going nowhere. Returning to the States, he took a job as an office
manager for Allis Chalmers. As an administrator, he was as
efficient as he was ruthless. As a friend put it: "He'd make
the perfect leader for a death march." But he was also
bored. So in 1964 he quit his $18,000-a-year job and, for
$128 a month, signed on as business manager of the San
Francisco Mime Troupe, a loosely organized band of Bay
Area radicals who were mounting avant-garde and guerrilla
theater productions.

The experience was an unhappy one for all concerned.
Graham, the toughminded, apolitical loner, did not mesh
well with the free-form, undisciplined ways of the Mime
Troupe. After a bitter year on the job, Graham quit. As a
parting gesture, he staged a benefit for the Troupe and invited several rock bands to perform in a loft the Troupe
had rented. The benefit was an enormous success: more
than three thousand people crowded into a space meant for
six hundred. A month later, Graham staged another benefit
and, at the suggestion of Ralph Gleason, mounted it in
more commodious quarters—a ramshackle dance hall in the
heart of the Fillmore ghetto—the Fillmore Ballroom. Graham knew little about rock—he invited the Family Dog because he thought they were a dog act, and wound up listing
them as a band—but he knew opportunity when he saw it.
The night of the benefit, a double line of kids stretched
around the block. After even larger crowds showed up for
the Trips Festivals he organized for Kesey, Graham sat
down with a yellow legal pad, drew a line down the middle
of the page, and listed the pros and cons of becoming a rock
promoter. The pro side had one notation: a large dollar
sign.

Soon he took a lease on the Fillmore and began staging concerts every weekend. They were remarkable affairs, giant in scope, massive in undertaking, meticulous in planning, not unlike Bill Graham himself. He was everywhere—checking the lines, selling tickets, cleaning ashtrays, sweeping up, tinkering with lighting, adjusting the sound system, ensuring the food was hot and the drinks cold, fighting with dealers, throwing people out, yelling and screaming, twenty hours a day, seven days a week. It was a never-ending battle. If it was not his patrons who were causing trouble, then it was the groups; if not the groups, then the Hell's Angels; if not the Angels, then the cops; if not the cops, then the acidheads (who, before Graham thwarted them, planned to douse the water supply one weekend with LSD); if not the acidheads, then his neighbors. One notable antagonist was the local rabbi, who spearheaded a petition drive to close the Fillmore. "Mr. Graham's people," the rabbi mourned, "they're urinating on my Holy Walls." It was too much for Graham. "What the *fuck* do you know about persecution?" he bellowed. "My family is buried in the camp, I came over here—walked across fucking *Europe* to get here at the age of eleven—and you're telling me about persecution! You asshole!" "I didn't know," the rabbi spluttered. "Your name is Graham. You're a Jew? Sit down." The Fillmore stayed in business.

What a business it was. Under Graham's manic management, the Fillmore, and later the Fillmore West, an even larger downtown ballroom to which he moved following the riots in the wake of Martin Luther King's assassination, became not so much music halls as shrines to which the faithful came each week, plunked down their three dollars, and paid their worship in dance. By 1968, Graham was staging nine concerts a week, and taking in an estimated $50,000.

His poster business alone was said to be grossing $500,000 a year. None of which endeared him to the Haight. Graham couldn't have cared less. "All that bullshit about vibes, feelings," he complained to Lydon. "Who needs it? Act! Do something, that's what counts. They think they're really something with their 'Hey, man, what's happening, baby?'— a lousy imitation of 125th and Lenox, where they do it so good I'll book it. Those hippies got to learn that we live in a business world. When you're involved with the public, artistic creativity can only survive in a sound business framework. Don't *accept* it, but accept the *reality* of it. I can do that. I go down to city hall, I put on a suit, so I can have my places open, which will do a lot more for changing the world than going there like a freak. You want to rebel, great, but rebel *for* something. Hippies couldn't do that. 'Oh, man, like trip out, man.' Bullshit! They call that changing the world?"

Hippies were one subject on which Graham and Wenner were in full accord. Both detested them. In Wenner's vocabulary, "hippie" was the epithet of ultimate derision. "We don't want to do that," he would say. "That's *hippie*." His contempt carried over to the magazine. There were no psychedelic graphics to be found in *Rolling Stone*'s pages, no items from the Underground Press Service, no ads for sexual emporiums, all of which sustained what Wenner called "the hippie press." His own magazine, he insisted from the beginning, had to be distributed "legit, like *Time*," not hawked on street corners as the "hippie" papers were. Hippies did not work, did not want money, and Wenner, like Graham, believed devoutly in both. "We want to run on a solid, commercial basis," Wenner told a reporter, when *Rolling Stone* was still in its infancy. "We also want to make money. We are in business and are not ashamed of it." Not long after his words appeared, Bill Graham arranged a ceasefire.

They needed each other just then, for San Francisco rock was undergoing a dramatic transformation. It was no longer a freaky cottage industry, but a five-million-dollar-a-year enterprise. A second Fillmore had opened in New York in 1970, and there were ersatz San Francisco rock palaces springing up across the country. One after another, the city's musical talents—Country Joe and the Fish, Earth, Wind and Fire, Quicksilver Messenger Service, the Airplane, Blood, Sweat and Tears, the Steve Miller Band—were being snapped up by the record companies, often for advances double what were being offered a year before. There were still free concerts in the park, but now amidst the longhaired fans were equally long-haired talent scouts from the record companies. With so much at stake, the bands fought for a chance to appear. A good concert could mean a contract; a contract could mean a hit record; a record could mean a national concert tour; a tour could mean everything.

For Graham and his concerts and Wenner and his magazine, it was a golden moment. For those less able to cope, including some of the bands themselves, it was a nightmare.

Wenner's friend Chet Helms was one of the latter. It had been Helms, the "inheritor" of the Family Dog, whom Wenner had first gone to with the idea of starting a music magazine. Although their talks never came to fruition, the two of them had remained close. Helms himself had become one of the cornerstones of the San Francisco music scene and, for a time, even teamed with Graham, alternating weekends at the Fillmore. The relationship ended after a few weeks, when both men tried to sign the Paul Butterfield Blues Band. Helms understood that Butterfield was to be his, but Graham, resorting to a most un-California-like tac-

tic, set his alarm for six o'clock in the morning—9 A.M.
on the East Coast—called Butterfield's manager first, and
landed the act. Helms was stunned. "Man," he said wearily
to Graham, "that's not where it's at." With that, Helms dissolved the partnership and leased his own ballroom, the
Avalon.

Helms seemed to have everything going for him. The
Avalon was far more accessible than the Fillmore, and the
Haight was rooting for him to succeed. Easygoing, idealistic,
at times almost ethereal, Helms was more visionary than
businessman. "I was interested in the scene's potential for
revolution, for turning things upside down, for changing
values," he said to *Rolling Stone*. "My motivations? Put
very simply, I liked to dance and that was a very free space.
It's where my body and my soul felt free." Rather too free,
as it developed.

So large was Helms's circle of friends, so loath was he to
trouble them for admission, that some nights at the Avalon,
a thousand people would be in attendance, three of whom
had paid to get in. Sighed his friend Charlie Perry, "Chet
ran it not so much as a business, as a church. He threw
open the doors. He invited one and all." The Haight loved
him for it, as deeply as they hated Graham, but love was not
paying the rent. Before long, Helms was hurtling toward
bankruptcy. "TCB, Chet, TCB," Janis Joplin, his old girlfriend, yelled at him—Take Care of Business. Helms responded by bursting into tears.

Graham, meanwhile, was eating him alive. Not only was
the Fillmore run more professionally, but the big-name acts
on which Helms depended preferred to play for Graham,
tantrums and all. His shows were better produced, drew
bigger crowds, and, unlike with Helms, there was never any
question that they'd be paid. After a few months, it became

a contest to see which would do in Helms first—bankruptcy or the law. The authorities won by a hair. Following numerous complaints about noise, Helms lost his permit to operate and was forced to close up shop. He moved his operations to a seaside amusement park some distance from town, and proceeded to lose even more money. Subsequent expansion to Denver finally brought his career to an end. Some of his partners in the Denver operation reportedly siphoned off most of the gate receipts, and a number of bands went unpaid. Helms himself was left $85,000 in debt. Distraught and disillusioned, he dropped out of sight for several years. When he reemerged in the middle Seventies, he was selling antiques out of the back of a pickup truck. "I found," he said, "that it is not enough to get up and make a statement."

The experience of the Grateful Dead, intimates of Graham and Wenner both, was nearly as harrowing.

The Dead were San Francisco's sentimental favorites. Other bands might sell more records and play to bigger crowds, but none better embodied the city's all-together-now spontaneity. "We're just interested in getting crazy," smiled their bushy-bearded leader, Jerry Garcia. "We dropped out, essentially, of what could be called a normal career in music." But by the Haight's standards, the Dead were doing just fine. While other bands were racking up tens of thousands on tour, the Dead were doing free concerts in the park. "Even if I were being paid five bucks a week," Garcia shrugged, "I'd still be doing what I am doing." That seemed to go for the rest of the Dead's 150-member "family" as well. In their rambling Victorian house in the Haight, they passed their days fooling with their instruments and playing host to the dozens of fans—"Deadheads," as they were known—who dropped by to chat, swig a beer, and, if the mood was mellow, share a joint. They were, as one critic put it, "a living hippie monument."

They had come on the scene in the early Sixties, as a folk group playing in small clubs around Stanford University. There, Ken Kesey heard them and introduced them to acid. Soon they turned in their banjos for electric guitars, switched to rock and moved to the Haight, where no less than Augustus Owsley Stanley became their patron. He designed a gargantuan sound system for them, a hundred speakers and amplifiers in all, an assemblage so large it required two trucks to transport it. Owsley himself was the only person capable of operating the rig, which made for complications since Owsley was stoned most of the time. To rectify this condition, Owsley brewed up a special batch of acid which, it was claimed, not only made the user high, but allowed him to function at the same time. With the Dead, it seemed to make no difference. Their music, a melange of rock, folk, blues, and country, fairly exploded out of their instruments. There was no telling when it would end—"Alligator," one of their most famous songs, could run to two hours—or when it would begin. They could be standing on stage half an hour or more, quietly tuning up their instruments, then all at once erupt into a cacophony of wailing sound. With the Dead, it was all a matter of feel, of sensing when, for reasons no one could explain, the time was right and everything in harmony. They were the perfect masters of the moment.

As businessmen, they were something else again. Graham was their manager, but they were unhappy with the way he was conducting some of his affairs, notably the Fillmore. With several other groups, the Dead decided to break Graham's monopoly by opening a ballroom of their own, the Carousel, in downtown San Francisco. The Carousel was as loose as the Fillmore was tight. The Dead provided office space free to various community groups, including the Panthers, and admitted one and all alike, junkies, dealers, Hell's Angels, and pillheads of various configurations. Brawling was common, arrests frequent. On one occasion, a group showed up and paid their admission with parts of a freshly butchered lamb. Another time, some overly enthusiastic music lovers built a small bonfire in the middle of the hall. The Carousel folded after thirteen weeks. The end came when a prankster affixed the words "Free Cunt" to the outside marquee. The cops arrived within hours and, on their heels, Bill Graham to take over the lease.

With the collapse of the Carousel in 1969 and the Avalon a year later, Graham now had the field entirely to himself. Wenner was not at all happy. Helms had been a friend; so, too, were the members of what Wenner called "the good old Grateful Dead." Now, thanks to Graham and their own foibles, they had been scattered in disarray. It seemed to Wenner that Graham was going for the jugular. It worried him. Virtually everything Graham had touched had been spectacularly successful. If, as persistent rumors had it, he entered rock journalism, the results could be perilous. Soon Wenner declared open warfare. Beginning in 1970, issue after issue carried predictions of Graham's imminent demise. All manner of plagues were said to be about to befall him: the city licensing authorities, a rebellion of his own performers, even Howard Johnson's, which, in a particularly dark moment, was said to be laying plans to replace the Fillmore with an ice cream emporium. None of the stories turned out to be true. For better or worse, Jann Wenner and rock and roll were stuck with Bill Graham.

It was an uneasy armistice which did not last long. Invariably, Graham did something to start the battle all over

again. A major provocation was his former management of
the Jefferson Airplane. The city never quite forgave Graham for what happened to the Airplane—dissolution and
disappearance—because the Airplane was no ordinary rock
group: they were a San Francisco institution. They had
been the first of the city's groups to sign with a major record
company, the first to record a million seller, the first to cut a
gold album. At one point during the Summer of Love, two
of their singles were among the Top Ten simultaneously,
and one of their albums was the second-best-selling LP in
the country, topped only by the Beatles' *Sgt. Pepper's.*
Several of their songs—including "White Rabbit" and
"Someone to Love"—were already Sixties classics. Other
bands wrote songs in tribute to them, and their slogan—
"Jefferson Airplane Loves You"—sprouted on buttons and
bumper stickers from coast to coast.

The Airplane's music was tight, hard-edged, searing.
Their lyrics captured it all: the alienation, the fascination
with drugs. "It doesn't matter what the lyrics say, or who
sings them," lead singer Grace Slick told an interviewer.
"They're all the same. They say, 'Be free—free in love, free
in sex.'"

The group was formed in 1965 by Marty Balin, a former
actor and folk club proprietor. There were six members at
first: Balin, lead guitarist Paul Kantner, vocalist Signe Toly,
bassist Jack Casady, Jorma Kaukonen, a guitarist of local
renown, and Skip Spencer, a guitarist Balin reassigned to
drums "because he looked like a drummer." Ralph Gleason,
who heard one of their first performances, waxed so enthusiastic in his review that representatives of every major record company in the country flew to San Francisco the next
day to sign them up. Then, in 1966, just as they were coming to prominence, the group underwent a shake-up. Signe

Toly was dropped and replaced with Grace Slick, former fashion model, Finch College graduate (she had been a classmate of Tricia Nixon's), and lead singer with a recently disbanded group called the Great Society. Grace's presence was electric. "Her voice," Charlie Perry wrote, "had an element of icy fury; when she reached for a high note, it was as if she was zeroing in on something in order to throttle it."

Her antics were as notable as her talent. During one outdoor performance in New York, Grace casually took off her blouse and, topless, licked a Popsicle. In Chicago, she responded to a call from the audience to "show us your chastity belt," by hiking her skirt to reveal that she wore none, nor, for that matter, anything else. But her most publicized stunt took place when Tricia Nixon invited all her former classmates to the White House for tea. Grace showed up in the company of Abbie Hoffman, only to be barred on grounds of being a "security risk." Grace was deeply disappointed. In her handbag was a large hit of acid, which she had planned to dump into the tea. Even her private life was a performance. Although married, she conducted a highly visible affair with Kantner and, when she became pregnant, announced that she would name the child "god." "Some people have animals around," she said nonchalantly. "I like animals, but I thought I'd try a human being, because they have more happening."

They were loose, Grace and the Airplane, as free as San Francisco itself. "We're not performing, we're making love," said Kantner. "The audience is our broad, and the stage is our bed." Then, in 1968, they met Bill Graham. Graham proposed to make them the biggest group in the country and, for a time, he succeeded. Within months, the Airplane's price for a single performance rose to $7,500, the highest commanded by any American band; in a single year, the group grossed more than $1 million. But success came at a price. Graham had them performing almost non-stop, one city after another, night after night—a total of 150 separate dates in the space of twelve months. After a year, they were worn out. They were also furious with Graham, who issued nearly as many commands as he booked engagements. When they complained, he protested that he was only protecting their interests. From a strictly business standpoint, Graham's dicta were hard to fault. But, as with everything, he carried them to excess. As one member of the band put it: "You always had to prove things to Bill, fight to convince him of everything." Finally, after eighteen months, the Airplane fired him.

The band was never the same after that. Their records kept selling, though with rare exceptions, not in the same numbers as before. Meanwhile, the Airplane indulged themselves with a variety of expensive toys. Grace bought an $18,000 Aston-Martin, and spent another $2,000 for a medieval torture rack, complete with winches, screws, and chains, which she had converted into a dining table and installed in a pillared Greek Revival mansion once owned by Caruso. Another band member contented himself with a small tugboat. After a year or so of Lear-jet living, the money began running out. At one point, $30,000 in debt, the band was forced to cut commercials for White Levi's to bail themselves out. The Airplane insisted the compromise was only temporary. They were determined, they said, to bring rock "back to the community," eliminate the commercialism, and, with their music, "spread the revolution." It never happened. The tension from years of performing finally took its toll. Individual members of the band were busted or went their separate ways. Kantner and Slick kept the group—now rechristened "Jefferson Starship"—alive, but the sound was different: angrier, slicker, devoid of the raw energy that had driven thousands to ecstatic frenzy.

Graham's doing or not, the crash of the Airplane was only the latest in a series of happenings, most beyond his control, that, in time, would lead to the demise of the city's music. By 1970 the big bands were gone, spending weeks, sometimes months at a stretch on tours away from town. In their absence, the music suffered. It was a fragile sound, vulnerable to sudden tremors, like San Francisco itself. Cut off from its roots, it began to crumble. Records could reproduce "the sound of San Francisco"—a phrase which an alert promoter had taken care to copyright—but they could not duplicate the feeling of what it had been like to be in Golden Gate Park on a sunny afternoon, or on the dance floor of the Fillmore on a foggy night, head full of acid, lights flashing, music roaring. There was no sense of community in a recording studio or at a stadium-sized concert a thousand miles from Haight Street. Jerry Garcia's proclamation—"Our music is only incidental to the celebration of life" —had tangible meaning in San Francisco. Said in New York, or for that matter, Des Moines, it sounded like an ad campaign. And therein lay the conundrum. For it was to New York and Des Moines and dozens of places in between that the music had to go, if it were to grow. It bothered artists like Garcia—"This is show business," he groused one night on tour. "It sucks,"—but there was nothing they could do. Their contracts bound them. Their ambition compelled them. It was too late to stop now.

To read *Rolling Stone,* nothing had changed; the grosses were only getting bigger. The "good old Grateful Dead" were still "the most beautiful band in the world." Jefferson Airplane, for all its troubles, had a "new smash," and, to all appearances, was "feeling no pain." True, Steve Miller had suddenly disappeared from town and Moby Grape was suing its former manager and Country Joe and the Fish had broken up and the Dead had blown all their money, and, yes, Led Zeppelin were destroying hotel rooms in frustration and one of The Who had defecated on stage to express his contempt, but in *Rolling Stone*'s retelling the incidents were no more than the "Random Notes" that Wenner headlined them. Pain was part of the business. "Success is a funny thing," the magazine quoted Graham as saying. "Some survive it gracefully, some don't." It was that simple. Besides, there were compensations . . . like the girls.

They were part of the traveling kit, like a guitar or an amp, and only slightly more animate. "Groupies," they called them: girls who got meaning for their lives from the bands they sexually serviced. "It's like collecting baseball cards," one lissome groupie explained matter-of-factly. "You know, like cutting notches in your belt for each cat you've balled."

They came in all shapes and sizes. There were solitary "star-fuckers," aloof and haughty, who slept only with the top acts; "good-time girls" who made it with anyone even remotely connected with the music; and still other groupies who did not sleep with the groups at all, but merely stayed on hand to do their bidding. Some groupies, like the GTO's (Girls Together Outrageously), traveled in formalized packs, gave out calling cards, and, in time, achieved a media celebrity of their own. There were also bizarre specialists, like "The Twins," who only worked in tandem, or the notorious "Plaster Casters," two Chicago girls who memorialized each encounter by making a plaster cast of a star's most notable sexual asset. And then there was the groupie who sent a letter to Jerry Garcia: "I want to know all about you," she wrote. "I want to know what kind of woman you prefer, I want to fuck with you when I get to San Francisco." She was eight years old.

So completely were the groupies taken for granted that, aside from a few songs (such as the Rolling Stones' "Stray Cat Blues") no one had ever bothered to publicly document their unusual avocation. *Rolling Stone* changed all that.

The idea of doing a story had been Baron Wolman's. Wolman, the magazine's chief photographer, had been with it from the beginning, and in that time had become a sensitive documentarian of the rock scene. Short, leprechaun-like in appearance, he possessed a shy, reserved manner that made it easy for him to slip between the cracks of situations and, once there, see things that others, including his boss, missed. So it was with the groupies. He had been traveling with various bands throughout most of 1968, and had befriended a number of the girls. A few had even offered him a taste of their manifold delights. Instead, Wolman asked them to pose. When he returned to San Francisco and showed the pictures to Wenner, accompanying them with a colorful narrative of some of their more notable exploits, Wenner immediately assigned a major story. Within days the project was under way.

The final article, compiled by Burks and reporters Jerry Hopkins and Paul Nelson, was nothing if not exhaustive. Fifteen thousand words long, it named names, cited preferences, recounted incidents, awarded ratings. "You look for certain things in certain towns," the magazine quoted singer Jimmy Page as saying. "Chicago, for example, is notorious for sort of two things going at once—balling two chicks or three—in combination acts." Groupies provided their own evaluations. Jimi Hendrix, it developed, was a particular favorite. "He balled seven different chicks in the space of three hours," Henri remembered. "Each chick knew what was happening, but it didn't seem to matter. He was Jimi Hendrix." Steve Miller took a more detached view. "They're on a whole fantasy trip," he observed, "and maybe they never see *you* through the whole fantasy, but that's groovy. Most rock and roll people are on a fantasy trip anyway, so it's natural that groupies and musicians should be drawn together. They're the same kind of people." By contrast, the girls seemed sad, almost wistful. "Being a groupie is like borrowing a series of lives from people and thinking you can be them," one young woman said poignantly. "Even when you're balling some cat, you're not really balling him and he's not really balling you, it's really just two different people on different planes, with different needs and different fantasies." On balance, however, everyone seemed to be getting everything he or she was after. "If you're a hit with groupies, you'll sell 15,000 records in L.A. alone," Frank Zappa, leader of the Mothers of Invention and a well-traveled expert on the subculture, told the magazine. "And it's good for the girls. Eventually most of them are going to get married to regular workers—office workers, factory workers, just regular guys. Those guys are lucky to get girls like these, girls who have attained some level of sexual adventurousness. It's good for the whole country. These guys will be happier, they'll do their jobs better, and the economy will reflect it. Everybody will be happier." Concluded *Rolling Stone:* "In short, a happy nation sucks."

There was an expectant buzz in the *Rolling Stone* office as the groupies issue was being readied for press. The article was the magazine's most ambitious undertaking to date, and the staff were excited, especially Wenner. "If this doesn't get noticed," he announced, "nothing will." But not even Wenner was prepared for the sensation the groupies issue provoked. In most cities the magazine was an immediate sell-out, and orders for additional copies poured into San Francisco. Then an unexpected piece of intelligence: *Time* was rushing into print with its own story on groupies— and the reporting was largely being lifted from *Rolling Stone*. Wenner, then in New York on a business trip, was delighted. "In 'the world,'" he crowed, *"Time* is the real thing . . . the kind of thing you find in the dentists' offices." His enthusiasm palled when he learned that *Time's* editors were not planning to credit *Rolling Stone*. Worse still, *Time* was running an accompanying music piece about guitarist Johnny Winter saying he had been discovered after a favorable review in "one of the underground papers." That paper, as it happened, was Wenner's own. "We gotta do something," he told Wolman.

The next thing Wolman knew, he and Wenner were in the offices of the New York *Times* and Wenner was writing out a check for $7,000, purchase price for the back page of the newspaper. Wenner composed the ad personally. Topped with one of Wolman's groupie pictures, it declared: "If you are a corporate executive trying to understand what is happening to youth today, you cannot afford to be without *Rolling Stone*. If you are a student, a professor, a parent, this is your life because you already know that rock and roll is more than just music; it is the energy center of the new culture and the youth revolution."

Wenner could barely contain himself waiting for the first edition of the *Times* to appear. He and Wolman wolfed down a congratulatory dinner at the Four Seasons, then bolted for the nearest newsstand. Jann ripped open the paper and read aloud the words he had written. "This calls for a celebration," he announced, snatched a dozen more copies, and climbed into the limousine he had rented for the occasion. They returned to his Fifth Avenue hotel suite and passed the rest of the night drinking champagne and plastering the walls with copies of the ad, giggling and joking all the while. "This is just the beginning," Wenner promised Wolman. "Just the beginning."

5

Super-Fan

Henri, the office groupie, couldn't stop laughing. Jann Wenner, the expert on groupies—it was just too funny. "Jann," she giggled, when her boss, triumphant, returned from New York, "you're the biggest groupie in the world!"

Even Wenner had to laugh. It was true. He was super-fan. No one liked rock better than he did. No one believed in it so devoutly. And, certainly, no one got higher, or felt such a rush, from hanging out with the stars, tasting their life and sharing their secrets. It was good for business, of course. The better Wenner knew his sources, the better-informed *Rolling Stone* would be. But Wenner's involvement with the music and the people who made it went beyond editorial considerations. There were moments when his editors, Burks especially, suspected that Wenner had started *Rolling Stone* simply so he could meet his gods. He was always talking about them, forever recounting how Boz Scaggs, the San Francisco rock-blues singer whose album Wenner was producing, had told him this, or Artie Garfunkel, a frequent tennis partner, had told him that. The staff joked about Jann's new friends, and no one with more relish than Gleason. "If Boz Scaggs farted in a windstorm," he cracked, "Jann would have it on the cover." Gleason was less amused when Wenner began living like a rock star, and in the case of the dark velvet suit and ruffled silk shirt he sometimes wore, dressing like one as well. Wenner was unconcerned. As if to prove it, he stayed at the Stanhope during business trips to New York, in the same suite the stars used, and tooled around town in a silver-gray Cadillac limo favored by the Rolling Stones, the one in which, as a courtesy, the driver provided the dope free.

He was enjoying himself immensely. The *Times* ad had made an important impression. A magazine that could afford to spend $7,000 on impulse was obviously no underground sheet. Here was a publication to be taken seriously, seriously enough in any case for both *Time* and *Newsweek* to feature Wenner in major stories within two months of the ad. "I suppose you could say I'm a *wunderkind*," Wenner boasted to one of the reporters—an accurate enough description, even if Wenner mispronounced it. He had ambitious plans on the drawing board. Soon, he revealed to *Time, Rolling Stone* would launch a British edition. What made the news all the more delicious was that Wenner's partner in the venture would be, as he put it, "my friend" Mick Jagger, leader of the Rolling Stones.

His editors never forgot the glow on Wenner's face the day he returned from meeting Jagger for the first time. "He was like a little kid who had just gotten everything he wanted for Christmas," remembered Burks. "He kinda floated in, giggling and smirking, like he was in the possession of some great secret. I'd never seen him happier. When I asked him what had happened, he said, 'Well, I finally did it.' 'Did what?' I asked him. 'Met Mick,' he said. He didn't stop talking about it for days."

It was hard to blame him. Jagger was a rock star of truly mythic dimensions. For a longtime fan like Wenner to meet him was extraordinary enough; to know him was all the more remarkable. But to be his partner—for Wenner this was the ultimate. Said Burks, "He was delirious."

For the next few months, Wenner spent much of his time in London, working out details of the new edition and basking in Jagger's company. They were heady times, filled with equally heady adventures. One of the most memorable occurred one morning as they were coming into the city in Jagger's chauffeured Rolls. Suddenly one of London's more notorious narcs pulled them over. Wenner panicked. He and Jagger had been sharing a joint, which now reposed, half smoked, in Jagger's ashtray. But Jagger was a man of considerable cool. Ordering the car's windows rolled up and the doors locked, he casually consumed the evidence while the stupefied lawman looked on in impotent rage. Such a man was impossible to resist.

No one knew it better than Jagger. A shrewd, calculating businessman, he was well aware of the benefits to be had from good relations with the trade press, and when Wenner had broached the idea of a partnership, he had gladly agreed. The deal made sense for both men. According to the terms of the agreement, Jagger was to put up most of the financing, while Wenner would contribute his editorial expertise, the *Rolling Stone* name, and copy lifted from the American edition. There was only one hook—a radical difference in style. It was apparent at the magazine's first staff meeting. "Okay, okay," said Wenner, calling everyone to order. "We're not here just to drink Mick Jagger's wine." "Hold it," Jagger shot back, "that's exactly why we're here. To drink my wine."

All went well at first. They leased luxurious offices on

trendy Hanover Square and, with great fanfare, launched
the magazine with a champagne christening party. Wenner
returned to San Francisco bubbling with optimism. But
trouble soon developed. Wenner had been counting on
Jagger to provide the magazine with overall guidance and
inspiration. However, after a first flush of enthusiasm,
Jagger lost interest. Other projects were also claiming his
attention, among them a Western in which he was to star,
directed by Jean-Luc Godard. When Jagger flew off to Aus-
tralia to begin location filming, *British Rolling Stone* started
coming apart. The staff, it developed, was more in Jagger's
mold than Wenner's. Disdainful of Wenner's nose-to-the-
grindstone business style, they were even less taken by
Wenner himself. One incident, recounted gleefully by the
Britishers, happened the day Wenner, in the company of
one of his editors, went on a shopping tour of Carnaby
Street. At one point Wenner turned to his companion and
said, clearly referring to himself, "There's not much for a
pop star to do in London except go and buy clothes, is
there?" For their part, the Brits turned out to be a playful
group, at times recklessly so. During the first office party for
advertisers, someone mischievously spiked the punch with
LSD, and two of the advertisers' wives wound up in the hospital. Matters were not much better on the editorial side. In
Jagger's absence, the office became a social center for London's hippies, unemployed musicians, and, as one editor
noted, "every two-bit hustler from here to Hong Kong."
John Goodchild, an English writer whom Wenner hired to
help shore up the enterprise, said later, "We worked two
and a half days a week, and the rest of the time it was just a
party. Sort of like Haight-Ashbury—pretty together, but totally irresponsible."

Watching these developments from afar, Wenner did

nothing at first. Every magazine underwent a rough shake-down cruise, and he assumed that once *British Rolling Stone* had completed its own, the quality would improve. When instead it worsened, Wenner issued a steady stream of increasingly exasperated letters. Soon the London staff began devising plans to get rid of him altogether. As Good-child put it: "It got to the point where there was no rela-tionship between Jann and the staff other than contempt."

The rebellion finally snapped Wenner's patience, and he fired off a letter to Jane Nicholson, *British Rolling Stone*'s editor.

"Your business practices are appalling," he wrote. ". . . Is this some kind of joke? . . . You're a bunch of amateurs and kids playing at the game of publishing . . . taking a ride on the established reputation of *Rolling Stone* and Mick's bank account . . . Suspend operations and payroll . . . have a chartered accountant audit the books . . . I hope that Mick and I will have a solution . . . restructuring from top to bottom."

The staff was in no mood to be ordered around. Defying Wenner's directives, they prepared to publish another issue, only to have Wenner shut off their bank account and with-hold the negatives from the American edition. Finally, after heated trans-Atlantic threats, Wenner relented and allowed the issue to go to press. It was the last that ever did. Even as the final copies were being published, Wenner folded *British Rolling Stone*.

He had few regrets. If his ego had been damaged, his treasury had not, since, per their agreement, Jagger had to cover all the losses. Nonetheless, his friendship with Jagger was still intact, and so was his appetite for celebrity. If any-thing, meeting Jagger had only increased it. Wenner was now determined to complete his acquaintance with rock's Holy Trinity: Dylan first, then the Beatles.

Reporters had for years been trying to get Dylan to talk; none of them had succeeded. Since breaking his neck in a near-fatal motorcycle accident in 1966, he had become a total recluse. Some stories had it that he was dead, others that he was confined to a psychiatric institution or had been rendered a vegetable. One of his fans, an eccentric Yippie and self-proclaimed "garbologist" named A. J. Weberman, had gone so far as to root through Dylan's trash looking for clues to his status. The yield was meager—a few unfinished songs, a half-written letter to Johnny Cash, instructions to his stock broker, a sizable collection of dog feces, and a number of back issues of *Rolling Stone*. So Dylan was alive, housebreaking a dog and reading Jann Wenner's magazine. But what had become of the rest of him? Who was Bob Dylan now?

The man whose music had influenced more young Americans than any other's, who seemed himself the embodiment of the Sixties ethos, was, deliberately, a figure of myth and mystery. Rail thin, intense, brooding, he had the fragile, waiflike look of a man not long for the world, a man who perhaps did not belong in it in the first place. "I see things other people don't," he once said about himself. "I dissolve myself into situations where I am invisible."

Dylan worked hard at maintaining his invisibility. A wall of faithful retainers and secretaries shielded him from inquisitors, and warned off the more persistent threats with lawsuits. Dylan himself leaked a series of details about his background designed to confuse and obscure. At various times he said he was born in Oklahoma, was an orphan, had frequently run away from home, worked as an itinerant carny, played bass for Bobby Vee, was Bobby Vee himself—none of which was true.

The actual facts were more mundane: born, Duluth, Minnesota, May 24, 1941; place of rearing, Hibbing, Minnesota, a small mining town; parents, very much alive, members of the middle class; adolescence, unexceptional; education, University of Minnesota (dropped out); career ladder, playing in college coffee houses, seeking the bright lights of New York, playing in Village coffee houses, becoming acquainted with Woody Guthrie, being spotted by a talent scout, then a meteoric rise to fame and fortune. Even his name was a cover. It actually was Robert Allen Zimmerman; "Bob Dylan" was a name he had made up in 1958 while playing in small folk clubs around the University of Minnesota. Was he Jewish? That, like so much else about him, was something about which Bob Dylan, nee Robert Zimmerman, was purposely vague. "Like Jay Gatsby, he arose out of some Platonic Conception of himself," wrote one student of his music. "He created himself, which is not unusual, but he was much more extreme than most of us; he created himself, name and all, from scratch and rejected all the elements in his past except those which fit into his carefully constructed personal mythology."

To probe behind that mythology was never easy. Dylan was always covering his tracks. Was he, as his reputation insisted, the greatest protest singer since Woody Guthrie? Not according to the man whose ballads, especially "Blowin' in the Wind," were on every civil rights worker's lips. "Hey, hey, news can sell, right?" he said mockingly to his friend and mother-protector Joan Baez. "You know me, I knew people would buy that kind of shit, right? I was never into that stuff." The more his fans insisted he *was* "into that stuff," the more determined Dylan became to break free of it, only to create an altogether new and, in its way, even more binding legend, the legend of rock and roll.

He had been thinking of making the change for some time. His success bored him. As he looked at his career in 1965, there seemed nowhere left to go. In a gloomy, depressed mood, he flew to England to do a concert tour, and there witnessed the success groups like the Byrds were having singing his songs to a rock beat. Their audiences were immense. But it was how they behaved that impressed Dylan most: where his folk singing evoked quiet reverence, the rockers drove people to frenzy. The potential for violence fascinated him. "That music," he said later, "is the only true valid death you can feel today off a record player."

When Dylan came home, he set about writing a different kind of song, rock in beat, cynical in tone. The first was "Like a Rolling Stone":

> *Once upon a time, you dressed so fine*
> *You threw the bums a dime*
> *In your prime,*
> *didn't you?*
> *People'd call, say 'beware doll, you're bound to fall'*
> *You thought*
> *they were all, kiddin' you*
> *You used to laugh about,*
> *Everybody that was hangin' out*
> *Now you don't talk so loud*
> *Now you don't feel so proud*
> *About having to be scrounging for your next meal.*
> *How does it feel*
> *To be without a home*
> *To be a complete unknown*
> *Like a rolling stone?*

"It wasn't called anything, just a rhythm on paper," Dylan later told writer Jules Siegel. "All about my steady hatred that was directed at some point that was honest. In the end, it wasn't hatred. Revenge, that's a better word. It was telling someone they didn't know what it's all about, and they were lucky. . . . Seeing someone in the pain they were bound to meet up with. I wrote it. I didn't fail. It was straight."

The new Dylan made his first public appearance at the Newport Folk Festival in 1965. There were gasps from the crowd when he walked out on stage, no longer the Village hobo but the London mod: black leather jacket, black slacks, dress shirt and pointed black boots with Chelsea heels. The electric guitar he was carrying was the final profanation. He paused only a moment, then struck into the first verses of "Like a Rolling Stone." "No one clapped and the boos and the hecklers' shouts rang through the Festival site," his biographer, Anthony Scaduto, reported. "Go back to the Sullivan Show!" someone shouted, and laughter rolled up from the audience. Dylan turned and stalked off. Some who were there behind the scenes said there were tears in his eyes as he made his way backstage, and tears in the eyes of Pete Seeger, who was standing off to one side while rock desecrated the hallowed Folk Festival ground. "He wasn't so much hurt as puzzled," Mike Bloomfield, one of the bluesmen who played with Dylan said later. "He couldn't figure it out. Here he had a hit record, and they were booing him."

After Newport, Dylan retreated into his shell more than ever. He moved to a country estate near Woodstock, in upstate New York, cut himself off from all but his closest friends, and married. Then came the motorcycle accident. The reports from Woodstock said that he had mellowed out during his recuperation and isolation. Much of the former rough-edged cynicism had been softened; even his voice had changed: it was more melodic, smoother now and easier, as, it was said, was Bob Dylan himself.

Such were the stories. Few people knew whether they were true. No outsider had come near Dylan in almost two years. It was a situation Jann Wenner meant to change.

He had been trying to talk to Dylan since *Rolling Stone*'s beginning. He bombarded Dylan's office with letters, calls and personal appeals. But always the answer was the same: Dylan was not giving interviews; however, he would consider the request. Dylan had been considering it now for almost a year, and there was still no word about when, if ever, he would talk. That did not dampen Wenner's enthusiasm. A talk with Bob Dylan, a conversation with the master himself, was, in the world of rock journalism, the ultimate scoop. To have his words in *Rolling Stone*—the magazine that had taken its very name from one of his songs—was an event worth waiting for. So it was that when Wenner, in the company of Boz Scaggs, stopped over in New York in November 1968 on his way to a recording session in Alabama, he made yet another call to Dylan's office. But this time the response was more promising. Dylan was in town, Wenner was advised. Indeed, he might stop by the next day.

Wenner was still asleep when a heavy knock on his hotel room door broke the early morning quiet. Groggily, he glanced at the bedside clock and registered shock at the indecent hour: 8 A.M. Still naked, he stumbled out of bed to discover who had roused him. He threw open the door, and there, standing before him, looking slightly nonplussed, was Bob Dylan. Wenner slipped on his pants, and for the next half hour, while Scaggs, unimpressed, dozed in the next room, they talked—about whether Dylan would agree to talk officially. Dylan had certain conditions—he wanted to see a transcript of his interview and personally edit it before it went into print—and Wenner readily accepted. "I got him," he announced happily to his friends in San Francisco. "I got Dylan."

Indeed he had. The interview that took place eight months later was, in terms of content, unremarkable. Dylan was his most laconic self, by turns elliptical, vague, seemingly bored by the earnestness of Wenner's queries, which he seldom answered in more than a sentence or two. All the same, "Dylan Speaks: The Incredible *Rolling Stone* Interview," as Wenner bannered the piece, was a publicity sensation. Wenner gloried in the attention. Not only did the story improve *Rolling Stone*'s fortunes—advertising and circulation both spurted in the weeks to follow—but it increased his own stature as well. If there was any lingering doubt that Jann Wenner was the most influential young publisher in the land, talking to Bob Dylan had removed it.

One thing had not changed: Jann Wenner remained very much the star-struck fan. Dylan had sensed it during their interview, and had toyed cruelly with him:

Wenner: Many people—writers, college students, college writers—all felt tremendously affected by your music and what you're saying in the lyrics.

Dylan: Did they?

Wenner: Sure. They felt it had a particular relevance to their lives . . . I mean, you must be aware of the way people come on to you.

Dylan: Not entirely. Why don't you explain it to me?

Wenner: I guess if you reduce it to its simplest terms, the expectations of your audience—the portion of your audience I'm familiar with—feels that you have the answer.

Dylan finally brought the fencing to an end. "I play
music, man," he told Wenner. "I write songs . . . I'm just
one person, doing what I do. Trying to get along . . . staying out of people's hair, that's all."

Dylan's coy modesty irritated Wenner. If Dylan himself
did not know his rightful place in the rock firmament,
Wenner certainly did. By his reckoning, a figure like Dylan
could no more be "just a singer," than could rock be "just
music." A superstar of Dylan's dimensions was to be something more: "The most visible and articulate voice of a
movement trucking along toward something—socially, politically, spiritually, whatever—but hopefully something better
than we started with," as Wenner put it in an introduction
to an anthology including the Dylan interview. When Dylan
refused to accept the role, Wenner wrote it off as a perverse
expression of the singer's "egomania." He continued to re-
vere the myth itself.

His staff was more cynical. "Star-fucker," some of them
began calling their boss after the interview: a journalistic
groupie on the make. "The girls screw 'em and Jann chats
with them," muttered Wolman, who was fast growing tired
of the rock scene. "Same thing, when you get right down to
it." But there was nothing calculating about Wenner's awe
of stars like Jagger and Dylan. His adulation was as genuine
as it was unabashed. "For most of us who have grown up
since World War II," he wrote in his introduction to the
Dylan piece, "rock and roll provided the first revolutionary
insight into who we are and where we are in this country;
our first discovery that behind the plasticized myth of what
we had been told was the United States, behind the Eisen-
hower/Walt Disney/Doris Day façade, was (damn!) a
real America: funky, violent, deeply divided, despairing,
exultant." Wenner meant every word of it. He owed a debt

to rock. Because of rock, he had an identity and a purpose, something nothing else had been able to give him. About many things, including the people who were close to him, he could be cold-blooded and ruthless. But in the face of rock, his resolve and, at times, his common sense, dissolved, and he was, once again—*oh, wow*—the fan. And for the fan, there was only one accomplishment left: the Beatles.

There was just one problem. By the time Wenner had sufficient fame to interview them, they were the Beatles no longer, but four separate musicians who had gone their highly disparate ways—George to eclectic Indian mysticism; Ringo to contented househusbandry; Paul to marriage and a group of his own; John to Dadaesque surrealism. The unthinkable had happened: the Beatles had broken up.

It was a by now familiar rock saga. Young musicians rise from obscurity, meet crafty manager, change image, make millions, feel pressures, become jealous, fall out. Essentially, that is what had happened with the Beatles. By 1968, they had broken every record, set every trend, tried every trip imaginable—acid, vegetarianism, mysticism, meditation. All the worlds had been conquered. There was no place left to go except down—and out.

The strains had begun to show as early as 1965, a year after their arrival in America and the launching of Beatlemania, a time when the Beatles were at the pinnacle of their fame. An album released that year, "Rubber Soul," was counted by many critics as the Beatles' best. But the songs on it showed that the legendary collaboration between Paul McCartney and John Lennon, an alliance once so close that Wenner had speculated that they were homosexuals, had begun to fray. As critic Greil Marcus noted for *Rolling Stone*, "Consistently, John's songs described struggle, while Paul's denied it; Paul wrote and sang the A sides, John the B's . . . John was already cultivating his rebellion and his anger; Paul was making his decision for Pop." Other things began to happen. For one, the Beatles tried acid, inadvertently the first time, when a dentist friend of George's slipped it into their coffee at a dinner party, but later more determinedly, and no one more so than John, who later claimed to have taken "hundreds of trips." Acid divided the Beatles, with John and George on the users' side, Paul and Ringo on the other. In the middle, keeping the peace and making the deals, was their manager, Brian Epstein, the former record store owner who had discovered them, when they were still wearing black leather jackets and calling themselves "The Silver Beatles." Epstein had cleaned up their act, dressed them in matching mod suits, given them their mop-top hairstyle, and, by dint of genius, energy and public relations wizardry, made them a household word around the world in the space of less than eighteen months. But for all his accomplishments, Epstein was a tormented soul, and in 1967 he committed suicide with an overdose of sleeping pills. Epstein's death devastated the group, and on George's advice they departed for India to share in the "inner peace" he claimed to have found at the feet of a highly publicized celebrity guru, the Maharishi Mahesh Yogi. They stayed a few months, listening to the Maharishi's lectures on the relation of smiling to cosmic consciousness, until word came to them that Mia Farrow, another member of the guru's star-studded clientele, had allegedly been assaulted by him. When the master refused to confirm or deny the report, the Beatles departed.

More trouble awaited them on their return to England. With the death of Epstein, McCartney asserted his leadership of the group. He set their recording schedule, directed their affairs, and laid plans to bring in a new manager, Lee Eastman, a New York music lawyer and the father of his girlfriend, socialite photographer Linda Eastman. The promotion of Eastman finally brought the friction among the Beatles out into the open. Lennon, resentful of what he deemed Eastman's snobbish condescension, successfully resisted his appointment, but at a cost of considerable bitterness from McCartney. The Beatles' business affairs were more complicated than ever, mired in lawsuits, claims and counterclaims. As a group, they had, for all intents and purposes, stopped functioning.

The final straw was Yoko Ono, who, beginning in 1967, became Lennon's lover and constant companion. The other Beatles did not take well to the addition of Yoko. She was, to say the least, a woman of great eccentricity. An artist and filmmaker of the surrealist school, she also fancied herself a musician of estimable abilities, a judgment in which the other Beatles did not concur. Lennon, married at the time (as was Yoko), was totally entranced by her; indeed, he seldom left her sight. Under her aegis his career took a series of increasingly bizarre twists and turns. He became involved in her art "happenings" (one of them involved appearing in public together shrouded in a large bag), conducted an eight-day "bed-in" for peace, and, strangest of all, starred in and produced a series of avante-garde films. One of them, fifty-two minutes in length, consisted exclusively of a close-up of Lennon smiling; another documented Lennon experiencing an erection. That, however, was about all that was rising for him. Between the bed-ins, the happenings, the filmmaking and brushes with the law (the U.S. Immigration Service was trying to deport him because of an old marijuana conviction in England), his career was falling off. Nor did being "constantly stoned," as he put it, help matters. He was, by 1969, almost totally estranged from the rest of the Beatles. Finally, in October of that year, during a stormy session with McCartney over upcoming concert plans, Lennon exploded. "I want a divorce," he declared. Stunned, McCartney implored Lennon not to make a public announcement of the rupture. That honor was left to McCartney, who six months later called a press conference to announce that "because of personal, business, and financial differences," *he* was leaving.

So the Beatles were finished. All that remained was a public accounting of the bloody details. For Wenner, it was a golden opportunity.

He needed a Beatles interview just now, more desperately than anyone imagined, for a series of financial miscues had brought *Rolling Stone* to the brink of bankruptcy. Costs had escalated dramatically. His own rock star life-style had drained more cash away. Circulation and advertising, meanwhile, had leveled off. A talk with the Beatles, even just one of them, might help turn the situation around. Wenner rapidly narrowed the choices. Ringo was charming but inarticulate; George was out of the country and lying low. Paul was at hand, but Paul was Paul: too nice to say anything liable to be newsworthy. Which left John: the "Bad Boy" himself.

John Lennon was nothing if not quotable. He had always been the most voluble Beatle, the brightest, wittiest, and most provocative. He was quick with a quip, a pun, a telling remark. His readiness to express his opinions had landed the group in trouble more than once. It had been John, for instance, who had whipped up the firestorm that followed his observation that the Beatles were "more popular than Jesus." A number of Southern radio stations banned Beatles records in protest, and one disc jockey had even inciner-

ated their albums in a public bonfire. Lennon was denounced from pulpits coast to coast; the Pope himself was
said to be upset. Lennon had ultimately apologized, but
hardly had that controversy subsided when he ignited another, by returning his Membership in the British Empire to
the Queen with a jaunty note explaining he was protesting
against "Britain's involvement in the Nigeria-Biafra thing,
against our support of America in Vietnam, and against
'Cold Turkey' [a recent Lennon release] slipping down in
the charts." He signed it: "With Love, John Lennon of
Bag." There was no one better qualified to tell the Beatles'
story, ugliness and all, than Lennon.

It had been more than a year now since Lennon had left
the Beatles, and in that time he had all but disappeared
from public view. When Wenner reached him in New York
and laid out his proposal for an interview—making no secret
of the effect he hoped it would have on *Rolling Stone*'s sagging fortunes—Lennon agreed ("as a favor," he told
Wenner) to cooperate. But, like Dylan, he had certain conditions. Yoko had to participate. And the interview would
be for the magazine's exclusive use; it would be put to no
further commercial purpose. Wenner agreed. "Okay," Lennon said. "Let's do it. I think I'll give you something you
can use."

The two-part *Rolling Stone* interview revealed that Lennon had lost none of his candor. He had barbs for virtually
everyone and everything: McCartney ("He's a good PR
man"); Dylan ("Dylan is bullshit, Zimmerman is his
name"); the Beatles' management; his producers; well-
heeled fans; Jagger ("Mick Jagger came out and resur-
rected the bullshit movement, you know, wiggling your arse
and that"); his early films ("just bullshit"); the Beatles

themselves. "Fuckin' big bastards, that's what the Beatles were," said Lennon. "You have to be a bastard to make it, that's a fact. And the Beatles are the biggest bastards on earth."

Looking back on his career, Lennon found little to be proud of. "We sold out, you know," he said to Wenner. "The music was dead even before we went on the theater tour of Britain. We were feeling shit already because we had to reduce an hour or two of playing . . . to twenty minutes of playing and go on and repeat the same twenty minutes every night. The Beatles music died then as musicians. That's why we never improved as musicians. We killed ourselves then to make it." Once they had made it, their fame had a momentum of its own. As Lennon put it: "Everybody wants the image to carry on. The press around with you, you want to carry on, because they want the free drinks and the free whores and the fun. Everybody wants to keep on the bandwagon. It's Satyricon. We were the Caesars. Who was going to knock us when there's a million pounds to be made? All the handouts, the bribery, the police, all the fucking hype, you know. Everybody wanted in, that's why some of them are still trying to cling onto this. Don't take it away from us, not a portable Rome where we can all have our houses and our cars and our lovers and our wives and our office girls and parties and drink and drugs. Don't take it away from us, you know, otherwise you're mad."

Wenner seemed unsettled by what he was hearing. Anxiously he kept trying to steer the conversation back to the Beatles' successes, their fame, their "place in history," as he called it. *"Do you think you're a genius?"* he asked Lennon. (Lennon: "If there is such a thing as one, I am one.") *". . . When did you first start getting . . . sort of spiritual reaction? . . . When did somebody first come up to you about this thing about John Lennon as God? . . . What was it like to go on tour? I read about cripples coming up to you? . . . What do you think the effect of the Beatles was on the history of Britain?"* All that came from Lennon, though, was bile. "The same bastards are in control, the same people are running everything, it's exactly the same," he shrugged. "They hyped the kids and the generation. We've grown up a little, all of us, and there has been a change and we are a bit freer and all that, but it's the same game and nothing's really changed. They're doing exactly the same things, selling arms to South Africa, killing blacks on the street, people are living in fucking poverty with rats crawling over them, it's the same. It makes you want to puke. And I woke up to that, too. The dream is over. It's just the same only I'm thirty and a lot of people have long hair, that's all."

Never before had a rock star given an interview so open and honest. And, as Wenner had expected, the impact of "The Working Class Hero" was enormous, and *Rolling Stone* eased back into the black. But Wenner did not leave it at that. Ignoring his promise to Lennon, he published the interview in book form, and *Lennon Remembers* became a minor best seller. Lennon, who shared in none of the proceeds, was furious. Briefly he considered suing Wenner, then settled by withdrawing his record company advertising from *Rolling Stone* for a year.

A few years before, the enmity of John Lennon, or of Dylan or of Jagger, all of whom, in time, fell out with Wenner, would have been fatal. Then, they *were* rock and roll, whole and indivisible. Now their estrangement barely mattered. The rock culture had become bigger than any single superstar or cluster of superstars, bigger than anyone, including Wenner, could have imagined. And all because of a rainy weekend near the small town of Woodstock, in up-state New York.

None of rock's Holy Trinity was there, not even Dylan, in whose veritable backyard the festival was held; it didn't matter. The weather was miserable, the concert site a sea of mud; it didn't matter. The food gave out, the toilets overflowed and the wells ran dry; it didn't matter. Traffic was impossible; the roads were backed up for twenty miles; so great was the crush that an estimated 100,000 people didn't make it to the concert at all, but gave up in disgust and went home; it didn't matter. The rip-offs were massive; water was being sold for a quarter a glass, bread at a dollar a loaf, hot dogs for $2.50; it didn't matter. By the time it was over, 5,000 people were given medical treatment for one ailment or another, and the New York *Times* was pro-claiming "Nightmare in the Catskills" ("little more sanity than . . . lemmings marching to their death in the sea . . . what kind of culture can produce such a mess?"); it didn't matter. None of it mattered—not even the fact that the festi-val wasn't held in Woodstock at all, but fifty miles away in Bethel. Woodstock created its own reality.

There was no easy way of reckoning what occurred the weekend of August 15–17, 1969, in the 600-acre alfalfa field a forty-nine-year-old dairy farmer named Max Yas-gur rented to the "Woodstock Music Festival and Crafts Fair." No one was prepared for it. The organizers had origi-nally hoped that perhaps 50,000 would come to listen to the assembled talent—Joan Baez, Country Joe and the Fish, Richie Havens, Jefferson Airplane, Crosby, Stills and Nash, Santana, Jimi Hendrix, Janis Joplin, the Band, Joe Cocker, The Who, Sly and the Family Stone, Canned Heat, Sha-Na-

Na, Ten Years After, Arlo Guthrie, the Butterfield Blues Band, John Sebastian. But by mid-Friday, the first day of the festival, 200,000 were already encamped and another 200,000 to 300,000 on the way. For one weekend, Max Yasgur's alfalfa field was the third largest city in New York State. "I don't know how to speak to twenty people, much less all of you," the bespectacled farmer stammered from the stage. "You are the largest group of people ever assembled in one place at one time . . . We had no idea there would be this many . . . You have proven something to the world . . . that half a million kids can get together for fun and music and have nothing but fun and music." And then, with tears brimming in his eyes, Max Yasgur shyly raised his hand and flashed the peace sign. The roar, it was said, could be heard ten miles away.

It was a dreamlike weekend, filled with dreamlike impressions. A vast hillside, aswirl in colors; from the air it seems like a living painting, ever shifting, ever growing, because the colors are people, 400,000 of them, 500,000, more; no one knows; no one cares. The moment is beyond comprehension. Announcements from the stage: ". . . Share: remember, the person sitting next to you is your brother . . . John, please come to the public announcement area; Donna has left her pills in the car . . ." Air Force helicopters in Vietnam camouflage fluttering out of the skies with supplies for the army of peace . . . Unarmed cops dressed in red T-shirts with the word "Peace" emblazoned across the chest, some with flowers in their hair, a few smoking joints . . . The ladies of the local Hadassah making 30,000 cheese sandwiches to feed the multitudes . . . A white boy and a black boy, naked, joining hands in the middle of a thunderstorm, dancing, others joining, the circle getting larger, larger . . . Dealing, out in the open, unbothered, a supermarket of psychedelia; "get your reds here, got acid, got mescaline, got whacha need, anything ya want, got it here" . . . Country Joe leading the audience in a college-style "Fuck" cheer: "Give me a F, give me a U, give me a C, give me a K, what's it spell?" . . . A dozen dairy cows looking on, oblivious, peaceful, chewing their cud . . . Skinny-dipping in the pond, people by the hundreds, all sizes, shapes, colors, innocent, childlike . . . The roads clogged, a Day-Glo Ganges, ever flowing, never ending . . . A box of Cocoa-Puffs passed from stranger to stranger: "Take a handful, pass it on" . . . Two antagonists, fists poised, about to fight, the crowd chanting "peace, peace, peace"; the fists came down; the mouths break into smiles; they shake hands; the crowd roars . . . Rain, torrential, blessed . . . And the people. So many, so beautiful, so unreal.

None of it was supposed to happen. Always before, bringing kids together in such numbers had been an invitation for trouble. But at Woodstock, there was no violence, not a single fight. Always before, kids were supposed to hate adults. But at Woodstock, the gap between the generations was closed. "This is the nicest bunch of kids I've ever dealt with," the local sheriff said. Young people helped them push their police cars out of the mud, lent a hand with traffic control, and brought casualties to the hospitals. "If these hippies bump into you," a local housewife said in wonder, "they actually say excuse me." A harassed telephone operator, one of those who had been buried by the avalanche of 500,000 long-distance calls, reported: "Every kid said thank you." Always before, rock had been threatening, unsettling. But at Woodstock, the music had an eerie, calming effect, as if the celebration was not a rock festival, but a religious rite.

Eventually, even the good, gray *Times* was moved. Days after its first editorial, it concluded that the festival was "essentially a phenomenon of innocence." As the paper put it, "They came, it seems, to enjoy their own society, to exult in a life-style that is its own declaration of independence . . . With Henry the Fifth, they could say at Bethel, 'He that outlives this day, and comes safe home, will stand a-tiptoe when this day is nam'd.'" At Woodstock, everything changed. For the three days of the festival, it was as if time stood still, and, in its suspension, none of the old rules applied. "A miracle," Margaret Mead called it; Max Lerner proclaimed it "the beginning of a cultural revolution." Even *Time,* putting aside its intolerance for rock, marked Woodstock "History's largest happening . . . the moment when the special culture of U.S. youth of the '60's openly displayed its strength, appeal and power." Woodstock, the magazine concluded, "may well rank as one of the significant political and sociological events of the age."

But no one was more startled than Jann Wenner.

He had seen the advance publicity, but had written off the glowing predictions as promoters' hype. For once, he had been caught thinking conventionally, measuring the promise of Woodstock by his own experience. Never before had there been a major American rock festival away from the West Coast. Never before had the biggest of these, Monterey, been able to draw more than 50,000 fans. And never before had anyone less than superstars, the figures he so ardently courted, been able to create the magic that was the music. Whatever their plans, he doubted that the East Coast promoters would break those patterns. The site of the concert itself—the East—made him instantly suspicious. He was very much a California chauvinist. Only here, in the West, in his San Francisco, was rock truly a revolution. Go to

Woodstock? Jann Wenner could not see the point. Where, after all, would Mick or Bob or John be? Not there. A subordinate could handle Woodstock.

Fortunately for Wenner, that subordinate turned out to be Greil Marcus. Ordinarily, Marcus' prose was dryly analytical, almost dispassionate. But even Marcus was overwhelmed. "It's like watching God perform the creation," he reported. " 'And for my next number.' " And there was that sense about the weekend: it was as if some force had been loosed, so awesome in magnitude, so vast in dimension, as to defy usual accounting. Ravi Shankar, whose sitar playing had brought the crowd to its feet in thundering ovation, had felt it. "Frightening," he said as he left the stage. "Frightening." Al Aronowitz, one of the thousand journalists present, had likened it to a wake. "You sit on the big stage watered by the blue spotlights while the Band plays Bob Dylan's 'I Shall Be Released,' " he wrote, "and you look out into the eyes of the monster." At Woodstock, it had been contained, beneficent. But Woodstock was merely the beginning, "a confused, chaotic founding," as Marcus put it, "of something new, something our world must find a way to deal with." He continued: "The limits have changed now, they've been pushed out, the priorities have been rearranged . . . To call it *over* was like saying that the entire population of Minneapolis had to pack up and leave right now . . . All over the nation, kids are moving to rock and roll. It's the most important thing in their lives. Janis Joplin's new album is more important than landing on the moon . . . Plan a festival like Woodstock for 150,000 and you'll get nearly a million. Plan next year for a million, and you'll get ten million. Plan and plan and plan and you'll go deeper and deeper into the hole. Ticket sales will not do it. Getting the bands to play for free will not do it, either. We are, for better or worse, beyond those sorts of solutions."

There were, in fact, no solutions, only trust that somehow it would work out. In the warm, self-congratulatory afterglow of Woodstock, trust seemed sufficient. It was not a time for questioning or for worrying. The few other cautionary voices, like Ellen Willis in the *New Yorker* ("rock . . . can be—and has been—criminal, Fascistic, and coolly individualistic as well as revolutionary") and Barry Farrell in *Life* ("It was a groovy show, all right, but I fear it will grow groovier in memory, when this market in our madness leads on to shows we'd rather not see"), were drowned out by the choruses of approbation. "One, Two, Many Woodstocks," *Rolling Stone* headlined, telling of the plans being laid to duplicate and make permanent the Woodstock phenomenon. Like the moment itself, it was an optimistic, confident story. The culture was at floodtide. Rock had finally been recognized for what Wenner had always insisted it was—"not just a particular form of pop, but the anthem of revolution . . . one long symphony of protest . . . basically moral . . . the proclamation of a new set of values." But they were not his feelings alone anymore. These were the words of the Establishment, speaking through its organ, *Time*.

"You see, I was right," Wenner grinned, pushing the *Time* story at Burks. "Now even *they* think so." For the moment, he was. How short that moment would be, how violently it would end, Jann Wenner could not know. No one could. But silently, inexorably, death was coming—and coming soon.

6

Let It Bleed

Free Rolling Stones: 'It's Going to Happen'

The cover headline on *Rolling Stone* was bold and black. Reading it over, Wenner felt an odd tingle of anticipation. His friend Mick was coming to San Francisco, last stop of the most successful tour in rock history, and this would be the climax—one massive free concert for the city that had put rock on the map.

It was December 2, 1969, four months since the birth of Woodstock Nation, and only days until the arrival of the Stones. But even at that late date, *Rolling Stone* reported, it was still not certain just where the concert would take place, only that, somehow, it would. Jagger was insisting on it. In fact, the magazine quoted him as saying, he had wanted to do his entire American tour gratis, as a way of showing his appreciation to his fans. "I'm richer than the rest of the fellas," he joked, "and I can afford it." But, in consideration of his manager's sensibilities, he had settled for a single, huge giveaway, a burst of munificence that, by the magazine's calculations, could cost him as much as $100,000. The money, though, did not matter nearly as much as the event. "It [will] be a Little Woodstock," the magazine predicted. "And, even more exciting, it [will] be an *instant* Woodstock."

Wenner was not the only one who was excited. When the story broke, the entire city fairly crackled with anticipation. Radio stations interrupted their programs with bulletins on the latest concert preparations; newspapers vied with one another in predicting the turnout . . . 100,000 . . . 200,000 . . . 300,000 . . . 400,000. The projections mounted as the concert date approached. So did the troubles. The city had denied the Stones a permit to use Golden Gate Park . . . an alternative site had been rejected by a Stones handler for "aesthetic reasons" . . . Sears Point Raceway, another site, had not been able to get insurance . . . everything was falling apart, except the mania itself: *Free Rolling Stones.*

They were the biggest, best, heaviest rock group in the world. Already, their tour had grossed nearly $2,000,000; 350,000 people had seen them (not counting the 250,000 who showed up at a free concert in London to see them off), and, had the seats been available, ten times that number probably would have. In New York, a single newspaper ad had produced 585,000 requests for tickets. Twelve of their fourteen albums were gold, and their latest, "Let It Bleed," had sold more than a million copies even before it was released. Altogether, they had grossed, in the space of six years, $72,000,000. Girls fell out of balconies trying to touch them. Pop bottles Jagger handled were accorded the same reverence as the relics of saints. Critics used up every superlative trying to describe them. In one brief, appreciative essay, *Rolling Stone* music critic Jonathan Cott compared them favorably to Arthur Symons, Rilke, the sixteenth-century Anabaptist commune at Munster, Salome,

and Jesus Christ. Jagger himself cracked half-seriously:
"The lines around my eyes are copyrighted."

Not even the Beatles, the Stones' chief rivals, commanded such fanatic adulation. They were rock's outlaws,
the group that broke all the rules. "Streetfighters for the
new sensibility," *Rolling Stone* associate editor David Dal-
ton called them. "An international conspiracy of rock and
roll punks determined to undermine Western civilization
with a combination of drugs, music, polymorphous sexuality
and violence."

They did their best to live up to their reputation. Both
Jagger and Keith Richard, the group's lead guitarist, had
done time in English jails on drug charges. So too had
Brian Jones, the group's original leader, whose visage on a·
London street had so moved Wenner three years before.
But Jones was no longer with the Stones. Shortly before the
American tour, Jones, who had been in and out of psychiatric institutions, was found dead at the bottom of his
swimming pool. The Stones mourned him only a month;
there was too much music to be made. And what music it
was. Other groups merely hinted at the pleasures of love-
making; the Stones left nothing to the imagination. The rest
of the culture sang of peace and love; the Rolling Stones
heard the sound of "marchin', chargin' feet." If the most the
Beatles asked was "to hold your hand," a convention of the
day went, the Rolling Stones came to pillage your town.

Adults, predictably, reacted in horror. Two of the
Stones' album covers—one showing a bulging crotch, complete with actual zipper—were censored, and a number of
stations refused to play their more sexually explicit songs.
In Chicago, Richard J. Daley went so far as to order the
city's radio stations not to air the Stones' "Street-Fighting
Man," for fear that young people, already aroused by the

Democratic Convention the summer before, might take its
revolutionary summons to heart. In Parliament, Conservative back-benchers warned that if the Stones were allowed
to come to the United States, irreparable harm might be
done to Anglo-American relations. Even the stately London
Times reported "there is no doubt that, in any poll for the
best-hated man in Britain taken among people over forty,
Mr. Jagger would be near the top." All of which only
swelled the Stones' stature. Every record banned, every lyric
censored, every arrest suffered, was another hundred thousand converts made. As Jagger himself put it: "Every time
somebody curses me, I think, 'Remember, that's what
makes me very rich.'"

It was not just that the Stones were so bad that made them
such heroes, but that they were so unrepentantly so. "We are
not old men," Richard sneered to a judge who questioned
him about the presence of a nude girl at a drug party for
which he was being sentenced. "We are not concerned with
your petty morals, which are illegitimate"—roughly what
many teenagers yearned to tell their parents. And when, at
length, Richard and Jagger were released from prison, their
next album began with the sound of a jail door slamming,
as if to say that nothing could hold them in. It was doubtful
whether anything could. Jagger challenged even the ultimate taboo. Seeing him prancing effeminately on stage, hips
shaking, sinuous mouth contorting, an audience could not
be sure what form of sexuality he favored—or, indeed,
whether it made any difference. He was all of Norman O.
Brown's unreadable theories of "polymorphous perversity"
sprung to throbbing life. Anything went. No holds were
barred. The Rolling Stones lived only according to their
own laws. If it felt good, produced an orgasm, promised a
high—do it. "The more successful you get the more you can

get away with," their manager explained. "What developed was total freedom."

And if, along the way, people got hurt, as people had a way of doing when the Rolling Stones were involved, there were always special dispensations. "When the Stones were at their most exploitative, wrote Jonathan Cott, in words Orwell would have understood, "they were at their most liberating."

The vision of the world they presented in their music, especially "Sympathy for the Devil," their most notable work, was of a universe gone mad, a place where, as *Rolling Stone* critic Jon Landau approvingly put it, "Cops are criminals, Saints are sinners, God is the Devil."

Jagger played the image out to perfection. By the 1969 tour, he had starred in three movies: in *Performance,* as a former rock star symbiotically linked to a professional killer; in *Ned Kelley,* as the legendary Australian outlaw; and in *Sympathy for the Devil,* a Jean-Luc Godard film, which used a Stones recording session as a metaphor for ongoing revolution. Small wonder, then, that on a previous visit to California, a radical group greeted "their satanic majesties" with the following proclamation:

Welcome Rolling Stones, our comrades in the desperate battle against the maniacs who hold power. The revolutionary youth of the world hears your music and is inspired to even more deadly acts . . .

We will play your music in rock-'n-roll marching bands as we tear down the jails and free the prisoners, as we tear down the State schools and free the students, as we tear down the military bases, arm the poor, as we tattoo

BURN BABY BURN! on the bellies of the wardens and
generals and create a new society from the ashes of our
fires.

Comrades, you will return to this country when it is free
from the tyranny of the State and you will play your
splendid music in factories run by workers, in the domes
of emptied city halls, on the rubble of police stations,
under the hanging corpses of priests, under a million red
flags waving over a million anarchist communes . . . THE
ROLLING STONES ARE THAT WHICH SHALL
BE! . . . ROLLING STONES—THE YOUTH OF CAL-
IFORNIA HEARS YOUR MESSAGE! LONG LIVE
THE REVOLUTION!

The irony was that, if the revolution ever did come to
pass, the first to go "up against the wall, motherfucker," as
a convention of the day went, would be the privileged
class to which the Rolling Stones belonged. They were,
for all their rhetoric about revolution, pampered children
of the middle class lusting after nothing so much as the
perquisites of the upper class. Their so-called politics, so far
as critic Robert Christgau could discern, amounted to "a
passionate commitment to sex, dope and lavish autonomy."
Jagger himself, far from being a demon, was, in person, intelligent, good humored, altogether likable—and, as Michael
Lydon discovered after spending some time with him, "as
bewildered by the events of his own life as I by mine." No
matter. The reality of the Stones—even the fact that much of
their "satanism" was carefully contrived commercialism—
counted far less than the myth that had grown up around
them. Rock did not deal with the way it was, but the way it
was supposed to be. And, in the eyes of the rock culture,
the Stones were nothing less than Nietzschean supermen.

Take away the costumes, change the beat, alter the lyrics, and what remained was the same nihilistic obsession with violence and power, the same fascist fascination with the criminal and the grotesque.

Even the Beatles, seemingly the most innocently fun-loving of the pre-acid rockers, had produced an album whose cover—before being pasted over on grounds of "good taste" —portrayed the "Fab Four" dressed in butcher's aprons, meat cleavers and knives in hands, surrounded by the dismembered remains of dolls. Later, Alice Cooper, the male rock star, went the Beatles one better and won notoriety by actually tearing apart baby dolls on stage. With different groups decadence took different forms. Jim Morrison, the lead singer of the Doors, claimed he could sustain an erection throughout the course of a two-hour performance. When that trick palled, he took to exposing himself at concerts. "I'm interested in anything about revolt, disorder, chaos, especially activity that has no meaning," he said. "It seems to me to be the road to freedom." All of it was supposed to be artistic, protesting the absurd grotesqueries of the parent culture with symbolic decadence. And, for a time, the fascination with the macabre made a bizarre kind of sense. Death was all around: on a Dallas street, in Vietnam, in a Los Angeles kitchen, every night on the evening news. Rock was a reflection of what was happening, and, since rock was art, it had to be allowed a certain license. But, in about 1969, life began imitating art.

A number of things happened that year, like red warning flags of the disaster to come. In May, meeting in Chicago, SDS, the student organization founded "to make a world in which love is more possible," exploded in factional chaos. Amidst shouting and fistfights, Weatherman was born, and immediately announced that the time had arrived to "fight

the pig in the streets." Two months later, the first Weatherman action took place in Chicago—the so-called "Days of
Rage." Armed with clubs and shielded by motorcycle hel-
mets, 200 Weathermen set off toward the Loop, trashing
cars and store windows on their way. Arrests totaled nearly
300; injuries were counted in the dozens. Berkeley, meanwhile, exploded again, this time with deadly results. When
the university announced its intention to turn an area of va-
cant land south of the campus regarded by the students as
"People's Park" into a parking garage, 6,000 protesters
marched to the site. The police met them with a hail of
gunfire. One young man died of buckshot wounds, another
was blinded, and dozens more were wounded. Governor
Ronald Reagan declared a state of emergency and dispatched a California National Guard helicopter to spray the
campus with CS gas, a chemical agent outlawed by the
Geneva Convention.

But there was no containing the violence any longer.
Across the country, students were firebombing banks, blow-
ing up power lines, trading potshots with the police and the
state militia. For the first and only time in its history, *Rolling Stone* was spelling America with a "k." "I am sick of
statistics and examples," Michael Rossman, one of the original FSM leaders wrote in a special issue devoted to "The
American Revolution, 1969." "I want to tell you about
what is happening in America, about why the violence will
increase, and about some real reasons for fear . . . During
pleasant nights in communes in San Francisco and Colorado, I watch friends oiling guns and learning how to load
magazines; they offer to teach me how to shoot . . . Let's
be frank and simple. Violence, as the good brother says, is
'as American as apple pie.'" Not even rock concerts were
safe anymore. A repeat of the Monterey Festival had ended

with 300 injuries, 75 arrests, and $50,000 in property damage. Another concert in Palm Springs produced extensive rioting, two wounded and 250 arrested. Then, in Los Angeles, came the grisliest event of all: the butchering of actress Sharon Tate, eight months pregnant with her first child, and four of her houseguests by a "hippie family" under the control of an ex-convict and would-be rock guitarist named Charles Manson.

Superficially, Manson and his family, save for their psychotic blood lust, were indistinguishable from many young people. Manson and most of his followers had lived in the Haight during the Summer of Love. They had tripped on acid (Manson claimed to have experienced the crucifixion of Christ during one acid experience, and afterward proclaimed himself "the god of fuck"), danced to the Fillmore's music, shared food with the Diggers, done, in short, all the things that young people did. "We slept in the park and lived on the streets and my hair got a little longer," Manson remembered after his arrest. "I started playing music and people liked my music and people smiled at me and put their arms around me and hugged me . . . It just took me away." Charlie and his music wove a spell that even his followers found hard to describe. "He had a guitar . . . and [he] began to play," Susan Atkins told the grand jury that indicted her for the murder of seven people. "He sounded like an angel . . . It blew my mind, because he was inside my head, and I knew at that time that he was something that I had been looking for . . . And I went down and kissed his feet." They believed him, as unquestioningly as they would believe a rock star, so much so that when Manson told them to kill, they stabbed Sharon Tate forty-nine times. "He is as good as he is evil, he is as evil as he is good," Susan Atkins said. "You could not judge the man."

After Manson's arrest he was canonized by some segments of the underground press. *Tuesday's Child,* a Los Angeles underground newspaper, named him "Man of the Year," and pictured him stretched out on a cross, with the word "hippie" printed above him. Weatherman issued an official communique congratulating Manson for having murdered "some rich, honky pigs." "Manson Power!" Weatherman proclaimed. Locked away in his jail cell, the object of all this attention passed his days writing rock and roll songs (he had a record in the works) and reading letters that poured in to him from youthful admirers, one of whom, as it happened, was a *Rolling Stone* editor sent to interview him.

Against this backdrop, the Rolling Stones made ready to come to San Francisco. As December 6, the date scheduled for the concert, approached, the logistical snarls that had entangled the idea from the start had yet to be unraveled, and the Stones were getting nervous. There was no possibility of backing out now; the premature publicity had forced their hand. Some of the underground press, never overly enamored of rock and roll, had begun to question the motivation behind the concert. After a little digging, they had sniffed out the fact that the Stones would be accompanied by a crew of filmmakers who planned to record the concert, as part of a *cinema vérité* feature on the Stones' American tour, a production that, once released, could be expected to gross millions. It also developed that the ticket prices that the Stones had been charging on the tour were the highest ever. As the stories of the Stones' avarice spread, critics pointed to Jagger's $250,000 townhouse, the 20-bedroom "country house," the fleet of Rollses, and wondered

how revolutionary "a man of wealth and taste," as Jagger
introduced himself in "Sympathy for the Devil," could be.
A token free appearance would still those critics. The concert, problems and all, was going to happen. For the Stones'
sake, it had to.

The hunt for a suitable site eventually took the Stones'
managers to Wenner. Wenner, despite the fiasco of *British
Rolling Stone,* had lost none of his affection for Jagger, and
he helpfully suggested several promoters. They, in turn,
brought the Stones to the flamboyant San Francisco trial attorney Melvin Belli, who at last succeeded in securing a concert site: a stock car track forty miles southeast of San
Francisco. The name of the place was Altamont.

As a staging ground for a rock concert, especially one expected to draw 300,000 people or more, Altamont could
hardly have been worse. The raceway, which had been teetering on the brink of bankruptcy, was small, cramped, and
difficult to reach. Its acres were littered with the rusting
hulks of junked automobiles and thousands of shards of
broken glass. In appearance, it had all the charm of a grave-
yard. Worst of all, though, the deal for its use had not been
sealed until the final moment. Whereas Woodstock had
taken months to prepare, Altamont had to be ready within
twenty-four hours.

One detail, however, had been worked out weeks in advance—security. Jagger had insisted on it. He was almost
neurotically insecure about his personal safety, continually
bewitched by premonitions of his own assassination. He had
reason to be worried. His concerts frequently ended in
brawls, fans not only punching and clawing each other, or
any cops within reach, but doing their best to get at Jagger
as well. During an appearance in Berlin, the concert hall
was ringed with barbed wire and armed police who finally

had to resort to tear gas to disperse the rioting Stones fans. In Zurich, 12,000 fans began tearing apart the seats in the local stadium until police piled in with clubs. In Warsaw, 8,000 teenagers crashed through police barriers and stormed the iron gates of the Palace of Culture. Police finally beat back the barrage of bricks and bottles with tear gas, dogs, steel-helmeted reinforcements, and two armored cars mounted with water cannons. Jagger had had an arm broken in one encounter, been punched in a second, and had a chair broken over his head in a third, leaving a small scar just above his eye.

There was something about him and the Rolling Stones that invited violence, something about the way they looked —streetfighters, outfitted in black, mean, malevolent, seemingly looking for a fight—something about the music they played—incessant, pounding, tension-filled, packed with images of blood and death—something about them—an aura of menace, of everything about to explode—that made their concerts not so much performances as assaults. There would be Jagger, bizarre, comical, absurd, deadly, waving an Uncle Sam hat, throttling the microphone, fucking it, whipping off his belt, flogging the stage, writhing in a frenzy of emotion, singing in the words of the hurt and the abused, damning all of them, offering himself in symbolic expiation. And then it would begin. The kids would come out of their seats, dance, shake, wave their fists, scream back at him, until, finally, with no recourse left, they would surge toward the stage to devour him. But still he would taunt. And so they would charge again. Back and forth, like waves of emotion crashing against an electric beach, ever building, threatening to engulf them all.

It was hypnotic to watch. The critic Albert Goldman likened a Stones appearance to a Hitler rally at Nuremburg:

"Dot good rock 'n' roll could warm the cockles of a storm-trooper's heart. OK. They don't give you a torch and an armband, like in the *real* old days, and send you down the Rhine to swing with the summer solstice. But you can still squeeze in hip by haunch with thousands of good Kamerads; still fatten eyes, ear, soul on the Leader; still plotz out while he socks it to you in stop-time, and, best of all, boys and girls, you can get your rocks off." The only question was how to control it. One of the Stones' managers in San Francisco, Emmett Grogan of the Diggers, came up with the ultimate solution. "We'll have a hundred Angels on hogs escort the Stones," he announced. "Nobody'll come near the Angels, man. They won't dare."

Hell's Angels. It was hard to conceive of a more unlikely alliance than that which existed between the Visigothic, swastikaed motorcycle gang and the children who came of age proclaiming the power of flowers. They seemed mirror opposites: the Angels, with their tattooed fidelity to Hitler and Jack the Ripper, superpatriots, who had offered their services as "a crack group of trained gorillas [sic] . . . for behind the lines duty in Vietnam," the free-lance terrorists who had beaten up peace demonstrators, an outlaw gang so violent that, as rumor had it, not even the Alameda County sheriff, whose jurisdiction included Altamont, would challenge them; and the peaceful, spaced-out denizens of the Haight. But the affinity was real. Hunter Thompson, who spent a year riding with the Angels before joining *Rolling Stone,* tried to explain:

> The Angels' aggressive, anti-social stance—their *alienation,*
> as it were—had a tremendous appeal for the more aesthetic
> Berkeley temperament. Students who could barely get up
> the nerve to sign a petition or shoplift a candy bar were

fascinated by tales of the Hell's Angels ripping up towns and taking whatever they wanted . . . The Angels didn't masturbate, they raped. They didn't come on with theories and songs and quotations, but with noise and muscle and sheer balls.

It had been Thompson, in fact, who had brought the two cultures together. Over beers one afternoon in 1965, he introduced some of them to Ken Kesey. "We're in the same business," Kesey smiled. "You break people's bones. I break people's heads." They spent the rest of the day together, the chief Prankster and his merry motorcycle men, drinking and smoking dope and swapping tales of how the System was out to get them. They had so much in common, it developed, that Kesey invited them, along with the entire San Francisco chapter of the Angels, to a Labor Day party in their honor at the La Honda ranch. There, to the sound of Allen Ginsberg playing finger cymbals and chanting mantras, Kesey introduced them to the wonders of LSD. Forty-eight hours of nonstop boozing, drugging and screwing later, the alliance was sealed. From there on, they were part of the scene . . . brothers, sisters. Ginsberg wrote a poem for them. Professors had them to dinner. Gleason proclaimed them "guardians of the flower children." Even Dylan had had them backstage at his last concert, given them free tickets, invited them to sing with him at Carnegie Hall: "You want to talk to people, say something to the nation?" he asked them. "Well, what's your act? . . . Do you have any songs? Can you recite poetry? Can you talk?" It was all so chic. Being at Altamont, guarding Jagger, would be the grooviest thing yet. Here was the perfect match-up: Hell's Angels and the Rolling Stones . . . outlaws meet outlaws. Besides, the price was right: $500 worth of free beer.

December 6 dawned dark and chilly in San Francisco. The clouds gathering to the east threatened rain. In his Pacific Heights mansion, Jann Wenner stirred, peered outside and considered the day ahead. It did not seem promising. Knowing that reaching Altamont would be a logistical nightmare, he had already chartered a helicopter to take him and a select circle of friends to the concert site. Now, he began to think better of it. Astrology had become his latest fascination, and one of the underground weeklies had pointed out that the moon was in Scorpio . . . a particularly bad omen. But something else bothered him, too. Festivals had never been to his taste. They were too uncontrolled. Anything could happen: a fight, a riot, God knew what. It sent a chill through him. He did not share his contemporaries' rapture with violence. The truth was, even the prospect of physical pain terrified him. As he thought the day over, the reasons for staying home mounted. Then, the unexpected happened. A hitch developed in the plans for the helicopter and the flight was scrubbed. That decided it. He would not go.

Even as Wenner was looking out his window, his premonitions were being proved right. At noon, the moment of the first scheduled set, the sound system was still not working properly. Meanwhile, the sanitary facilities had started to overflow. Even the weather was deteriorating. The only thing going according to plan was predictions of huge numbers of young people. Nearly 300,000 were on hand, and from the look of the clogged roads leading to the site, another 100,000 or 200,000 were still on their way. They were not · like the well-behaved, well-heeled crowd that had trooped to Woodstock. This was a harder, blue-collared bunch, scruffier and tougher looking than the usual rock audience. The mood was tense and apprehensive. There was none of the fun, camaraderie and good-natured sharing of

Woodstock. Instead, there was continual jostling and shoving for position, and, not infrequently, raised fists and muttered threats. A number of people were drinking heavily to
stave off the cold. To Baron Wolman, who arrived early,
the vibes were all wrong. It scared him. He left, hours before
the Rolling Stones appeared. Thousands of others did the
same.

The Angels began arriving around 11 A.M., one caravan
after another, their tattered colors identifying their home-
town allegiance . . . San Francisco . . . San Jose . . .
Oakland . . . San Berdoo . . . Angels by the score. Their
appearance elicited a small cheer, then a mad scramble as
kids frantically tried to get out of the way of their spinning
wheels. One young woman was nearly run over. She cursed
at the departing Angel. He skidded to a stop. From the back
of his bike, the Angel's girlfriend alighted, swaggered forward, and punched the girl in the face. The crowd did
nothing.

No one wanted to tangle with the Angels, especially
when they were so well fortified, not only with alcohol and
drugs (one of their Berkeley friends had thoughtfully provided them with 1,000 tabs of speed-laced acid, and the
Angels themselves had brought along cases of cheap "Red
Mountain" wine, plus a large bag of barbiturates, which was
dumped onto the stage for communal consumption), but
with chains and weighted, sawed-off pool cues specially imported for the occasion. The Stones' management had given
them their marching orders: keep people away from the
stage. "We don't give a fuck how you do it," Sam Cutler,
the Stones' touring manager, told them before the concert.
"Just keep those people away." Now, drunk and stoned, the

Angels prepared to carry out their instructions with a vengeance.

"Ladies and gentlemen, we give you Santana. The first band in the best party in 1969." It was Cutler, razor thin, beak-nosed, beady-eyed, announcing that Altamont was, at long last, underway. The crowd roared back, and for five minutes, while Carlos Santana and his band delivered their Latin, voodoo rock rhythms, Cutler's promise seemed to be coming true. Sol Stern, Wenner's old boss at *Ramparts,* felt his fear ebbing. "It was almost pure ecstasy," he remembered later.

> Turning around all I could see were people as far back as the clear blue horizon. In front was the music, evil but beautiful, coming from huge, perfect amplifiers at the side of the stage, enveloping us in a protective coat of mind-shattering sound. It was like being in the eye of a hurricane, with energy and turmoil all around . . . I thought everything was going to be all right, that the power of the music would keep it all in balance. Then suddenly we went over the edge. Ugliness and meanness erupted all around.

A grotesquely obese man started the trouble. Stripping off his clothes, he stumbled toward the stage in a stupor. Women began screaming. Then, a fight. And in the next moment, only a blur, as three Angels, pool cues at the ready, dove off the stage and into the melee. The fat man went down while the Angels pummeled him. There were shouts of "peace, peace," but the beating continued. A young man leaped up and attempted to go to the fat man's aid. He, too, was struck down, clubbed, kicked and gouged.

Half a dozen times more during the next forty-five minutes, variations of the scene took place. A commotion, some shrieks, then the Angels. Santana later told a reporter, "It all happened so fast, it just went right on before us and we didn't even know what was going on. There were lots of people just fucking freaked out . . . I could see a guy from the stage who had a knife and just wanted to stab somebody. I mean, he really wanted a fight. Anybody getting himself in the way of anybody had a fight whether he wanted it or not. There were kids being stabbed and heads cracking the whole time. We tried to stop it as best we could by not playing, but by the time we got into our fourth song, the more we got into it, the more people got into their fighting thing."

By the conclusion of Santana's set, the first casualties were streaming into a makeshift field hospital: broken arms, opened scalps, smashed ribs, and, on cot after cot, victims of bad trips, screaming of terrors for which there was no first aid. So many bad trips, that within hours the supply of tranquilizing Thorazine was exhausted, and an emergency ration choppered in. Getting the trauma victims out was more difficult. The choked roads made passage for ambulances next to impossible, and a helicopter the Stones had promised for the purpose failed to materialize. As the trickle of patients turned into a torrent, two of the doctors began fighting with each other.

Outside, the music and beatings went on. Jefferson Airplane had taken the stage and tried, without success, to calm everyone with a rendition of "We Can Be Together." But even as they were playing, a beer bottle sailed through the air and impacted directly on the head of a female musician. She collapsed, unconscious, then struggled to her feet and collapsed again, her skull fractured. The Airplane played on, "Revolution" now, with its refrain "Up against the wall, motherfucker." Just behind them, on the stage it-

self, the Angels were stomping a black man. Marty Balin
stopped playing and tried to intervene. An Angel sent him
down with a fist to the jaw. For a brief moment, art became
life, horrifying and real.

It went on that way the rest of the afternoon, a dull,
numbing routine broken only by the sight of the looming
shape of a helicopter, locust-like, slowly dropping out of the
sky onto the concert grounds. "It's Jagger!" The word
flashed like wildfire through the crowd, and as it did, kids
got up, yelled, and started running, bursting past the Angels
to get close to him. Jagger emerged, smiling, waving, calling greetings, with Timothy Leary at his side flashing the
peace symbol. Then, as his phalanx of security men started
hustling him toward a trailer, a long-haired youth lunged at
him. "I'm gonna kill you! I'm gonna kill you!" he screamed,
and, with a well-aimed hook, punched Jagger in the jaw.
The blow bruised Jagger and his head snapped back. Eyes
wide, he pushed through the crowd and rushed for the security of the trailer.

The beatings resumed. One hysterical girl, topless, hurled
herself onto the stage and was hurled off again by the Angels. A young man who had been punched and kicked unconscious by the Angels lay in a bloody heap in front of the
stage for more than an hour before help could arrive. A
photographer, moving in to record the carnage, was told by
an Angel to stop taking pictures and turn over his film.
When the photographer kept shooting, the Angel smashed
the camera into his face, opening up a gash that eventually
required thirteen stitches to close. As he lay crumpled on
the ground, the Angel reached down, retrieved the camera,
emptied it of film, them kicked his victim a final time. Finally, the photographer got up, ran a short distance into the

crowd, and collapsed. The Stones' cameramen were getting it all down on film. When the producer spotted one of them shooting a naked fat girl freaking out behind the stage on a bad acid trip, he pulled him aside. "Don't shoot that," he ordered. "That's ugly. We only want beautiful things." "How can you say that?" the cameraman shot back. "Everything here is ugly."

By now it was five o'clock in the afternoon and the skies were rapidly darkening. Crosby, Stills and Nash, the final warm-up group for the Stones, had cut short their set and hurriedly departed by helicopter. Long moments passed, and still no sign of Jagger. Then Cutler took over the microphone. "The Rolling Stones are here to play, but they won't play until this stage is cleared and that means Hell's Angels, too." The Angels didn't budge. One of them, dressed in a wolf's head, strode up to the microphone and began to play a screeching solo on a flute. No one dared make him stop. "We hated them, hated them and envied them at the same time," Stern wrote later.

> For all their brutality and ugliness, they had a definition of themselves and their purpose that showed us up. We had all talked about a counter-community for years—and now, with that community massed in one place, we couldn't relate to anything. In their primitive way, and without talking much about it, the Angels were so together that less than 100 of them were able to take over and intimidate a crowd of close to half a million people. We had talked about solidarity, but they, not us, were willing to go down for each other in a showdown. We had the music but they had a purpose, and everyone in that atomized, alienated mass in front of the stage knew it, and that was their incredible power over us.

A half hour slipped by, then another, and another, and Jagger had yet to appear. Cutler kept making announcements, telling people to cool down so the Stones could play. Actually, he was stalling, waiting for complete darkness to envelop the valley. Jagger wanted the night.

Then, in one blinding flash, the stage exploded in red light, and there, surrounded by a coven of Angels, was the man who called himself Lucifer: Uncle Sam hat atop his head, black and orange cape draped over his shoulders, legs sheathed in silver pants and high black boots, and, across his chest, a black shirt emblazoned with the Greek letter Omega—the end.

Whirling and fluttering across the stage, he crashed into his first number, "Jumping Jack Flash." The crowd roared and leaped to its feet; even the Angels seemed entranced. Another number—"Carol." And then Jagger's trademark— "Sympathy for the Devil."

Suddenly, bodies bunching in front of the stage, falling, disappearing into a pile. The music abruptly stopped and, squinting into the glare of the spotlights, Jagger grabbed the microphone: "Brothers and sisters, come on now! That means everybody just cool out! We can cool out, everybody! Everybody be cool, now. Come on." He paused a moment more, still straining to see what was happening beneath the stage in front of him. Then he spoke again: ". . . Everyone just cool down. Is there anyone there who's hurt? Okay, if we're cool, I think we can groove. We always have something very funny happening when we start that number." He started over, but only for a moment. Whatever was happening in front of the stage was still going on. "Why are we fighting?" Jagger demanded. "Who wants to fight, who is it? Every other scene has been cool . . . We gotta stop right now. You know, if we can't, there's no point . . ."

Richard cut in—"Either those cats cool it, man, or we don't play"—only to have an Angel grab the mike out of his hand and shout at him and the 300,000 others present: "Fuck you!" Finally, it became apparent that something terrible had happened; in front of the stage, people were holding up hands covered with blood. "We need a doctor here, now!" Jagger yelled. "We're trying to help someone who's hurt." How badly, he still could not tell. Only later, long after the music was over and he looked at the films his camera crew had taken, would the horror be fully revealed.

In the viewfinder, a young black man appears. There is a glint of gun in his hand. The Angels move in. One of them flashes out with a knife: once, twice, three times, four. The black man goes down, and the Angels close in, kicking and stomping. *Rolling Stone* later quoted an eyewitness: "There was a big hole on his spine and a big hole in the side and there was a big hole in his temple. A big open slice. You could see all the way in. You could see inside . . . at least an inch down, you know. And then there was a big hole right where there's no ribs on his back . . . the side of his head was just sliced open . . . all of us were drenched in blood." He died within the hour.

Jagger, meanwhile, had resumed singing. There was terror in his eyes now. He sang like a man possessed, better, it was said later, than he had ever sung before. On through his routine they went, hit after familiar hit, concluding in grand crescendo with "Street-Fighting Man." And then, mercifully, it was over.

John Burks, who had been at the concert, called Wenner early the next morning, waking him, and laid out the broad outlines of what had happened. The story, as Burks related it, was a chronicle of unrelieved horror: one murdered,

three others killed by accident—two by a hit-and-run driver
coming home from the concert, another drowning in a
drainage ditch; scores of injuries; bad trips by the hundreds.
Burks's narrative was emotional and angry. "These fuckers,"
he said over and over to Wenner, describing the Angels and
the Stones. "We gotta tell people what these fuckers did."
Wenner tried to calm him. He told Burks to gather everyone on the staff who had been at the concert for a meeting
to plan what to do. In the meantime, he'd do some checking
on his own. Wenner hung up and glanced at the morning
papers. The stories did not jibe with Burks's rendition of
events. According to the Sunday *Examiner-Chronicle,* Altamont had been an even more successful replay of Woodstock, the Stones playing their most brilliantly, a good time
being had by all. Cutler was quoted as saying that the proof
of how well the festival had gone was the fact that three ba-
bies had been born. (In fact, there were none; the closest
thing to a live birth was a stoned young man who comman-
deered an ambulance and insisted on being driven to the
hospital, claiming he was about to have a baby; at a freeway overpass along the way, he got out, stripped off his
clothes, and plunged over the side, critically injuring himself.) Dick Carter, the owner of the raceway, was reportedly
already drawing up plans for another festival, three days in
length, for half a million fans, with the Beatles as star performers. "The will of the people will win out," he was saying. "They want the Beatles, we'll give them the Beatles."

Wenner was still dubious when he reached the office. He
listened skeptically as Burks and the rest of the staff began
to relate stories of the violence. It was the testimony of
Greil Marcus, whose judgment Wenner deeply respected,
that changed his mind. Altamont had been "the worst day
in my life," Marcus said quietly. As far as he was con-

cerned, he didn't care if he never heard another rock and
roll record again. Gleason, once one of the Stones' and the
Angels' most enthusiastic supporters, also joined the chorus.
"Is this the new community?" he asked. "Is this what
Woodstock promised? Gathered together *as* a tribe, what
happened? Brutality, murder, despoliation, you name it
. . . The name of the game is money, power and ego and
money is first and it brings power. The Stones didn't do it
for free, they did it for money, only the tab was paid in a
different way."

Wenner needed no more convincing. A summons went
out for every photographer who had been at the concert;
eventually, nearly fifty of them were rounded up. A similar
sweep collected copy and firsthand recollections. Some
eleven reporters contributed to the final effort, which ran to
nearly 15,000 words. Edited by Burks, with top-editing by
Wenner himself, the story was something less than a model
of coherent, well-organized prose. But as an exercise in
first-person, emotional reporting, it was a masterpiece. Detail after grisly detail, "rock and roll's all-time worst day,"
as the magazine called it, was all there, beginning with a
lengthy, eyewitness account of the murder and its aftermath, continuing through a meticulous recounting of how
the concert was organized, and concluding with a powerful
indictment of the concert's organizers and the Rolling
Stones themselves. Cutler emerged as the chief villain. It
had been Cutler who had arranged for the security, Cutler
who had given the Angels their violent charter, Cutler who
had been on stage throughout the entire affair. "Now fifty
per cent of the people will dig what they did," he shrugged,
"and fifty per cent will not dig what they did. I don't need to
get into a positive-anti kind of thing . . . I didn't dig, in
fact, what a lot of people did."

   No one wanted to pass judgment. "Those cats are on a

different trip," David Crosby of Crosby, Stills and Nash said
of the Angels. ". . . I ain't gonna put them down, I'm not
gonna put them up. Remember," he continued, "the Angels
were asked to be there. If it's not that kind of scene, they
don't get into that kind of bag. I don't dig everybody blaming the Angels. Blame. Blame is the dumbest thing there is;
there isn't any blame." *Rolling Stone* could not leave it quite
at that. Someone, something had to be responsible: that rich
downtown lawyer ("Fuck Melvin Belli"), Jagger ("What
an enormous thrill it would be for an Angel to kick Mick
Jagger's teeth down his throat"), bad planning, hotheads,
the lack of space, the low stage, even the moon being in
Scorpio—anything but the culture itself.

Part of it bothered Wenner, though: the murder part. A
considerable portion of the *Rolling Stone* story was taken
up with recounting the brief life story of the young man
who had been stabbed to death at Jagger's feet. His name
was Meredith Hunter. Just eighteen, he turned out to have
been a typical rock and roll kid, dancing to the music,
grooving, doing everything most of *Rolling Stone*'s readers
did, only carrying a gun with him when he did it. Since his
death, no one from the Stones' organization had contacted
his family. They were in trouble now. Meredith had been the
only male breadwinner, and with his murder the bills had
begun to mount up. To make matters worse, his mother had
suffered a nervous collapse in the wake of her son's killing
and had been hospitalized. Still the Stones had done nothing. It upset Wenner. Late one night in his office, not long
after Altamont, he wrote out a draft for $500 to Hunter's
family and slipped it in the mail.

Months went by before the full implications of Altamont
finally sank in. In the interval, the Stones, now returned to
London, prospered. In March, *Rolling Stone* reported that,

thanks in large measure to the killing, the Stones' film "Gimme Shelter" would wind up a box office smash. The story added that the Angels were allegedly demanding a total of $54,000—$6,000 for each of their nine chapters—from the film proceeds "or else." Cutler, however, would not be seeing any of the cash. The Stones had fired him, and he had returned to San Francisco in a bitter mood. "What had gone down" was actually someone else's fault, he insisted. There was no blaming him; he had not made a penny. Mick had taken it all. "Jagger," he claimed, "has not acted honorably."

The same conclusion gradually began to dawn on Wenner. In the months after Altamont, he seldom saw Jagger; and as the years passed, the two of them became estranged entirely. Later Wenner would mutter darkly that he knew things about his old friend that "could put him in jail." In truth, Wenner had few causes for complaint. *Rolling Stone* profited handsomely from the Altamont affair. In 1971, the magazine's story, along with its account of the Manson murders, was singled out by Columbia University for receipt of the prestigious National Magazine Award for Specialized Journalism. The accompanying certificate praised *Rolling Stone* in particular for "challenging the shared attitudes of its readers."

After Altamont, those attitudes began to change rapidly. The Angels lost their status as the protectors of the flower children, and slipped back to what they always had been—a mechanized brigade of violent sociopaths. There was a mysterious shake-up in the Angel hierarchy, and the suicide of one Angel who had been particularly close to the rock scene. A few weeks later, the Alameda County sheriff arrested Alan David Passaro, a twenty-four-year-old Angel with a long criminal record, for the murder of Meredith Hunter. Sonny Barger, the Angels' leader and former confidant of Kesey, failed to see what all the commotion over Altamont was about. He and the Angels had never made any pretense about who they were. "I'm no peace creep by any sense of the word," Barger told a radio interviewer. "Ain't nobody gonna kick my motorcycle. And they might think because they are in a crowd of 300,000 people that they can do it and get away with it. But when you're standing there, looking at something that's your life, and everything you've got is invested in that thing, and you love that thing better than you love anything in the world, and you see a guy kick it, you know who he is. And if you got to go through fifty people to get him, you gonna get him."

They never used Altamont for a rock concert again; "too much bad Karma," a member of the Grateful Dead explained. With minor exceptions, the festival scene itself disappeared entirely. There were a few sporadic attempts to rekindle the Woodstock feeling—Warner Brothers went so far as to form a rock band, "Stoneground," which traveled from concert to concert in a caravan of buses, recorded all the while by movie cameras, in hopes, never realized, of duplicating the success of *Woodstock* and *Gimme Shelter*—but the impulse that had brought young people to listen to the music, share their dope and call strangers "brother" and "sister" had been a casualty of Altamont. Now, when young people gathered, violence was too often the result. A concert at Grant Park in Chicago ended in a full-scale riot. At least 91 policemen and 119 civilians were injured, and Grant Park was left in shambles. At Randall's Island in New York, 10,000 paying fans and another 20,000 gate-crashers showed up to listen to Jimi Hendrix, Joe Cocker, and Jethro Tull. When four of the five headliners failed to show, another riot ensued. Other cities banned concerts altogether. Not even the musicians wanted to play festivals anymore. "Holding a rock festival now," Paul Kantner of the

Airplane told a reporter in 1971, "is like inviting someone
to a party, then charging him $20 and hitting him over the
head with a baseball bat every ten minutes while you give
him some grass so it doesn't feel so bad."

It was Rock Scully, though, one of the Grateful Dead's
roadies and himself a part of the team that planned Altamont, who said it best. "Anyone should have seen this
would happen," he mourned. "This whole trip, man—if
somebody tried to buy another Woodstock. We should have
seen it, but we couldn't see that."

After Altamont, everyone saw it. To a culture given over
to casting events in apocalyptic, symbolic terms, Altamont
was Götterdämmerung. Never after Altamont would
Wenner proclaim that "rock and roll can set you free."
Never after Altamont would rock have its same mystic
power. Altamont was the killer of the dream. "Woodstock
Nation never existed," Wenner wrote, two years after the
concert, in an editorial marking *Rolling Stone*'s fourth anniversary. ". . . Free is a complete myth . . . If you're doing
public art and communication in America—if you even *live*
here—you're dealing with money, and you're in business
. . . As long as there are printing bills to pay, writers who
want to earn a living by their craft, people who pay for gro-
ceries, want to raise children and have their own homes,
Rolling Stone will be a capitalist operation . . . Rock and
roll obviously will not 'save the world,' nor is it for everybody 'the music that will set you free.' The notion of a coherent counterculture is [a] myth."

The suddenness with which the world had turned upside
down dazed even Jagger. Long after Altamont, the once satanic prince of darkness, face sallow and dissolute, uttered
Woodstock's epitaph. "All this stuff about my leading and
perverting them," he mused, "we just sort of went along together, didn't we?"

7

The Gonzo Prince

Jann Wenner was freaked.

Not worried or upset in the ordinary way, the way his editors had become used to, but *freaked*. Here it was, 1970, and to believe the notices he was getting in the straight press, *Rolling Stone* was at the very height of its powers, the readers and advertisers pouring in. His money problems had been solved, his enemies vanquished; a storm of approval fairly thundered in his ears. "The young publishing genius," *Parade* was calling him, editor of a magazine that, according to the *Columbia Journalism Review,* has "spoken for—and to—an entire generation of young Americans." "*Stone* has become solvent and earned the trade's respect," *Time* concluded. Even the conservative Los Angeles *Times* was singing his praises. "*Rolling Stone* is the only intelligent voice speaking naturally and easily to an audience which has so far been identified principally by its tendency to buy rock and roll records," the *Times* declared. "Wenner finds himself in charge of a unique and valuable medium."

From the look of it, everything seemed golden. Wenner knew better. Something was wrong. *Rolling Stone* was reading—and feeling—a little flat.

The problem, in a word, was music. It was a puzzling

phenomenon. Superficially, the business had never been healthier. More records were being produced, more groups being formed, more money coming in than ever before. But something important was missing. Giants, some said; incontestably, there were fewer of them to be found. Hendrix, Joplin, and Morrison were burnt-out cases, not long for the world. Dylan had gone into one of his periodic funks. The Rolling Stones, bogged down by tax problems, and with Altamont still fresh in their minds, had cut back their public appearances. As for the Beatles, their reincarnation was a promoter's fantasy. "There is a lack of excitement in the air," Landau complained in *Rolling Stone*. "There are no legends, no passion, no glamor and no stars." Michael Lydon was even blunter. "The star trip of the Sixties is over," he declared. The decade was finished. What had begun, added critic Albert Goldman, was "the new depression."

The music showed it: a jangling, heavy, metallic sound, as empty as it was loud. Innovation had disappeared. The culture had grown older, and in growing older, had lost its fire. Instead of rebellion, there were laments for lost love; instead of change, there was numbing repetition. "It is too rational, too business-like and too orderly," Landau warned. "And if something doesn't break loose soon, it will kill off what energy is left for a good long time."

But nothing was happening. Like a needle stuck in a groove, rock was content to repeat proven patterns. And why not? The audience had never been larger or more adoring. Elvis had come to Vegas; the frug had invaded the White House. With the dawning of the Seventies, there was no hamlet, however small, that did not support a Top 40 station; no gathering, however chic, that did not throb to the beat of the music. Rock and roll had exploded. No longer was it the refuge of the young and the rebellious. Now it belonged to everyone.

That, of course, was the trouble. Rock was not meant to be accepted. By its nature, the music was supposed to be alien and threatening. Rock and roll belonged to the young. It was their medium, their *only* medium, Wenner kept saying through the Sixties. But now the Sixties were over. The protesters were headed for law school. The culture, *Time* reported, with an almost audible sigh of relief, had cooled off. *Rolling Stone,* so dependent on music for its energy, desperately needed a new gig.

And then, one memorable Friday afternoon in April, *he* walked in. The Solution.

Wenner had been warned in advance that the man he was about to meet was a bit "out of the ordinary," as one of his editors gently put it. But he was altogether unprepared for the apparition who appeared that Friday and proceeded to tell him with bizarre if utter certainty that he was about to be elected Sheriff of Aspen, Colorado, and that he wanted to write a story about it. It was not just what he said, or the way he said it, or how he was dressed (tennis shoes and white chino shorts, topped by a multicolored Mexican shirt), or the six-pack of beer he had brought along (and, amidst numerous belches, consumed in the next two hours), or even the gray woman's wig he was wearing. It was simply everything taken together, the entire weird persona, that was so overwhelming. When at length his visitor excused himself to make use of the facilities, Wenner, who had been gradually slinking beneath his desk, straightened up, took a deep breath, turned to one of his editors, and said, "I know I'm supposed to be the spokesman for the counterculture and all that, but what the fuck is *this?*"

This was simply Dr. Hunter S. Thompson, the Mad Dog Prince of Gonzo Journalism. Wenner's reaction was understandable. On first meeting, one never knew quite what to make of Dr. Thompson (the title was self-bestowed), whether he was a genius or a madman or maybe both. His background seemed conventional enough: Born, Louisville, Kentucky, 1938, the son of an insurance agent; adolescent stick-up artist and troublemaker; honorable discharge, United States Air Force (which relieved itself of his presence, two years before his enlistment was up, after his commanding officer reported that "his flair for invention and imagination" combined with "rebellious disregard for military dress and authority . . . sometimes seems to rub off on the other airmen"); sportswriting stint in Florida; a stint as foreign correspondent in Latin America; tours with *Time,* the New York *Herald Tribune* and the *National Observer;* two unpublished novels, one minor best seller, *Hell's Angels,* and, as a direct result thereof, one smashed-in face and three broken ribs. Nothing, in short, that would set him apart from any other journeyman writer with a fondness for drugs, motorcycles, and anything else that promised his own destruction. Indeed, when he took the wig off Thompson even looked straight: short-haired, balding, trim, like a family man with a mortgage to pay. It was easy to be fooled. During the 1968 New Hampshire primary, for instance, Richard Nixon had taken Thompson for a sports fanatic, and had spent an hour privately chatting with him about their mutual obsession, pro football. Of course, when Nixon deposited Thompson at the airport, he nearly killed the next President, not to mention himself, by leaning over the open gas tank of Nixon's private jet with a lighted cigarette dangling from his mouth. Not that Thompson would have harmed Nixon on purpose. "He's a very gentle soul," *Roll-*

ing Stone managing editor Paul Scanlon was to say of him. "When he's not working, he sits at home in Woody Creek and shoots at a tree with a .45."

But when he sat down at his typewriter, Hunter Thompson was someone else entirely. Then he became the dark Prince of Gonzo, the demon of fear and loathing, out to do rhetorical battle with the enemies of truth, justice, and, as Hunter perceived it, the American way—be they Hell's Angels, Vegas hustlers, Super Bowl fans, or conniving politicians. The prose that issued forth under those conditions—along with Thompson's own accounting of the substances employed to fortify him ("Two bags of grass, seventy-five pellets of mescaline, five sheets of high-powered blotter acid, a salt shaker half full of cocaine, and a whole galaxy of multicolored uppers, downers, screamers, laughers . . . a quart of tequila, a quart of rum, a case of Budweiser, a pint of raw ether and two dozen amyls")—led many readers to suppose that his genius lay in his craziness.

The truth was that Hunter Thompson, aside from certain eccentricities (such as occasionally employing a giant-sized medical syringe to inject a pint of gin directly into his stomach) was utterly sane. The "crazy" Hunter Thompson—the "Raoul Duke" (a character Thompson invented for the purpose of saying things that Thompson thought ought to be said, but had found no one to say), who, as his official biography had it, "lives with . . . an undetermined number of large Dobermans trained to kill, in a fortified retreat somewhere in the mountains of Colorado"—was a cover, an elaborate disguise devised to conceal a warm, generous, rather insecure young man who wanted nothing so much as to be a writer, and concluded that great writers had to be, by their very nature, a little larger than life.

That Hunter Thompson reverenced writing, the way

other men worship a god or a rock star, and he worked at it
—hard. Years before, as a clerk for *Time,* he had spent evening after evening laboriously copying pages of Faulkner
and Fitzgerald, trying to unravel the genius of their
rhythms, wanting to feel their talent coursing through his
fingertips. Later, he traveled west, to California, learning on
the road, because that is what Kerouac had done, and he
wanted to be like Kerouac. He worried over his own talent,
and confessed to his doctor that if he didn't use drugs, he
would have the mind of a "second-rate accountant." But,
when it came time to write, he put away most of the drugs
and concentrated on his craft, sculpting each sentence and
paragraph with a care and precision that belied his seemingly crazed stream-of-consciousness prose.

Thompson called the style "Gonzo." It was not so much a
manner of writing, as an assault on it, a rhetorical light
show of images, flashes, and truths, squawks, hisses, and
grunts, obscure literary references, fragments of autobiography, confessions of failure, and continual reminders to
the reader that all of it, like life itself, was "madness, gibberish, shit." Gonzo recognized no limits. It could be som-
ber and sane one moment, bizarre and fantastic the next. As
with Thompson, one was never certain how much of it was
contrived and how much was true. The genius of the style
was that, after reading it, one didn't care.

It had begun by accident. As Thompson recounted the
story, he was having dinner one night in 1970 in Aspen
with novelist Jim Salter, who casually suggested that the
two of them attend the upcoming Kentucky Derby. Thompson, at the time, was writing competently, if conventionally,
as a free-lance for *Scanlon's,* a feisty, short-lived weekly
launched by Warren Hinckle after the death of *Ramparts.*
As they continued talking and drinking, the idea of going to

the Derby became increasingly appealing. Finally, at 3:30 in the morning, and by now quite drunk, Thompson called Hinckle in San Francisco and announced that the Derby was "the greatest spectacle in the country," and that to do it justice required his special talents. Hinckle groggily agreed, said he would dispatch British illustrator Ralph Steadman to accompany him. With that, Hunter was on his way.

He arrived in Louisville only to discover that the deadline for press passes had expired three months before, and that there were no hotel rooms to be had in the entire city. Undaunted, he cajoled, threatened and lied his way in, informing the Derby officials that *Scanlon's* was a world-famous Irish magazine and that he and Steadman had come to produce illustrations that would hang in the British Museum. Impressed, Derby officials granted Thompson and Steadman admittance to the press box. It was a blunder of huge proportions.

For Thompson, in addition to his usual drug paraphernalia, had brought along a can of Mace to Churchill Downs. As post time approached, Thompson grew restless. He wanted action, then and there. Absently he peered over the balcony, and spied a collection of dignitaries sitting directly beneath him—the governor, his wife, all manner of notables and officials, smug and self-assured, not knowing the weirdness that lurked over them and their mint juleps. In that instant, the race became secondary. While a horrified Steadman looked on, Thompson reached into his pack, retrieved the Mace, leaned over the balcony again, aimed at the governor, and pressed . . . once, twice, three times. "Let's get the hell out of here," Thompson suggested with as much calm as the situation would allow. "Nobody Maces the governor in the press box. It's just not done."

Thompson repaired to his hotel room to await inspiration. But his mind was somewhere else: Ohio National Guardsmen had shot and killed four students at Kent State. In panic, he flew to New York, hoping that a change of scenery would unblock him; instead, he was even more paralyzed. Deadline was nearing; the rest of *Scanlon's* was either printed or on the press in San Francisco; all that was missing was his story, the cover piece.

Encamped in a strange New York hotel, Thompson reposed for hours in his bathtub, guzzling White Horse scotch from the bottle, convinced that his writing career was at an end. "The pressure," he remembered, "began to silently build like a dog whistle kind of scream . . . You couldn't hear it, but it was everywhere." After three days of anxious, drunken stupor, Thompson decided that something, *anything*, had to be sent in. Ferociously, he ripped the pages out of his notebook and began feeding them into the telecopier. He then collapsed in front of the television, waiting for the worst. Instead, *Scanlon's* New York editor wanted more. Thompson, incredulous, phoned Hinckle, only to find him chortling over how wonderful Thompson's "story" was. With that, Thompson proceeded to send in the rest of the notebook, page after crazed page.

He returned to Aspen worn out and depressed. He had always come close to Missing Deadlines, but this time he had gone over the line. What he had done, he thought, was produce, but in "the foulest and cheapest way, like Oakland's unclean touchdown against Miami—off balance . . . all wrong . . . six seconds to go . . . but it worked." *Scanlon's* wound up printing his notebook word for word. That cheered him only slightly. Hinckle, after all, was even whackier than he was. Thompson still fully expected to be impaled by the readers and the reviewers. What resulted instead was a hurricane of critical acclaim, letters and calls by the dozen, writers calling it "a tremendous breakthrough in journalism," "a stroke of genius."

One of the letters came from Bill Cardoso, a writer whom Thompson had met during the '68 primary in New Hampshire, and who was then editor of the *Boston Globe Sunday Magazine*. "Gonzo" was a word Cardoso had picked up during his tours of neighborhood Irish taverns. Gonzo wasn't so much a fact as a state of mind. If someone was still on his feet drinking long after everyone else had dropped, he was "gonzo." If a rock song was great, that was "gonzo" too. And, as far as Cardoso was concerned, it was precisely the right adjective for Thompson's Derby piece. "That was pure gonzo," he wrote. "You've broken through. Stay with it." And thus, however improbably, was the legend born.

In later years, Thompson claimed that gonzo's high-speed comic-book-style excitement—people didn't speak in Thompson's world, they hissed, sputtered, snarled, snorted, "eeeeeched" and "aaaarrrgged"—was the natural outgrowth of his years as a sportswriter. "You get, in sportswriting, the opportunity to use verbs and adjectives naturally," he explained. "You know, where the Eagles would squash somebody and the Penguins would rip somebody and somebody else would stomp somebody. You want the feeling of the grass, the atmosphere of the crowd, the tension, the excitement. You get a tremendous leeway with the usage of words. As a matter of fact, the wilder you get, the better it is." It was the perfect preparation for politics. "Sportswriters are used to being lied to," Thompson went on, "so you come in a little angry. It's a whole horrible con job, just like politics, and either you accept it, or you don't. I chose not to."

That was Hunter Thompson's great weakness: he didn't

like being lied to. His curse was to be an old-fashioned moralist trapped in a world that, by its very immorality, continually threatened to destroy him. Until the Chicago convention, he had tried to ignore it, pretending he didn't care about politics. But the night of April 24, 1968, changed everything. Thompson was in the streets; he had no business being there, wanted not to be there, but off with Norman Mailer at a cocktail party three blocks away. Suddenly the police were everywhere, flailing wildly with their nightsticks. A girl went down in a bloody heap and Thompson moved forward to pull her away. Then he went down as well. He saw one of the cops standing over him, face contorted in dumb rage, then the blur of a club whistling toward his head, and then, only blackness.

For weeks afterward, he could not talk about the experience without crying. Yet he could never bring himself to write about it; the vision of kids being brutalized while "good Democrats" decried the "immorality" of the protesters, the memory of Hubert Humphrey smiling, Dick Daley snarling, giving them the finger, whirled in his head like a dervish. The violence with which he wrote was his only defense. He lived with a sense of doom, a conviction that he should never have lived past thirty, that he and the rest of his generation were simply existing on borrowed time.

Try as he might, Thompson could never get out of the world on schedule. He committed unspeakable crimes against his body, pumping it full of all manner of stimulants and depressants, combinations which, in the hands of anyone else, would have brought death. In Thompson, though, they had no effect. If anything, the punishment only made him stronger. He had the look and physique of a professional athlete, catlike grace and bone-crushing strength, like a hopped-up tight end for the Oakland Raiders. He could take the most lunatic chances, and somehow, against the odds, in the face of all that was reasonable, manage to survive. When he brushed with death, as he did one day in a Texas motel room by unthinkingly jabbing a needle full of speed into a vein, he neither welcomed it, nor fled from it, but watched it coming, with detached, professional fascination: "The tile was white, the curtain was white—but in the corner of my eye in the mirror I looked down and saw a hell of a lot of red. Here was this tiny puncture, like a leak in a high-powered hose . . . You could barely see the stream. It was going straight from my leg and hitting the shower curtain at about thigh level, and the whole bottom of the curtain was turning red. I thought, 'Oh Jesus Christ, what now?' I went in and lay down on the bed and told the people in the room to get out without telling them why; then I waited 20 minutes; all I could think about was those horrible Janis Joplin stories: O.D.'ing in a motel . . . Jim Morrison . . . Jimi Hendrix . . . needles. And I thought, 'oh fuck, what a sloppy way to go' . . . I thought, 'oh God, it's going to come all at once.'" But of course it didn't; it never did. The bleeding stopped and Thompson lived on, almost embarrassed that he had.

It was that way with him, always testing the limits of the possible. He boasted once that "there are very few things that can really beat driving around the Bay Area on a good summer night—big motorcycle, head full of acid—wearing nothing but a T-shirt and a pair of shorts and getting on Highway 1 and going 120 miles an hour . . . A rush of every kind . . . head, hands maintaining control . . . and seeing how far I can go, how weird I can get and still survive, even though I am seeing rats in front of me instead of cops. Rats with guns on." He knew that one day he would go over the edge, that there would be a moment, like the one years before, heading too fast into a rain-slicked curve, suddenly feeling control slipping, letting go, powerless, riding with it, then hearing nothing, as a deer on a hillside or a man on a battlefield hears nothing the moment he is killed; everything exactly as it had been then, only this time there would be no waking up. It did not stop him. Something about him was incapable of putting the brakes on. He tried to explain what it was once by telling a story about jackrabbits:

> People who know jackrabbits will tell you they are primarily motivated by Fear, Stupidity, and Craziness. But I have spent enough time in jackrabbit country to know that most of them lead pretty dull lives; they are bored with their daily routines: eat, fuck, sleep, hop around the bush now and then . . . No wonder some of them drift over the line into cheap thrills once in a while; there has to be a powerful adrenalin rush in crouching by the side of the road, waiting for the next set of headlights to come along, then streaking out of the bushes with split-second timing and making it across to the other side just inches in front of the speeding front wheels. Why not? Anything that gets the adrenalin moving like a 440 bolt blast in a copper bathtub is good for the reflexes and keeps the veins free of cholesterol.

Gradually, it occurred to Thompson that his surviving all these things, Hell's Angels, drugs, motorcycles, had to have a meaning, that there was some purpose to his being continually spared, that he had a mission: to tell the world the end was coming, and that the moment for repentance was at hand.

"Hunter Thompson's Disease," Kurt Vonnegut called it:

an incurable, fatal malady suffered by those "who feel that Americans can be as easily led to beauty as to ugliness, to truth as to public relations, to joy as to bitterness."

Would Wenner back him up? Sitting in the exposed-brick confines of the editor-in-chief's office, Thompson could only wonder. Across the desk, Wenner straightened himself, chewed his nail for a moment, then looked at him and flashed a broad smile. "Like it," he pronounced. "Story's great. Do it." Thompson emitted a final belch, got up, and stretched out his hand. Wenner took it, and immediately blanched in pain. The grip was vise-like. Thompson chuckled to himself; the warning had been delivered.

What Hunter Thompson could not know at that moment was that Jann Wenner needed him as much as he needed Wenner. Thompson was, even then in 1970, already a cult figure among younger readers, largely on the basis of *Hell's Angels;* and Wenner was desperate for star quality. For, to add to his problems, some of his best writers and editors were deserting, and all because of John Burks. Burks had long been a problem. His competency had not been at issue; in the two years since Wenner had installed him as managing editor, Burks had taken virtual command of the magazine. He had professionalized its operations, commissioned meaty reporting on the youth culture, and assembled a first-rate staff personally loyal to him. And therein lay the difficulty: control of the magazine.

Initially, Wenner had been content to let Burks assume command of *Rolling Stone*'s day-to-day operations. He was away much of the time, scurrying between New York, London, and Los Angeles, trying to put the magazine on a more solid financial footing. His absenteeism, coupled with Burks' strong-willed ways, made a confrontation inevitable. Behind his back, Burks sneered that Wenner's sojourns were not so much business expeditions as "the boy publisher out riding in his limousine." Burks was also upset by Wenner's coziness with the record industry, notably the increasing emphasis Wenner put on music coverage after securing advertising advances from various record companies. "Jann had a rule of thumb," Burks said later. "When in doubt, put the Beatles on the cover." Financially, there was no arguing with Wenner's logic. The Beatles sold. Politics and pop sociology—Burks's special interest—did not. As the months wore on, relations between Burks and Wenner deteriorated. Older than his boss, and vastly more experienced, Burks made no secret of his growing contempt for Wenner. Matters were made worse by Burks's stature: at six feet six he towered over Wenner by nearly a foot. Wenner, always sensitive about his size, was nervous when Burks was in the same room; he tried whenever possible to have Burks sit while he stood. Burks was well aware of Wenner's insecurity and played on it unmercifully, describing Wenner to the staff as "the kid." Wenner tried to ignore the taunts.

Then, in April of 1970, the United States invaded Cambodia. At Kent State, National Guardsmen killed four students. With Wenner out of town, Burks decided to put out a special issue, entitled "On America: 1970: A Pitiful Helpless Giant." The reporting in that issue, like the events it described, was highly emotional, and Burks and his colleagues had been anxious to follow it up with more of the same. They were also determined to settle, once and for all, who was running the magazine—its absentee owner, or the people who were putting it out week after week. Meetings had been called and Charlie Perry drew up a manifesto. It was Berkeley all over again.

Wenner's loyalists alerted him that a putsch was in the making, and he hurried home to take charge. His first move was to call the staff together and reaffirm *Rolling Stone*'s reason for being. In a word, it was music. "It was a bizarre meeting," Burks remembered. "Jann was incredibly nervous. He kept chewing on his fingernails. His head was down and he was mumbling so low you could barely hear him. He kept quoting the Beatles' 'Get Back.' He must have said 'get back' about six times." Get back Wenner did. For the rest of the year, there was a nearly unbroken string of music covers. Politics was, if not forgotten, put safely into cold storage. In the meantime, Wenner proceeded to get rid of his rivals. Several were fired outright. Others had their paychecks trimmed or were shifted to obscure positions. Burks lasted only a few more weeks, while Wenner devised ways to get rid of him. In the end, it turned out to be easy. In late June, Princeton University awarded Bob Dylan an honorary degree, an event Wenner deemed worthy of major attention, while Burks wanted to consign it to "Random Notes." Wenner seized on the incident. "Obviously," he told Burks, "we have different ideas of what this magazine ought to be about." "I guess so," Burks replied, shrugging, and thereupon tendered his resignation.

Now came Hunter Thompson, like a Day-Glo life raft heaving into view. Hardly pausing to consider what he was getting into, Wenner quickly scrambled aboard. Thompson was delighted. He needed *Rolling Stone*'s cash badly just then, and its publicity even more. For, even if no one else thought so, he was taking his campaign for Sheriff of Aspen most seriously. "The green heads, land-rapers and other human jackals," as Thompson characterized the developers, were taking over Aspen, committing all manner of nefarious crimes, and Thompson had decided it was up to him to stop them. If elected, he promised, he would tear up the streets of Aspen, replant them with sod, change the name of

the town to "Fat City," and punish bad-dope dealers in
"proper public fashion" by imprisoning them in stocks on
the courthouse lawn. Whether it would come to pass, he
said, depended on "how many Freaks, heads, criminals,
anarchists, beatniks, poachers, Wobblies, bikers and weird
persuasions will come out of their holes and vote for me."
Alas, it was not to be. Thompson lost the election (though
not by much; "We ran an honest campaign," he explained
to the press after his defeat, "and that was the trouble"),
which was fortunate for Wenner. If Thompson had had to
enforce the law rather than break it, he could hardly have
become the superstar he quickly became for *Rolling Stone*.

Thompson's impact was immediate. "The Battle of
Aspen: Freak Power in the Rockies," followed by "Strange
Rumblings in Azatlan," a fiercely detailed, angry inquiry
into the killing by sheriff's deputies of Los Angeles *Times*
reporter Reuben Salazar, loosed an avalanche of approving
mail. But neither compared with the two-part story which
Thompson eventually transformed into a best seller: *Fear
and Loathing in Las Vegas*. Tom Wolfe, whose own writing
was not unlike Thompson's, proclaimed *Las Vegas* "a
scorching, epochal sensation." "The funniest piece of American prose since *Naked Lunch*," added the New York *Times*.
"The final word, a brilliant vision, a terrible, magnificently
funny telling," the *Village Voice* declared, "of what happened to this country in the 1960's."

Fear and Loathing in Las Vegas was all of that, and a lot
more. It was a deceptively simple story, a running chronicle
of how Thompson and his lawyer, a 300-pound Chicano
named Oscar Acosta, set out from Los Angeles for Las
Vegas on "a savage journey to the heart of the American
dream," intending to cover a marathon motorcycle race and
winding up indeterminate days and many mishaps later in

the ballroom of Caesar's Palace, honored guests at the National District Attorneys Association's Third Annual Institute on Narcotics and Dangerous Drugs. Very little of what went on at either event emerged in Thompson's book. Instead, virtually the entire work was given over to retelling Thompson's exploits staying one step ahead of the law, rental car agencies, Jesus freaks, hotel clerks, addleheaded editors, and his own lawyer, who, in between chewing blotters of acid, throwing up, seducing unsuspecting maidens, and pilfering 600 bars of Neutrogena soap, seemed intent on killing him with gun and knife. Thompson, naturally, survived, to tell a tale that was at once savagely manic and oddly elegiac, a last stoned lament for the freedom that had been the Sixties. "Vegas," he said later, "was sort of a final fling. I had a sense that Nixon and Mitchell and all those people would make it impossible for anybody to behave that way and get away with it. It wouldn't be a matter of a small fine. Your head would be cut off."

While the fun lasted, Thompson made the most of it. He emerged in the pages of *Fear and Loathing in Las Vegas* as an existential prankster, reveling in his tricks, yet never so completely, even in his most drug-deluded moments, as to forget the consequences of what he was doing. Sooner or later, the piper would have to be paid. All Hunter Thompson could do was dodge, weave, thumb his nose, spit in his eye while fear and loathing inexorably closed in. His "felonies," as he grandly referred to his acts of petty mischief, had a bad-little-boy quality to them: the Weathermen planted bombs; Thompson wrote dirty words on the hull of the America's Cup yacht. Neither had any effect. Every day, Thompson returned to his garish Vegas hotel room, smack dead in the double-knit heart of the American Empire, to see how hopeless it was. There, on the flickering

screen in front of him, Walter Cronkite told him what the
real felons were up to: bombing Laos, invading Cambodia,
shooting students, paying attention to Hunter Thompson
and his madcap antics not in the slightest. *Of course* Hunter
Thompson drank. *Of course* he took drugs. *Of course* he
was crazy. How else could he have remained sane?

The underlying message of *Fear and Loathing in Las
Vegas* was never apparent to Wenner. Like most readers, he
took it at face value. What he wanted from Thompson was
more of the same—more adventures, more madness. They
were great for circulation. But Thompson had a more ambitious project in mind: nothing less than turning his manic
talents loose on a presidential campaign.

Thompson first broached the idea of covering the campaign
in December 1971 at a *Rolling Stone* editorial conference
in Big Sur. The opposition from the other editors was nearly
unanimous. Freak politics was one thing; a straight presidential campaign was something else entirely. Personally,
they were, like most young people, turned off by politics.
Professionally, they didn't see how it would fit in *Rolling
Stone*'s format. But Thompson was a powerful advocate.
More important, he had Wenner, still in wide-eyed thrall, as
an ally. If Hunter wanted politics, Wenner told the staff,
then, rock magazine or not, politics it would be.

In the early days of the campaign, that rock image hin-
dered Thompson. Most of the other reporters either
snubbed him or nervously steered clear of him. The candidates' staffs, with the exception of McGovern's, who shared
his after-hours interest in getting high, shunned him. Edmund Muskie banned him altogether, after being heckled
and harried through Florida by a drunken hippie who had
sneaked aboard his campaign train using press credentials

Thompson had obligingly provided. It was difficult to blame them. Thompson was not the usual variety of political reporter. Serious reporters did not, as he did, show up for their first assignment—following McGovern through New Hampshire—toting six-packs of ale and a fifth of Wild Turkey, babbling about "eating acid" and "shooting up," and loudly suggesting that the only way to enliven the proceedings was "sex, dope and violence."

Shut out and cut off, Thompson grabbed his interviews where he could (one memorable session with McGovern was conducted while standing at the next urinal), absorbed what was going on around him, and left the rest to his imagination. Other reporters might *think* that Hubert Humphrey "campaigned like a rat in heat," or that Edmund Muskie betrayed the desperation of "a farmer with terminal cancer trying to get a loan on next year's crop," but only Hunter Thompson wrote it. While his colleagues pondered the collapse of Muskie, the man they had unanimously adjudged to be the front-runner, Thompson came up with the only reasonable explanation: the man from Maine had been poisoned by "Ibogaine," a little-known drug, Thompson reported, drawn from the roots of the "Tabernanthe Iboga, a shrub indigenous to West Africa." Extracts from the root, Thompson went on, "are used by the natives while stalking game. It enables them to remain motionless for as long as two days while retaining mental alertness."

By the Wisconsin primary, word of Thompson's abilities had come back to the press corps from various front offices demanding to know why *they* hadn't discovered that Muskie was an Ibogaine addict. (The explanation was easy enough: Thompson had made up the entire story.) Then, during one swing through Wisconsin, George McGovern spotted Thompson in a crowd of reporters and called out to him

that his last piece was "brilliant." Suddenly, Thompson was
one of the boys. Even the Secret Service came to accept
him, after Thompson blundered into their hotel suite one
night to discover half a dozen embarrassed agents and the
distinct odor of marijuana lingering in the air. Knowing that
Thompson wouldn't reveal them, the staffs of the various
candidates began to relax with him. Once the campaigning
was done, they would gather in someone's room, crack open
a bottle, take the mirror down from the wall, chop the cocaine fine, and let the craziness of the race go away.
Thompson, whose tolerance for drugs was higher than anyone else's, got a lot out of the sessions. With their guard
down, and their heads full of coke, the staffs said things that
would have remained unsaid, had anyone but Hunter
Thompson been in the room.

In time, Thompson won their respect not just for his
Gonzo life-style, but for his shrewdly analytical observa-
tions. He was always giving advice, badgering McGovern
and his aides to do this or that, and, if they seldom took it—
Thompson's notion of a winning formula was to make
McGovern a middle-aged freak, dress him up in a Led Zeppelin T-shirt, put a beer can in his hand, and photograph
him wandering Miami Beach—they at least listened. Thompson gave them little choice. After McGovern's nomination,
and his cozying to the party establishment, Thompson
stalked the campaign headquarters for weeks, determined to
uncover the "villain" who had tricked McGovern into selling out.

His own politics were difficult to define. Thompson himself claimed he was "basically an anarchist" who, of necessity, emerged from his closet from time to time "to deal
with reality." By his life-style, he would have seemed a radical. But his philosophical beliefs were deeply moral, almost

conservative. He cared not at all for the Democratic Party; indeed, he would have destroyed it personally if he could, in revenge for what he claimed was Larry O'Brien's reneging on a promise in 1968 to make him governor of American Samoa. But he was unwilling to opt out entirely. In Chicago in 1968, he had learned that "you couldn't afford to turn your back on the bastards because . . . they . . . would run amok and beat the shit out of you—and they had the power to do it."

Thompson was still looking for the villain when the campaign drew to a close. He wrote his last piece in a liquor-soaked orgy of depression.

> This may be the year when we finally come face to face with ourselves; finally just lay back and say it—that we are really just a nation of 220 million used car salesmen with all the money we need to buy guns and no qualms about killing anybody else in the world who tries to make us uncomfortable . . . What a fantastic monument to all the best instincts of the human race this country might have been, if we could have kept it out of the hands of the greedy little hustlers like Richard Nixon . . . Jesus! Where will it end? How low do you have to stoop in this country to be President?

When the story was finished, Thompson made a final bet: $100 on McGovern to win. It was the only one of the campaign that he lost.

Thompson was determined not to let it happen again. If politicians would not behave the way he wanted them to, he would take matters into his own hands. He, Hunter Thompson, would summon the great political wizards of the country—the men he knew and admired (and, in several cases, had shared dope with) from the McGovern, McCarthy, and Kennedy staffs, and together they would deliberate the future course of America, set the agenda, as it were, determine which issues were important and which were not, then put down the sum of their conclusions in a work so powerful, so brilliant, so absolutely compelling that, as Thompson put it, "whatever candidate's office you would walk into, you would see that book on his desk." Let the party haggle over the candidates. Thompson would decide the issues.

Wenner agreed to finance the conference, and, amid great secrecy, the summonses went out. The guest list was an impressive roster. There was Dave Burke, Ted Kennedy's chief of staff; Richard Goodwin, veteran of assorted liberal wars; Pat Cadell, the polling *wunderkind;* Adam Walinsky, Robert Kennedy's chief speechwriter; McGovern strategists Rick Stearns and Frank Mankiewicz, and some lesser known, but no less important, lights from the McCarthy campaign. To Wenner's considerable surprise, all accepted. What made their appearance all the more remarkable was that Thompson had invited them not to Bermuda or Hilton Head or some other corporate watering hole, but to Elko, Nevada, a cow town Thompson had passed through during his hegira to Las Vegas. Elko (pop. 8,617) in the dead of winter, Thompson figured, was the last place anyone would seek such notables. And to Thompson, security was crucial. These were going to be heavy doings—no less, he said, than the creation "of a new Federalist Papers."

And so the greats convened, armed only with their own imaginations and clublike tirecheckers Thompson had provided to punctuate their points. For two days and nights they talked, drank, smoked dope, and attempted to chart the future course of the nation. The passage proved to be meandering. Everyone had their own ideas of how to elect

the next President, and what his agenda should be. Cadell
wanted more polls, Stearns more TV. At one point, someone mentioned the weather, noting that the English growing
season had shrunk six weeks since 1940. This sparked a pro-
tracted discussion of meteorology, crop conditions, and the
dynamics of world hunger. Eventually, as Thompson put it,
the conference "descended into gibberish." Two other meetings were scheduled for the future, but they never came off.
When the transcript of the first meeting was later examined,
it was deemed unfit for publication.

But Elko was not a total loss. Wenner's willingness to
underwrite such a scheme increased Thompson's regard for
him. He had been wary of Wenner at first, especially when
the editor vetoed some of his pet requests, such as renting a
white Cadillac convertible to transport himself around Las
Vegas ("How do they expect me to cover the American
Dream in a Volkswagen?" he complained to no avail) or
writing off cocaine for sources on the Oakland Raiders as a
business expense. Yes, Wenner could be tightfisted; Thompson had only to look at what had happened during the 1972
presidential campaign to realize that. Wenner had put him
on a ridiculously modest retainer of $1,000 a month and, to
make matters worse, insisted that all his expenses be paid
back out of royalties from *Fear and Loathing on the Campaign Trail*. The result was that Thompson finished his most
productive year deeply in the hole. But it was more than
money that made Thompson uneasy. He worried, sometimes, that there were two Jann Wenners: the "nighttime"
Wenner, warm, generous and loose, and the "daytime"
Wenner, uptight, greedy, vindictive. Now, in the aftermath
of Elko, his resistance softened. Wenner had come through,
done everything Thompson asked of him, spent a consid-

erable amount of money on a will-o'-the-wisp with no com-
plaining. In Thompson's eyes, he had proven himself.

They grew closer after that. During Thompson's rare
forays to San Francisco, he was a guest in Wenner's home,
as was Jann in his, when Wenner visited Aspen to ski.
Wenner possessed a well-developed if cynical sense of
humor and delighted in Thompson's continual put-ons, even
if they sometimes could get out of hand—as on the night
when Thompson blew a mouthful of lighter fluid over an
open Zippo in his direction, creating a whooshing, rolling
fireball that nearly brought his career to a premature end.
And that, in a sense, was the only problem he had with
Thompson; he didn't know where to draw limits. It was one
thing to nearly incinerate him, it was quite another to, as
Thompson did late one night at his home in San Francisco,
rouse him from sleep with a point-blank blast from a fire extinguisher full in the face. Wenner would never forget that
incident: how he awoke, sputtering and choking, in a cloud
of gray glop, stumbled directly into the glass patio doors,
and finally wound up on his knees, tears in his eyes, shaking
his fist at Thompson, vowing to get him if it took the rest of
his life, only to have Hunter blast his French poodle with
the extinguisher, sending the hapless beast careening across
the room. Yes, being Hunter Thompson's friend was a positive hazard. But Wenner couldn't help it. He needed him. He
liked him. Hunter Thompson was the only writer who truly
was his friend.

As time went on, the bond between them grew tighter
and tighter. They wrote each other long letters, and talked
late at night for hours on the phone, planning their exploits.
Wenner said that when he became President, Hunter could
be his press secretary, even his Secretary of State. The more

they talked, the more it seemed crazily possible. Why stop
at rock, Wenner mused one night on the phone. Why stop
at publishing? There was a whole country out there, waiting
to be led. They could have it. They could have anything.

8

Mr. Wenner Goes to Washington

Wenner's announcement caught people by surprise. There were a number of them, in fact, who simply wouldn't believe he was serious. "Bullshit," a senior editor had said, using the same word Wenner had always used to describe what he was promoting now. But it was true. And Jann Wenner was adamant. "Politics," he informed his editors, "will be the rock and roll of the Seventies."

Something had happened. Thompson had gotten to him, some of the staff speculated. No, it was the star trip all over again, others argued, just dressed up in different clothes. "You know Jann," one of them shrugged. "He's into people who get their names in the papers. Rock stars, politicians, well, you know." But they didn't know, not then, in 1974, not how seriously their boss meant it, not what it would mean for all of them, not how close Wenner was to the truth: that politics was rock and roll.

At first, none of it made sense. Jann Wenner, the young man who had, like all of them, avoided political involvement all his life, shunned it almost as a matter of principle—

not only shunned it, but attacked it as a kind of grown-up evil that menaced the very meaning of rock and roll: Jann Wenner, the Berkeley sophomore who had badgered his employers that "the real revolution" was in the Haight; Jann Wenner, the editor who had fired Burks precisely because of his interest in politics; Jann Wenner, the stoned rock and roll freak who said "more people listen to the Beatles . . . more people got some kind of philosophy or some kind of thinking from the Beatles or the Stones or Bob Dylan." Now this same Jann Wenner was going against all of it.

It was strange. And the more the staff considered Wenner's history, the stranger it became. How, after all, were they to reconcile statements like the one Wenner had written in the aftermath of Martin Luther King's assassination, declaring his murder "meant little or nothing to the majority of the American people," or the editorial tongue-lashing he had delivered to the radicals who were planning a rock concert to lure young people to the 1968 Chicago convention? "It looks like a shuck," Wenner had written, "as corrupt as the political machine it hopes to disrupt." He had told them to forget it, that protest and politics were hopeless, that "rock and roll is the *only* way in which the vast but formless power of youth is structured, the only way in which it can be defined or inspected." Occasionally, the sheer weight of national events had forced him to deal with politics, and, as after the murder of four students at Kent State, he had been forced to pay at least passing obeisance to the political realities of the day. "Like it or not," he had written, politics could no longer be ignored. "It threatens our daily lives and our daily happiness," he went on, ". . . and, willingly or not, we are in it." *Willingly or not;*

that was the key phrase for Jann Wenner. When it came to politics, he was most unwilling.

Wenner's distaste reflected an old split in the youth culture, a bitter, sometimes bloody cleavage between two revolutions, one of life-style, the other of politics. It was difficult to discern at first: superficially, the two cultures were identical. They dressed alike, took the same drugs, listened to the same music, and, for the most part, shared the same political outlook. No one liked the war, racism, cops or college administrators. The difference was what they did about them; whether, in the end, they ignored them, or fought them. Through the early Sixties, music further obscured the rupture. Many of the songs, like Buffalo Springfield's "For What It's Worth," and Country Joe MacDonald's "Fixin to Die Rag," were protest. But when Dylan dropped folk singing and "went electric" in 1965, the style rapidly began to change. The "folkies" either died out or followed suit. Protest lyrics were abandoned in favor of a more commercial rock sound. And the youth culture suddenly discovered that, as *Rolling Stone* critic Greil Marcus put it: " 'Shooby shooby doo wah' heard in the right mood has more meaning than a flat-out protest song ever does."

As the number of "shooby-doobies" increased, the Movement became first alarmed, then hysterical. Before long, political ideologues like Paul Johnson, editor of the *New Statesman,* were describing the "bottomless chasm of vacuity" rock produced, as if music had become yet another Establishment plot. Go to any rock concert, Johnson had written and the evidence would be there: "Their huge faces, bloated with cheap confectionery and smeared with chainstore make-up, the open sagging mouths and glazed eyes, the hands mindlessly drumming in time with the music, the broken stiletto heels, the shoddy, stereotyped 'with it' clothes: here, apparently, is a collective portrait of a generation enslaved by a commercial machine."

The rock revolutionaries volleyed back. Kesey showed up at a Berkeley Vietnam Day Committee rally dressed in a Day-Glo orange World War I army costume, played "Home on the Range" on the harmonica, and advised the 25,000 assembled: "There's only one thing to do. . . . And that's everybody just look at it, look at the war, and turn your backs and say . . . Fuck it." Dylan had another idea: How about balloons? he suggested—balloons and signs with bananas painted on them; that would be a political statement that would blow people's minds. When someone asked Country Joe MacDonald his program for social justice, he replied, "Free concerts in the park."

"Politics has failed," Ralph Gleason declared in one of his columns. "The Beatles aren't just more popular than Jesus, they are more potent than SDS. . . . Jimi Hendrix playing the Star Spangled Banner while screwing his guitar is a revolutionary act as important as getting arrested at a Hubert Humphrey rally."

There were sporadic attempts to unite the two cultures, weld the galvanizing energy of rock and roll to the hard tasks of political organizing. The San Francisco *Oracle,* an underground newspaper that lived and died with the Haight, threw open its pages to both sides, the result being that one issue featured twin cover stories on concentration camps *and* masturbation. In Detroit, one frankly political rock band, the MC (Motor City) 5, briefly appeared and, for a time, attracted considerable attention. The MC 5's members belonged to "The White Panther Party," popularizers of the slogans "Revolution for the Hell of It" and "Armed Love." "We have no 'problems,'" they declared in their manifesto.

Everything is free for everybody. Money sucks. Leaders
suck. Underwear sucks. School sucks. We will do anything
we can to drive people crazy out of their heads and into
their bodies. Rock and roll music is the spearhead of the
attack because it's effective and so much fun. We have developed organic, high-energy guerrilla bands who are
infiltrating the popular culture and destroying millions of
minds in the process. . . . With our music and our eco-
nomic genius we plunder the unsuspecting straight world
for money and the means to carry out our program, and
revolutionize its children at the same time.

But the MC 5's genius was not as great as the White Panthers had hoped. The band was subjected to continual legal
harassment, and one of its leaders, John Sinclair, was eventually sentenced to a long prison term on drug charges. Finally, the MC 5 gave up their political music-making in
favor of straight commercial rock and, before long, disappeared altogether.

Not even Abbie Hoffman, the clown prince of the Movement, could turn rock to his devices. At Woodstock, he succeeded in convincing the festival's canny promoters to do-
nate $10,000 to finance political organizing, but few others
to listen to what he had to say. As it turned out, when
Hoffman took the stage to deliver his message, he managed
to provoke the only violent incident of the entire festival:
just as he was getting into his political rap about John
Sinclair and Pig Nation and all the rest, the microphone
went dead, and Peter Townshend, leader of The Who,
whacked him over the head with his guitar. Down dear
Abbie went, and with him any fantasies about rock as revolution.

It was a doomed vision to begin with. Political organization required determination and dedication, qualities

which, in the estimation of Charles Reich's *The Greening of America,* were strictly Consciousness II. All that rock demanded, by contrast, was copious free time, and, if at all possible, a stash of drugs. Given the choice between years of grim organizing toward a goal that, in all probability, would never be reached, and an instant turn-on, the result was inevitable. No one knew it better than Hunter Thompson, who had tried, without success, to walk both sides of the youth culture divide. After his defeat in his bid to become Aspen's sheriff in 1970, he wrote:

> Somewhere in the nightmare failure that gripped America between 1965 and 1970, the old Berkeley-born notion of beating The System by fighting it gave way to a sort of numb conviction that it made more sense in the long run to Flee, or even to simply hide, than fight the bastards on anything resembling their own terms. So most of the freaks felt that voting wasn't worth the bullshit that went with it . . . This sense of "reality" is a hallmark of the Drug Culture, which values the Instant Reward—a pleasant, four-hour high—over anything involving a time lag between the Effort and the End. On this scale of values, politics is too difficult, too "complex" and too "abstract" to justify any risk or initial action. It is the flip side of the "Good German" syndrome.

So it was with skepticism, if not utter astonishment, that the news of what *Rolling Stone* was about to become was greeted by the men and women who worked for Jann Wenner. "You're shitting," one of his editors challenged him. "Protest? All that politics bullshit?" No, Wenner said. "Politics politics."

At last, it sank in: Jann meant to be with the heavies, not the Hoffmans and Rubins and Dellingers, but the people who practiced "politics politics": the Kennedys and McGoverns and Humphreys, the *real* politicians, the grown-ups. Now it made sense. Whatever Wenner's history, his new-found love for politics conformed to what they knew about him. He was a man always searching after gods, the larger-than-life figures who got their names in the New York *Times* and *Time* magazine. He liked being with them, sharing their company, basking in the attention they lavished on him, hoping that the approval they received would, by his very proximity, rub off on him. And, at that moment in 1974, politics had captured center stage. There was, for those few fleeting moments, no superstar so shining, no celebrity so great, as a quietly tortured academic, who, with a few volumes of stolen papers, had taken the imagination of the country. Daily, Wenner read the name in the headlines: Daniel Ellsberg, purveyor of the Pentagon Papers. He had to have him.

The invitation Wenner proffered was straightforward. He would like Ellsberg to be his weekend houseguest in San Francisco. There, while a tape recorder rolled, Wenner would interview him; the result would be, he promised, a major milestone in the history of *Rolling Stone*. Ellsberg agreed and, on the appointed day, Wenner was the essence of the awed fan. One of his questions said it all. *What was the Pentagon like, as an experience, to run around with five-star generals passing in the hall?* Ellsberg's entire answer: *"It's a job."*

He was, as always, more than slightly star-struck, still the little boy with his nose pressed firmly against the candy-store window. The tone was painfully evident to Wenner's own editors, who, after reading the transcript of his conversation, gently suggested that Wenner might want to edit the interview very carefully. Wenner was unmoved. The

60,000-word interview (along with a cover portrait of Ellsberg that made him appear remarkably like a Greek god)
took up much of the next two issues of *Rolling Stone*.
Wenner thought so much of his work that he later turned
the piece into an expensively printed booklet, which he sent
to reporters as a representative example of the magazine's
finest work.

It was, at the very least, an indication of just how completely Wenner had become enraptured with politics. The
bug had bitten him, and once he was infected, the interest
spread like a contagion. There was no stopping Wenner
now. He regarded himself as a political seer and strategist of
the first rank, talents he quickly sought to demonstrate in
electing a figure of his choosing as Governor of California.

The politician thus favored was William Matsun Roth, a
liberal San Francisco shipping magnate then attempting to
secure the Democratic nomination. Roth, despite his
money, was adjudged by most political analysts as having
only a slight chance to win the nomination. Their opinion
did not deter Wenner. He joined the Roth campaign, first as
an ad hoc adviser, then as media expert. If he had had his
way, he would have been the campaign manager. Once
Roth was elected, Wenner confidently told his friends, he
expected to be appointed a regent of the University of California, a system from which he had failed to graduate.

It didn't work out that way. Roth was trounced in the
election, and the nomination went to the then Secretary of
State, an ambitious young man named Jerry Brown—though
not before Wenner had succeeded in bedeviling most of
Roth's staff. Roth himself was more tolerant. He had been a
family friend of the Wenners in Marin, and had known
Jann since childhood. He took Wenner into the campaign
on the advice of Pat Cadell, one of the Elko participants,

who was then serving as Roth's pollster. Cadell also brought
along the Elko papers, which Roth read with rapt attention,
especially the portions having to deal with the disillusionment of voters. The solution, the Elko conferees had decided, was for candidates to project the image of being out-
siders from the political process, men of integrity who had
made their mark and established their reputations away
from politics—a description that fit Roth perfectly. That was
not the image, however, that Wenner wanted to project. He
wanted something more dramatic. An excellent commercial,
he suggested to Roth's advertising director, would be one
that showed something *powerful* happening: a fist, perhaps, coming down to smash a model of the state capitol.
Roth's other advisers listened, stupefied. As pleasantly as
possible, Maxwell Arnold, Roth's advertising director, told
Wenner his ideas didn't make any political sense. Irritated
but persistent, Wenner tried his hand at writing radio commercials. A senior staffer of Roth's who read them bluntly
informed Wenner that they were nonsensical. That couldn't
be, Wenner protested; he was, he claimed, the best writer on
Rolling Stone.

The wrangling continued for weeks, with Wenner becoming increasingly upset. He tried to take charge of the media
aspect of the campaign himself, and, when that failed,
sought to have Roth's advertising director fired. "Let's get
rid of all this fuzzy shit," Wenner said, as Arnold sat by.
"Bring in Dave Garth. He's the best." Once again, Wenner
was overruled. As the campaign wore on, with no signs of
getting anywhere, Wenner withdrew from the other staffers,
and spent most of his time with Cadell. One night, at dinner, the two of them, a little tipsy, got into an argument.
Cadell boasted that he owned a Mercedes. Wenner rejoined
that he had two. "Yes," Cadell said, "but they're smaller."

No matter, Wenner replied, he would be a millionaire first.
Oh no he wouldn't, Cadell replied; *he* would. On and on the
dispute continued over who was wealthier and more successful, until it came time to pay the bill; then, each man
thought the other should pick up the check.

Meanwhile, Roth's staff kept pressing Wenner as to when
Rolling Stone would provide some actual publicity for the
campaign. But Wenner was evasive. "Well, when this thing
gets off the ground," he would say. "Then we'll see." The
Roth campaign never did get off the ground, nor did it receive any notice in *Rolling Stone*. By election day, Wenner,
still not able to have his way, had faded out of the campaign
completely.

By then, he had bigger plans in mind. Since the conclusion of the 1972 presidential campaign, he had wanted to
extend and regularize *Rolling Stone*'s political coverage.
Thompson had pointed out that there was no chance of
that, so long as the magazine's chief political pundit,
namely the good doctor himself, was ensconced in Woody
Creek, Colorado, while the magazine itself remained 3,000
miles away from the scene of the real action: Washington, D.C. To be taken seriously, *Rolling Stone* had to come
to Washington itself. The mere physical presence of an office, though, was not enough. Someone had to lead it. A person of stature. Someone who, by his reputation alone, would
demonstrate just how serious *Rolling Stone* was. Wenner
had just such a person in mind: Richard N. Goodwin.

Dick Goodwin was a man who attracted controversy almost by his very being. Abrasive, tough, possessed of an
almost animal allure, Goodwin, by the time he met Wenner,
had long since established a reputation for brilliance
equaled only by a propensity for making enemies. The
Kennedy loyalists thought him a traitor for staying on to

work with Johnson. Johnson, whom Goodwin left because of the war, flew into rages at the mention of his name. The State Department, which had suffered Goodwin's experimentation with Latin American policy during the Kennedy administration, still hadn't gotten over him. Eugene McCarthy, for whom Goodwin briefly worked before jumping ship for Robert Kennedy's presidential campaign, gently allowed as how Goodwin was "an honorable traitor." His friends and former friends despaired at his excesses, the brusqueness of his manner, the pushiness, the complete arrogance of the man—not to mention his forgetfulness about paying bills. "I have never known a man with so many ex-friends," author William Saroyan, an ex-friend himself, told a reporter. Even his appearance was hostile—"an Italian journalist with a hangover," journalist Bo Burlingham described him. "Pockmarked skin, a slightly bulbous nose, and scraggly dark hair that threatens to overrun his body. His mouth expresses his moods and whims—one moment a sneer, the next a radiant smile—when it is not occupied by a cigar. Other people smoke cigars; Dick Goodwin eats them." Despite all that—perhaps *because* of all that—he was an imposing presence, a rough-cut, larger-than-life figure, at once appealing and forbidding, a handy man to have, either in the Oval Office or in an alley on a dark night. Wenner, like everyone who encountered Dick Goodwin, couldn't help but be impressed. One look at his résumé established that Dick Goodwin, warts and all, was a most formidable talent: *summa cum laude,* Harvard Law; clerk for Felix Frankfurter; speechwriter for two Presidents; Latin American expert; an architect of the Great Society (the phrase had been Goodwin's); friend of the Kennedys, mover, fixer, man about town, a person who had, as

Felix Frankfurter told Lyndon Johnson, "politics in his blood."

They first met in 1972, during a McGovern campaign stopover in Nebraska. They chatted about politics and *Rolling Stone*, Goodwin confessing that he had never read the magazine. But the idea of combining rock and politics, Goodwin allowed, sounded interesting. For the next year, Wenner pursued the relationship, dropping Goodwin notes, telling him of his plans to increase *Rolling Stone*'s political coverage, and asking whether Goodwin would like to contribute. Goodwin, who by then had read several issues, replied that he didn't see how his style of writing would fit in a rock format. Wenner kept pushing, Goodwin kept demurring. Gradually, however, Goodwin's resistance softened. Wenner had begun talking about considerable sums of cash that might come his way, and Goodwin, then deep in debt, desperately needed a lucrative income. Finally, they worked out a deal. Goodwin would open a *Rolling Stone* office in Washington, and recruit writers whose work, along with Goodwin's essays on the state of the nation, would appear in a special section of the magazine to be known as "Politics." If all went well, "Politics" would be spun off into a separate magazine: a "non-boring *New Republic*," as Wenner envisioned it. In return, Goodwin was to receive a six-month salary of $50,000, expenses and a townhouse in Georgetown, for which *Rolling Stone* would pick up most of the rent.

Goodwin came to work in the summer of 1974. While the search went on for suitable Georgetown headquarters, his friend Ethel Kennedy, then out of town, let him use Hickory Hill as a base from which to recruit writers. One of those he approached later recounted the scene for *Esquire:*

We went out on a Sunday afternoon and drove up to the
house. Rock and roll music was blaring. We just followed
the sound. In the back of the house, we saw a small crowd
gathered around the swimming pool in front of an enormous photograph of Bobby Kennedy. Goodwin greeted
us. Hunter Thompson was sitting in a chair, drinking beer
and telling stories. Babes in bikinis were lounging around
the pool listening to Hunter. . . . I had the sense of being
at a fraternity rush.

Amid such surroundings, it did not take Goodwin long to
make his presence known. The résumés from writers and
reporters rained in on the *Rolling Stone* office, including
one from a then-unknown reporter whose career was in decline at the Washington *Post*. Thompson, then on detached
duty to the Washington office, would have hired him, as, indeed, he was prepared to hire, as he put it, "every good
writer in the country." But Wenner and Goodwin were
more cautious, and thus it was that the *Post* reporter, an intense young man named Carl Bernstein, was passed over.

Bernstein was not the only instance in which Wenner's
instinct for talent operated at lower-than-usual capacity.
One member of the *Rolling Stone* Washington bureau had
previously experienced severe trouble in getting Wenner to
take his abilities seriously. That was Timothy Crouse. A
Harvard-educated Peace Corps veteran, and the son of Rus-
sel Crouse, the Pulitzer Prize-winning playwright (*Life with
Father; State of the Union; Anything Goes; Call Me
Madam*), Crouse had taken up rock criticism after his return to the United States in 1969. Before long, his work attracted the attention of Jon Landau and, for the sum of $50
per month, Crouse became one of the magazine's East
Coast stringers. When Crouse tired of music ("I just

couldn't take it anymore. It was getting to be the same story over and over again"), he set out to cover the 1972 presidential campaign. Thompson, meanwhile, had also decided to cover the campaign. Wenner resolved the conflicting ambitions by assigning the two of them to the same story, the result being that of the six reporters following McGovern through the early days of the New Hampshire primary, two of them were from the same rock and roll magazine. As far as Wenner was concerned, though, Crouse was very much the junior partner in the arrangement. His only function, he instructed Crouse, was to babysit for Thompson: get him up in the morning, put him on the plane, do his legwork, make sure, in short, that the Great Gonzo functioned and that the copy came in on time. Wenner belittled Crouse's own abilities, telling other editors that "not only can he not write a story, but wouldn't recognize one if he tripped over it." The taunts hit hard; Crouse was as insecure as he was noncombative. He stuttered badly, and after his conversations with Wenner his nervousness and stammering noticeably worsened.

But Crouse hung in. He enjoyed being on the campaign, and learning from Thompson, who, for all his supposed craziness, was a dogged reporter, always eager to show a younger man the ropes. All went well until the Wisconsin primary. Thompson was covering Muskie, the expected winner, while Crouse was to report on McGovern's concession statement. By early evening, however, it was apparent that McGovern would be a landslide winner and that Thompson, as a result, would have no story. Over drinks at Milwaukee's Phister Hotel, Thompson arrived at the only possible solution: Crouse would write the story. When Crouse informed Wenner of the change of plans by phone, Wenner went into a tirade. "The only thing you're there for is to be Hunter's legman. Don't write a fucking word." The threats continued for a few more minutes, with Wenner warning that he would fire Crouse for "insubordination." Finally, Crouse hung up, returned to his hotel room, and, with a drunken Thompson cheering him on, proceeded to do exactly what Wenner had told him not to. The resulting piece ran almost unchanged and no word of firing was ever mentioned again. Crouse's stuttering immediately dropped off.

The Wisconsin primary was the last purely political story Crouse reported during the campaign. Thompson had come up with another idea. Resentful of how the other reporters had been treating him, Thompson had devised a vengeful ploy. "Watch those swine day and night. Every time they fuck someone who isn't their wife, every time they pick their nose, every time they have their hand up their ass, you write it down. Get all of it. Then we'll lay it all on them in October."

So Crouse began watching, and the more he saw, the more entranced he became. Years before, his father, who had worked as a reporter with Hemingway, had told him story after story of the romance of journalism, the adventures, the swashbuckling, fascinating lives reporters led, and now it seemed to be coming true. Crouse took in all the screwing, nose-picking and ass-scratching Thompson had predicted, but also much more: the whole rich tableau of people and process, a drama vested with color, glory, pathos, and tragedy, a story, in its way, as important as—and certainly more interesting than—the campaign itself. Soon, he reported to Thompson that he would have to abandon the idea of shafting the reporters; instead, he wanted to focus on the reporters themselves, "the boys on the bus," he called them, a phrase that wound up as the title of his best-selling book, and in the political lexicon forever after. Crouse's portraits of the men who reported, and often made, the news was the first recognition of what had long been an unspoken fact: that journalists were celebrities, media stars whose perceptions of events were as important as the events themselves.

The "Kid," as Crouse was patronizingly known, had it all: the late-night, drunken conversations, the frustrations with editors thousands of miles away, the wild variance between what reporters said in private and what they wrote, the pretensions and foibles of the men themselves. Reading about themselves, his subjects were chagrined. They never had suspected that so slight a figure, a man-child of such exaggerated politeness, could waylay them as he had. They were not happy.

No more so, as it happened, was Jann Wenner. Back in San Francisco, Wenner could barely contain himself when, to lavish reviews ("The best writing about journalism I have ever read," David Halberstam enthused; "the best thing on the *campaign*," John Kenneth Galbraith corrected him), the book version of *The Boys on the Bus* appeared and became an immediate best seller. One editor recalled that, as Wenner read an especially favorable review, his face tightened with every paragraph until, at last, he flung the paper into the wastebasket. But Wenner's jealousy passed quickly. When the Washington bureau opened, Crouse was named senior correspondent. Wenner couldn't help but be appreciative. By extension, Crouse's fame was his fame—and in Washington, fame was the name of the game.

Other notables were quickly signed on. Frank Mankiewicz, McGovern's campaign manager and press secretary for Robert Kennedy, was given a $500-per-month retainer as a free-lance advice-giver. Mankiewicz also tried his hand at several articles, including one, written just before the 1976 New Hampshire primary, correctly predicting that Ronald Reagan would lose. Wenner, more impressed by what he was reading in the New York *Times,* killed it, and shortly thereafter Mankiewicz received a curt note from San Francisco, firing him.

The truth was that the magic of politics was beginning to wear thin. Wenner's staff, which had been opposed to the Washington venture from the beginning, poked fun at Goodwin's turgid essays on the state of the nation, one of which was pinned on the bulletin board with the mock headline, "Stating the Obvious." Some of the reporting Goodwin had commissioned, especially from Joe Klein, a Boston reporter whom Goodwin lured to Washington, was first-rate. The trouble stemmed from the idea of trying to join two essentially antithetical cultures: *Rolling Stone* was a reflection of the easy, laid-back climes of San Francisco; the thinking that went on in Georgetown drawing rooms was an altogether foreign environment. Crouse, who lived in Georgetown with Goodwin and his wife-to-be, Doris Kearns, regarded Washington as "a place for grown-ups. You always had to be on your best behavior there," he complained, "like you always had to wear a tie." Klein, who was used to the arms-and-elbows street reporting of Boston, became "confused and frightened" by the "steady parade of famous, facile people with good teeth and chestnut hair shooting clever things to each other across the dinner table." When Klein asked Goodwin what he was supposed to do, Goodwin replied: "Get your feet wet. Take people to lunch."

It turned out that everyone was taking everyone to lunch, and the bills were beginning to mount up. Rent on the offices that Goodwin had secured for the magazine a block from the White House (CREEP was headquartered in the same building) alone accounted for nearly $7,000 per month. And when Goodwin entertained, which was frequently, it was in *grand luxe* style. Matters finally came to a head over what came to be known at *Rolling Stone* as "the foreign ministry dinner."

The original idea was noble enough: Goodwin wanted to expose Wenner to some members of the Establishment-in-exile, the Tony Lakes and Dick Holbrookes and some of the crowd from Brookings. What resulted was a graphic demonstration of the chasm between Washington and San Francisco. One participant remembered: "Everything went wrong from the start. First, Goodwin didn't invite Klein and [*Rolling Stone* editor] Marianne Partridge. They only came because Wenner insisted on it. Marianne, who had been told to wear a long dress, showed up in a blue nightgown, the only long dress she owned. Jann almost didn't show at all, and when he did come in, he was wearing jeans and a checkered shirt. Anyway, all these guys were sitting in the drawing room, smoking pipes, and talking about what *Rolling Stone* should cover, things like the gold market and shoe-import quotas. At one point, someone said, 'If we can just forget about hunger for a moment, and concentrate on the larger issues.' Well, the evening went like that. Jann was sitting off in a corner, and his eyes were rolling up to the ceiling."

They all but bugged out when a thousand-dollar bill from the caterer arrived. Wenner refused to pay it. "It would have been cheaper to take everyone to Sans Souci," he exclaimed. Goodwin, not a man to be trifled with, thereupon offered to represent the caterer in a lawsuit against *Rolling Stone*. Wenner finally paid up. But it was the beginning of the end. Wenner, who had long defended Goodwin against the criticisms of the staff, began to cool toward him. As a token of his displeasure, he took away Goodwin's air travel card and closed his charge account at the Class Reunion Bar. Goodwin, for his part, was none too happy with Wenner. Despite assurances that he would have final say in editorial matters regarding Washington, he found that Wenner continually undercut his authority. Writers whom Goodwin had hired sometimes discovered that when their bills went to San Francisco, they went unpaid, or more often, were paid only in part. One writer collected his $2,000 fee only after Goodwin provided him with a sworn affidavit.

Goodwin had intrigued Wenner at first, not so much because of his writing, which Wenner had found difficult going, but for the cachet his name gave to the magazine. Goodwin, it seemed, knew everyone, and was in turn known by them—all the important, famous people Wenner wanted to know. In the beginning, Goodwin had shared his celebrity. He had taken Wenner to lunch with Jacqueline Onassis (when one of his editors asked what had transpired Wenner replied "I don't think I'm in a position to reveal personal confidences"), an experience that, as one of his editors put it, "took Jann to heaven for months." But Goodwin's independence—the fact that he was a power in his own right, with or without *Rolling Stone*—was worrisome. Then there was Washington itself. Wenner had never felt comfortable in the town. His one great dream, an exclusive *Rolling Stone* interview with Ted Kennedy, with him, Jann Wenner, posing the questions, had not come off. What remained did little to attract his interest. He was, for a man in his position, woefully ignorant of public affairs. Even years later, when he commissioned Richard Avedon to photograph the political, cultural and business greats for a special

Rolling Stone issue, many of the names Avedon suggested drew a blank. Andrew Young, Carl Albert, Earl Butz, Emmanuel Celler—Wenner knew none of them. To Goodwin, Wenner seemed almost boastful of his anti-intellectualism. Goodwin did little to help matters. He regularly patronized Wenner, not only about political affairs, but about concerns closer to Wenner's heart, such as his stereo system, which Goodwin (who, among his other talents, could take apart and rebuild amplifiers) inspected and, to Wenner's chagrin, pronounced "five and dime stuff." "Washington was not Jann's turf," Thompson put it. "He'd come to town and no one would pay any attention to him. People in the office wouldn't even pay any attention to him. Goodwin treated him like he was a necessary evil, like he was a little rich kid who didn't know anything—and, of course, he didn't."

Nonetheless, plans for the new political magazine still seemed to be going forward in the fall of 1974. Wenner had agreed to put up $500,000 to get the venture off the ground. In return, Goodwin was expected to make a three-to five-year commitment to the project. Former Democratic National Committeewoman Anne Wexler had been hired to publicize the magazine. Then, even as the final papers were being drawn up, Goodwin quit. He was weary, he said later, of the constant tension that came from dealing with San Francisco, the petty intrigues and "minor league hustling" that came from working with Wenner. He doubted, frankly, "whether Jann had the guts to be a big entrepreneur." Said Goodwin, "I simply decided that there were more important things I wanted to do."

Bitter as the experience with Goodwin had been, coming to Washington had not been a total write-off. Simply being there had enhanced *Rolling Stone*'s reputation, if not with its readers (who, the surveys showed, cared for politics not at all), then with the straight press whose favor Wenner so ardently courted. Goodwin's employment had sparked a raft of stories heralding *Rolling Stone*'s "quest for respectability," the "new seriousness" of its purpose. Jann Wenner was now a power to be reckoned with—"a crucial fulcrum," as one account described him, "at the interface of two cultures." So Wenner's instincts had been right, even if the execution had failed. There was profit to be had from politics, profit in the forms of power and prestige. *Politics* might be dead, and Richard Goodwin departed, but political reporting would continue in *Rolling Stone*.

As always, Wenner's tastes were quixotic. Months would sometimes pass with no political stories at all; then they would come in a flurry: Crouse reporting the Watergate Hearings as soap opera; Tom Hayden, weighing in with a favorable assessment of Jerry Brown; John Dean, dooming Earl Butz with his reporting of Butz's joke about the alleged proclivities of blacks. They were disconnected stories, jarring, unpredictable, but, somehow, holding together, like rock itself. "We've become pretty used to the confusion," Wenner confided to his readers in the magazine's two-hundredth issue. " 'Hey, what gives?' is the invariable question. 'Is *Rolling Stone* into music and politics or sociology or what?' . . . The fact is, from the very first issue *Rolling Stone* has been dedicated to the covering and uncovering of the rock culture, with the consistent belief that the rock culture encompasses all of the above. What we're talking about, really, is not a generation but an event—the greatest mass alteration of personal consciousness since the country began."

The politicians instinctively understood what Wenner was talking about: Kids were different. Whatever their "consciousness" was, they had to be taken seriously, especially in that they had the right to vote. A pool of four million possible voters between the ages of 18 and 21 was there for the taking. All that was required was figuring out a way of tapping into it. *What interested young people? What did they want? Just what would turn them on?* The polls pondered and ultimately came up with the same answer their Movement counterparts had years before: rock and roll.

McGovern had tried it in 1972, and the concerts Warren Beatty had organized (Simon and Garfunkel; Grateful Dead; Peter, Paul and Mary) had raised $1.5 million and helped bring him the nomination. As the 1976 presidential campaign approached, there was even more reason to turn to rock again. Congress had set tough new strictures on campaign financing. Individual contributions of more than $1,000 were banned, and a complicated registration required for any donations more than $10. There was nothing in the new law, however, which precluded gathering ten or twenty thousand donors in one spot, and having each of them ante up $5 or $10 apiece. When federal matching funds were figured in, such an event could potentially raise $25,000, or even $50,000 or $100,000, in a single stroke. But what kind of event would draw such numbers? A rock concert. Of course.

By the onset of the primary season, the competition for the endorsement of rock stars was as fervid as the wooing of Richard Daley. Jerry Brown had Linda Ronstadt, Jackson Browne, Chicago, and the Eagles. Sargent Shriver replied in kind with Neil Diamond and Tony Orlando and Dawn, while Fred Harris cadged Arlo Guthrie and Harry Chapin. Birch Bayh was not about to be left out; Stephen Stills sang for him. Even Hubert Humphrey managed to cadge a rock star of sorts, soul singer James Brown. But no candidate wooed the stars—and their magazine—with more guile and effect than Jimmy Carter.

Carter's chief ally was an old friend of Wenner's: Phil Walden, president of Macon-based Capricorn Records, the label of, among others, the Allman Brothers Band. Like Carter, Walden was a poor Southerner who liked to stress the humbleness of his origins, a racial moderate long before tolerance was fashionable in the South ("I was one of your early nigger-lovers," Walden boasted), a wrong-side-of-the-tracks outsider who was, like Carter, quietly resentful of being one. "It bothers me a little when I think about it," one of their mutual friends said during the campaign, "but there is a lot of Jimmy in Phil, and a lot of Phil in Jimmy."

Walden's rise had been as improbable as Carter's. He had started Capricorn on a shoestring and the talents of one Macon artist. That artist, however, happened to be black blues-rock singer Otis Redding, who, under Walden's tutelage, became one of the most commercially successful talents in the country. Then, in 1967, just as Redding's popularity was at its peak, he was killed in a plane crash. As quickly as it had begun, Phil Walden's Capricorn Records seemed about to come crashing down. But Walden had already sensed that the fascination of white teenagers with black artists was on the wane and, at the time of Redding's death, he had begun planning his move into the world of white rock and roll. He spotted a guitarist at a recording session whom he thought showed promise, signed him to a contract, and instructed him to gather a band around him. The guitarist was Duane Allman. With his brother Gregg, he formed the Allman Brothers Band. Within two years, they were the largest-grossing, best-selling band in the land —and Capricorn the largest independent record company in the world. All at once, the poor boy with the flashing smile and curly flowing hair found himself an exceedingly rich young man.

He bought a mansion on nine acres of Macon land, and filled it with expensive art and equally expensive antiques. There was another "country house" outside Macon similarly outfitted, and another at Hilton Head, where Walden entertained the stars and opinion-makers of the music industry, among them his friend Jann Wenner. Around town, he traveled in a white Rolls-Royce once owned by Debbie Reynolds, or, when the mood moved him, in a six-door limousine outfitted with bar, television, video-tape recorder and stereo tape deck. For sportier occasions, there was a brace of $24,000-a-copy Mercedes 450 SEL's at his disposal. The Capricorn offices were similarly lavish: Delft porcelain toilet, cockatiels chirping in the lobby, antiques and Wyeths filling up the walls, a fire crackling in the Napoleonic fireplace. From here, Walden controlled a varied empire with a combined yearly gross of $20 million. There was the Walden shopping center, the Walden amusement park, the Walden apartment complex, the Walden rock and roll club, even the Walden liquor store, which came in handy, since its owner began most business meetings with hefty amounts of J&B Scotch. Taken together, they gave Phil Walden a net worth estimated at $5 million. *Fortune* magazine could write, with only slight exaggeration, that "Phil Walden Turns Rock into Gold," and could quote the "hip southern impresario" (after all, he wore blue jeans to the office) as saying: "If you can make money and have fun and power, that's what it's all about."

Quiet, conservative Macon—"the biggest country town in the world," the city billed itself—took none too kindly to the hip life-style of his stars and hangers-on. So Phil Walden, the rock promoter, became Phil Walden, the politician. He arranged for the Allman Brothers to perform a series of benefits that raised $100,000 for various civic projects. He hired Macon cops and stationed them, in uniform, at his rock club to keep away troublemakers. But most of all, he courted the town's mayor, a gun-toting rightwinger named "Machine Gun" Ronnie Thompson. One thing Walden did was to become the largest single financial contributor to Thompson's campaign. Another was to indulge former gospel singer Thompson's love of music by letting him cut demo tapes at the Capricorn studios. In gratitude, Ronnie named one of the city's bridges in memory of Otis Redding. Walden himself was named to the city planning commmission, which approved zoning changes for houses one of Walden's companies was restoring downtown.

There were other, less noticeable perks. Walden's executives, for instance, could park all day in the no parking zone in front of Capricorn's offices and be confident that their cars would never be ticketed. And whenever one of Capricorn's stars got into a scrape—such as exposing himself at the town's best restaurant, getting drunk or into a fight—the police had a way of looking the other way. Nor did it seem to matter that the various headquarters of the Allman Brothers were veritable storehouses for drugs (one visitor to the Allman farm was impressed to discover that the kitchen equipment included a large-size Hellman's mayonnaise jar filled with cocaine). For some reason, they were never raided. Everything, as the saying went, was cool in Macon, so cool that a visitor to Walden's office was not overly surprised to discover Walden casually sharing a joint with one of the town fathers.

Walden enjoyed the power, and he wanted more of it. In an expansive moment, he told a woman friend that he had two ultimate ambitions: "Become the governor of Georgia, or control the President." That was shortly before he met a man with even bigger ambitions, the governor of Georgia himself, Jimmy Carter.

It was 1973, and Carter was in his third year as governor. He had come to Macon during a "stop and listen" tour of the state, and had dropped by the Capricorn offices to meet the man who by all accounts was the town's biggest booster and leading citizen. Carter left impressed, and promised to keep in touch. A year later, Walden invited him to be the guest of honor at an Allman Brothers concert in Atlanta. Carter accepted and, shortly thereafter, made a tough law against tape piracy, one of the plagues of the recording industry, a part of his legislative package.

When Bob Dylan came to Atlanta on a concert tour a few months later, Walden suggested that the governor host a reception in his honor. Carter agreed, and Dylan, to Walden's surprise, accepted. The party broke up about two, without the appearance of Gregg Allman. He finally showed up at four o'clock in the morning, mumbling apologies, and coked to the gills. Carter, who had to be roused from bed, didn't seem to mind. He greeted Gregg in jeans, an old sweatshirt and bare feet, and the two of them stayed up talking, alone, until dawn. As Allman later summed up the evening, the governor of Georgia was "really far-out."

Walden and Carter drew closer after that. Whenever he was in the area, Carter dropped by Walden's offices, usually to talk, but sometimes to simply listen to the music, as he did for an hour one afternoon during a recording session with the Allmans' lead guitarist, Dickie Betts. It was during that visit that Carter informed Walden that he intended to run for the presidency. Walden offered to do whatever he could. Walden's chance to help came late in the fall of

1975, when a worried Jimmy Carter called him to say that unless the campaign could quickly raise $50,000, he would probably have to stop running. The result was a concert in Providence, Rhode Island, on November 25, 1975, featuring the Allman Brothers and Grinder-switch, another Walden group. With federal matching funds, the concert raised nearly $100,000 and put the Carter campaign back into operation. More Walden-arranged concerts and one enormously successful telethon followed, bringing almost $800,000 into the Carter coffers at the moment it was needed most. "If it hadn't been for Phil, Jimmy would have been dead," a senior Carter aide said afterward. "We were just about through when Phil came along. Phil made everything possible: Iowa, New Hampshire. That was concert money, a lot of it. Jimmy owes Phil an enormous debt."

There seemed no limit to Walden's influence. In addition to his fund-raising, he began to offer political advice. For a time, there were rumors that Walden himself would take over management of the Carter campaign. Carter's aides were worried about his chancy alliance between the non-drinking, born-again Christian candidate for President and the hard-living, non-believing record executive. The association with Allman increased the risk. Allman's drug addiction was notorious, so much so that the joke in the rock community had it that if Carter was elected, the reward Allman would ask for would be appointment as head of the FDA. Carter did not seem worried. "Phil Walden," he said, "is my one-man campaign organization."

With everything working so well, the questions soon died away. And during the general election campaign, Walden more than rewarded Carter's confidence. Thanks to his concerts, another $2 million was pumped into voter registration work. Carter himself, togged out in Capricorn T-shirt, took time out of his schedule to drop by Walden's annual company picnic. He went out of his way to proclaim his appreciation of rock, telling reporters like Thompson of the hours he spent back in Plains, listening to Dylan and Led Zeppelin. Bob Dylan, he said "is a friend of mine," a "poet" whose records had taught him "to appreciate the dynamism of social change." One of Dylan's songs, "Maggie's Farm," had enlightened him about "the proper inter-relationship between the landowner and those who work on a farm." (Actually, "Maggie's Farm" describes the exploitation of a performer by the record industry.) So highly did he think of Dylan's work that he quoted from "Song to Woody" in the opening to his autobiography, *Why Not the Best?,* and cited him again in his acceptance speech to the Democratic Convention: "We have an America that, in Bob Dylan's phrase, is busy being born, not busy dying."

The young people who read *Rolling Stone* couldn't help but be impressed. Certainly Hunter Thompson was, especially after Carter invited him to the governor's mansion for breakfast, and greeted him at the door, as he had Allman, wearing jeans. Hunter carried a tape of Carter's "Amazing Law Day Speech" around with him two years after that, playing it for anyone who would listen, reminding them of how much Carter was "into Dylan." It required a cynical, non-stoned representative of the Establishment, journalist Steven Brill, writing for *Harper's,* to probe the full measure of Carter's commitment. Flying back to Atlanta with Carter during the campaign, Brill asked Carter to name his favorite Dylan song. "He smiled and smiled and said, 'I hate to offend Bob by just naming one,'" Brill related to *More.* So Brill asked him to name several. "Carter smiled some more and said, 'Rosalyn and I listen to him all the time, but the lyrics and the titles blur.'" "Well then," Brill replied, "name a few albums, even one album." The smile disappeared from Carter's face. "Why don't we talk about something else?" he said coldly.

"It looks like a shuck," Jann Wenner had written in 1968, referring to an entirely different kind of politics. He was more tolerant this time. This time he threw a party. After it was all over, and Carter was in the White House, Jerry Rubin, one of the Chicago organizers whom Wenner had so excoriated, asked Wenner why he had changed his mind, how it happened that *Rolling Stone* had joined the Establishment. "We're not going with losers anymore," Jann Wenner said. "We want winners."

9

Solid Gold

Jann Wenner had scant patience for the Jerry Rubins of the world. They were hopelessly naïve. Rock and roll was not a revolution anymore; it was a business, a very big business. If others could not see that, he did—and he would tell them. "One is tired of the eager attacks on any music enterprise (whether a group, ballroom, newspaper or record company) because it makes money," he lectured in one editorial. "The music business, corporate and otherwise, has spread more pro-life propaganda in the last five years than any other commercial institution that quickly comes to mind." And Jann Wenner believed it. He had to. If it had not been for the record companies and their ever-burgeoning advertising revenues, *Rolling Stone* would not have existed. Jann Wenner depended on them, and they on him, far more than Jerry Rubin—or *Rolling Stone*'s readers—could imagine.

It was a curious business, the record industry. Given the hundreds of records released each week, the very few that made it to the top, or even onto a radio station's play list, the wonder was that anyone would want to be in it. "The chances for making a profit," commented one industry magazine, "are better at any race track." Yet, there was no lack of companies willing to take a gamble. The reason was obvious: nine out of ten records released might fail to make money, but there was always that one that came in. There were the Eagles, who, at one point, with two records on the charts, were selling 500,000 units *per week,* or Carole King, whose single album, *Tapestries,* sold 9,000,000 copies. By the middle Seventies, there were dozens of others—at least fifty—who annually earned between $2 million and $6 million, an amount, *Forbes* dryly noted, "from three to seven times more than Harold Geneen, the highest-paid executive in the country, makes." A producer with a good ear could literally make a fortune overnight. There was Berry Gordy, the Detroit auto worker who borrowed $700 from a relative to found Motown—a record company whose profits in 1972 were $30 million. Or the four young plungers who started Dunhill Records in 1966 with a $75,000 cash advance from ABC, grossed $4 million on their third try, and sold back to ABC the contract of one of their acts, the Mamas and the Papas, for $2.5 million—all in the space of eight months.

American capitalism had seldom witnessed such explosive growth. In 1945, the year before Wenner's birth, gross sales from records totaled $99 million; by 1968, a year after *Rolling Stone*'s founding, they had increased more than tenfold, climbing to more than $1 billion. That year, Americans purchased 183 million singles and 196 million long-playing records—approximately two records for every man, woman, and child in the United States. And it was only the beginning. Five years later, the sales gross had topped $2 billion—over three times what Americans spent on football, hockey, basketball, and baseball *combined*—making recorded music, for the first time in history, the most lucrative and popular of all art forms.

Such success did not occur by accident. Hits were manufactured as well as made. One notable example was David
Cassidy, one of the stars of TV's *The Partridge Family,* and
a young actor with no apparent musical talent. That did not
deter promoter Wes Farrell from turning him into a rock
star overnight. With the help of 60 songwriters and 300
specially commissioned possible tunes, Farrell finally settled
on one of them as a potential hit—"I Think I Love You."
Within a year, the single had sold 3.6 million copies, and
Cassidy was on his way. Many of the same talents went into
creating the Monkees, a look-alike Beatles imitation contrived to tap the teenie-bopper market in the late 1960s.
The ploy worked brilliantly. The Monkees' television show
shot toward the top of the Nielsen ratings, and the group itself—once they had been taught to sing and play the guitar—
sold millions of records. Sad to say, they began to believe in
their own myth and, before long, not only acted like rock
stars, but began to live like them as well. One of the group's
members, Mike Nesmith, earned $3 million between 1967
and 1969—and spent every cent of it. When the Monkees
folded, he wound up owing $60,000 to the IRS, and was
forced to vacate his $500,000 mansion in Bel Air for a run-
down two-room house.

Such tales deterred the record companies only slightly.
To make money, they spent money—and in lavish amounts.
Grunt Records, a relatively obscure label, once laid out
$120,000 for a single promotion party. Atlantic countered
by flying a planeload of guests to a company anniversary
party in Paris, at about the same time RCA was flying another jetload of critics to London as part of its $100,000
build-up for David Bowie's first release. ABC invested
$68,000 to produce *one* record by Richard Harris. Within

six weeks, the company had made more than a quarter of a million dollars on its investment.

And then there was advertising.

Until the appearance of *Rolling Stone,* the major record companies advertised their wares in the underground weeklies. But corporate types who ran the record business had never been entirely comfortable with the undergrounds, what with their image-tarnishing scatological journalism, questionable business practices, and bothersome habit of disappearing from week to week. (CBS President Frank Stanton reportedly brought Columbia's advertising in them to an end, after noticing a Columbia ad in *Evergreen* directly opposite a full-page color shot of interracial lesbians making love. The editors at *Evergreen* were nonplussed. Said one of them: "I saw a Columbia ad one time right next to a description of a blowjob in another publication, and they didn't do anything about that.") Then along came *Rolling Stone,* which, to the record companies' delight, looked and read like a professional publication. And there was no denying the magazine's demographics. The average nineteen-year-old *Rolling Stone* reader had more discretionary income for leisure-time activity than his parents. Every year, he (more than 90 per cent of the early *Rolling Stone* readers were male) spent $600 on record albums, another $300 on stereo equipment. As one Roper study put it: *"Rolling Stone . . .* comes out on top . . . delivers more musicians, together with more young people who are heavily into music than any other media anywhere—a total potential market of more than one million." They were the sort of words that were literally music to a record executive's ears.

In the magazine's early days, Wenner personally flew to Los Angeles every week to visit the company media buyers.

Stan Cornyn, executive vice president of Warner's, remembered him then as "a short, nervous, anxious publisher who always seemed just a step or two ahead of his creditors." Cornyn would keep Wenner waiting in his outer office half an hour or more. When Wenner finally gained admittance and made his pitch, Cornyn couldn't help but be impressed at the combination of bullying and pleading that issued from Wenner's lips. Despite his age and inexperience, Wenner thought like the companies did. Warner's, one of the first of the major labels to enter rock, quickly signed up.

Wenner proved to be most cooperative. While his page rates (then $300, versus the 1977 price of more than $6,000) were higher than those of comparable publications, he was careful to call the companies and negotiate every increase. The executives showed their appreciation. As *Rolling Stone*'s influence grew, Wenner gained admittance to the executive suite more easily. No longer was he kept cooling his heels in some outer office. Now he talked business with the executives over lunch, at dinner, and, more often than not, in their homes. In time, he developed close personal relationships with Cornyn, Earl McGrath of Atlantic and Jack Holtzman, president of Elektra/Asylum. They and the others whose company he kept had become more than advertisers; now "Clive" and "Ahmet," as he referred to the presidents of Columbia and Atlantic records respectively, were friends.

For Jann Wenner, Clive Davis turned out to be a most handy friend to have. Clive J. Davis was king of the hill. The company he led—Columbia—was the industry giant, with 1972 sales of $300 million worldwide, a full 25 per cent of the market. He paid out the biggest advances—$4 million for Neil Diamond, $2 million for Laura Nyro, hundreds of thousands for lesser-knowns, simply on a hunch—

and attracted many of the biggest stars—Dylan, Streisand, Joplin, Donovan, Chicago, Simon and Garfunkel, a whole galaxy of talent. "A decent man," Bill Graham said of him; "brilliant," pronounced David Geffen; "the greatest executive in the history of the record business," lauded Nilsson, one of his artists; "brains and ears, style and class."

All of it was true, which made his success even more remarkable, because, in his own way, Clive Davis was as improbable as the industry he dominated. His training had been as a corporation lawyer, and his knowledge of rock and roll prior to becoming Columbia's president reflected it. When he first heard of Simon and Garfunkel, he joked later, he thought they were a law firm. Tall, balding, middle-aged, patrician in bearing, with a fondness for pinstriped, three-piece suits, Davis seemed the very antithesis of a rock and roll mogul. "Mr. Dignified," they called him in the CBS executive suites: "incorruptible Clive."

He had grown up in Brooklyn, loving the Dodgers and hating Frank Sinatra ("I just didn't like all that screaming") and keeping his nose to the grindstone. "I was your basic, garden-variety, ambitious, upwardly mobile, hardworking Jewish boy," he recounted in his autobiography. "I was *bound*—and so were the kids around me—to go beyond my parents. It was simply the way things were. Our parents had worked hard, but we had to work harder." Young Clive worked very hard indeed, hard enough to win a scholarship to NYU and, afterward, to Harvard Law. He did well, kept his grades high, and in 1960, after a brief stint at a New York law firm, joined CBS as assistant counsel in the second division.

Columbia, at the time, was enjoying solid if unspectacular success with a line-up of talent weighted heavily toward middle-of-the-road "easy listening" sounds. Dylan,

Simon and Garfunkel, and a few other rock artists were on board, but were overshadowed, in Columbia's estimation, by the likes of Johnny Mathis and André Kostelanetz. The company's chief talent scout was Mitch Miller, whose "sing-along" albums had made millions. Miller despised rock and roll. When a promoter named Colonel Tom Parker had come to him in the mid-Fifties with some tunes by a former Mississippi truck driver, Miller had turned them down out of hand. "No singer is worth an advance of more than $25,000," he sniffed. RCA thought otherwise, and thus it was that Parker's truck driver—a swivel-hipped young man named Elvis Presley—found fame and fortune elsewhere. The loss of Presley did little to chasten Miller. "You carefully built yourselves into the monarchs of radio," he lectured a convention of 850 disc jockeys in 1958, "and then you went and abdicated your programming to the 8- to 14-year-olds, to the pre-shave crowd that makes up 12 per cent of the country's population and zero per cent of its buying power—once you eliminate the pony tail ribbons, Popsicles and peanut brittle. Youth must be served—but how about some music for the rest of us."

But the demographic and financial equation had changed radically since then. As the Sixties slipped by and the full weight of the postwar baby boom made its presence felt, it changed even more. Before the decade was out, there would be 10 million more Americans between the ages of 15 and 26 than there had been twenty years before—43 per cent more in the 18 to 25 age group. And, Miller's scornful assertions to the contrary, all of them would be buying. Between 1959 and 1969, expenditures by teenagers alone would double, increasing from $10 billion to $20 billion. When young people in their twenties were included, the figure rose to $45 billion. For Miller and Columbia, the trend lines were ominous.

Columbia's competitors were already aggressively pursuing the youth market. Warner's had dispatched Cornyn to the Haight, and he came home to a report that "it didn't uptight us too much." At least not enough to prevent Warner's from, as one company executive put it, "going after as many acts as we possibly could that we thought would relate to this age group." Warner's also hired "company freaks"—"kept hippies," as one of them described himself, ". . . Judas leading the lambs to slaughter"—to "destraighten" the company's image, a task in which bright advertising in *Rolling Stone* also assisted. Columbia, meanwhile, was lying dead in the water. By 1966, it had been passed by Warner's in pop record sales for the first time ever. It was painfully clear in the upper reaches of Black Rock that a change had to be made. The man CBS summoned was Clive Davis.

Davis bided his time at first, waiting for the office politics to sort themselves out. By 1967, with his power secure, he began making his moves. First, he trimmed costs and dropped marginal performers. Then he broke the single pricing structure that had existed throughout the industry for decades. Soon there were growing grumbles that brusque, brash Clive was a "revolutionary." They had no idea, though, just how revolutionary he would be. Until Monterey.

Lou Adler, a friend and colleague of Davis, had invited him to the Monterey Pop Festival, of which he was a board member. Adler told Davis it would be an excellent opportunity to see some of his acts perform and witness firsthand the still nascent "San Francisco Sound." Davis accepted—

and was completely smitten. "It was the first glimpse of a new world," he wrote. "I was a believer."

The good vibes were still washing over Davis midway through the festival, when a group called "Big Brother and the Holding Company" took the stage. Davis had never heard of them. No one outside San Francisco had. Their music was still uneven, and they had yet to cut a record. All they had going for them was a straggly little girl from Port Arthur, Texas, dressed up in a silver lamé pantsuit. But what a girl. And what a voice. "My eyes riveted wherever she went," Davis recalled. ". . . She just couldn't contain herself, and you didn't know how to take it all. It was ebullience thrust at you in the most basic, primitive ways . . . trembling . . . shaking . . . almost a violent tremor when she got extremely *into* what she was doing. She seemed bursting with emotion; and it was so *pure*. I knew immediately that I had to go after her." Her name was Janis Joplin.

For Davis it was the climax of a crusade to drag Columbia, pinstripes and all, into the strange new world of rock and roll. One after another he signed them on: Santana, Sly and the Family Stone, Loggins and Messina, Dr. Hook, Mott the Hoople, Poco, Spirit, the Chambers Brothers, Electric Flag, New Riders of the Purple Sage, Aerosmith, Ten Years After, and a dozen more, so many groups, so quickly, that Columbia, once the most staid and conservative of all the majors, now called itself, with fitting justification, "The Rock Machine." If there were any remaining doubters, they were drowned out by the sound of ringing cash registers. In three years, sales doubled—to $200 million, with pre-tax profits of $25 million. Thanks to Clive Davis and rock, Columbia was now almost as large as its two biggest competitors combined.

The key to Davis' success was spotting good talent and, once he spotted it, turning it to good advantage. He was that way with his artists—"he always had the limousines and flowers right on time," one of the Mamas and the Papas marveled—and he was that way with his friend, Jann Wenner. Ever alert to budding promise, Davis commenced Columbia's advertising in *Rolling Stone* with issue number eight. Some of the ads were self-consciously hip ("Know who your friends are," the copy on one of them advised. "And look and see and touch and be together. Then listen. *We* do"), others downright offensive ("The Man Can't Bust Our Music," Columbia proclaimed in the aftermath of the Columbia University strike), but they worked and, for Wenner, they were literally money in the bank. Best of all, the other companies soon took notice and began placing ads of their own. Columbia itself eventually contracted for a minimum of 52 advertising insertions per year.

The ads, however, were only the beginning.

In 1968, during one of the magazine's periodic financial crises, Davis advanced Wenner $20,000 against future advertising. "I was anxious to help *Rolling Stone*," he explained. "What was good for them was good for the business, and what was good for the business would inevitably be good for Columbia." Other favors started coming. To fatten the magazine's circulation, Columbia had its salesmen distribute *Rolling Stone* through record stores, a mutually lucrative arrangement that accounted for more than 15 per cent of *Rolling Stone*'s single-copy sales. Davis also steered Wenner to a management consultant to straighten out the magazine's confused financial operations. Meanwhile, Columbia's art department designed a direct-mail campaign for the magazine. When Wenner needed still more cash in 1970, Davis stepped in again, this time with a bailout of $25,000 against future advertising. So close did *Rolling Stone* and Columbia come that, at one point, advertising salesmen were working directly out of the CBS building. Wenner was appreciative. One Christmas he sent Davis a giant-size blow-up of a *Rolling Stone* cover, with Davis on it. The headline read: "Should the music industry appoint an emperor?" In 1971, when Wenner went to Columbia University to accept the National Magazine Award, he invited one guest from outside the magazine to go with him: Clive J. Davis.

Davis had Wenner's ear whenever he wanted it, which turned out to be often. He frequently called Wenner to lambaste him about what he considered unfavorable reviews or stories about Columbia artists. "You don't understand the nature of the business." As Davis himself recounted in his autobiography:

> The hide wasn't so thick. I always took it personally when the paper made a snide comment about Columbia or took one of its artists to task. Despite my anger I recognized that *Rolling Stone* did this as a service of sorts to its allegedly anti-establishment readership. I occasionally wondered how they could accept consulting and advertising assistance from Columbia—and then poke fun at us . . . or say downright nasty things. Then I'd cool down and realize that this was part of the game. Jann knew his readership, and his loyalty obviously had to be to them. Nice notices for Columbia made him vulnerable to charges of "selling out." I began to realize that he blasted us occasionally just to protect himself against this kind of problem.

Davis had nothing to fear from *Rolling Stone*. The threat to his empire stemmed from another source: the United States government.

For years, it had been an open, if quiet, secret inside the industry that records found their way onto the play lists and to the top of the charts not always by dint of mere talent alone. Sometimes the way was greased. Whether it was a color television set, a plane ticket to Europe, an ounce of coke, or outright cash, the name for it was the same: payola. The first scandal had broken in 1960 and had revealed a whole array of unsavory practices involving some of the industry's most prominent talents, among them Dick Clark and New York disc jockey Alan Freed, coiner of the term "rock and roll" itself. After months of lurid headlines, Freed died, a number of companies signed consent decrees, and the controversy fizzed out. But payola lived on. It took a different form now. The outright cash payments for record play gave way to stacks of albums, which a DJ could sell to a friendly record store at cut-rate prices. There were refundable plane tickets to company conventions, which radio station executives were never expected to attend, along with other "love gifts"—a hooker, a night on the town, a gram of coke. In Los Angeles, one record company promotion man spent $2,100 a week for cocaine, then distributed it to other promoters, who, in turn, wrote off the expense as "one bass guitar rental, $100." Everything was cool. Only the people in the business knew what was going on, and they hardly talked about it; hardly, in fact, even thought about it. It was simply the way business was done.

No one ever suspected Clive J. Davis, the man they called Mr. Straight, of such dealings. Hirelings handled those chores. At Columbia, his name was "Mr. Gotcha." "Gotcha got whatever an artist wanted," one of Davis' employees explained. "If an artist came to town and wanted a hooker, or grass, or whatever, he went to him." Davis himself seemed unassailable. CBS, in appreciation of the wonders he was working on corporate earnings—Columbia's profits rose 600 per cent in six years, while the price of CBS stock more than doubled—had named him a member of the board, given him salary and benefits totaling nearly $350,-000. But rumors still spread. "Industry, undisguisedly envious, predicts he will go too far and fall," *Time* reported in February 1973. "[Davis] seems unworried." Three months later, the prediction came true.

Davis had just finished his regular morning bowl of corn flakes and was beginning to sort through the day's mail when the call came through summoning him to the office of CBS President Arthur Taylor. Their meeting lasted two minutes; Davis was fired, effective immediately. "We'd like you to return to your office," Taylor said, "and take whatever you'd like to take with you and leave immediately." Davis could only mumble "I'm in shock." When he emerged from the meeting, two CBS security people were waiting for him. They served him with papers informing him that CBS was suing him for $94,000—the amount, the complaint alleged, that Davis had misappropriated from company funds, to (among other things) redecorate his apartment ($53,000) and host a lavish ($20,000) bar mitzvah for his son. Back at his office, Davis discovered that his belongings had already been crated and packed. A company limousine took him home. Half an hour after his arrival, CBS called, asking for the car's return.

There was more trouble to come. Within weeks of Davis' dismissal, CBS hired a law firm and a battalion of investigators to probe into his business deals. As the probe continued, apprehension mounted over what, if anything, Pasquale Falcone, a reputed organized crime figure and manager of two of Columbia's acts, might be telling the authorities since his arrest a few months before on charges of conspiracy to import and distribute heroin. Finally, the other shoe dropped. The New York *Times* reported that the Federal Organized Crime Strike Force in Newark was in the midst of a massive investigation of payola and drug-dealing, with Columbia Records at its center. A close associate of Davis, the newspaper went on, was reported to have told the FBI of distributing $250,000 a year in payola payments to black disc jockeys around the nation. The day the story broke, Clive Davis went into seclusion.

Wenner was vacationing in Rome (in the company, ironically, of an Atlantic Records executive), when he heard what had happened. His immediate reaction was disbelief. When he returned to San Francisco and the taunts of Gleason, who needled him mercilessly that the "bible of rock" had been scooped on the industry's biggest story by the good, gray New York *Times,* he hurriedly began his own investigation. He summoned David Hamilton, a former *Newsday* reporter and then the magazine's music editor, and issued a stream of orders. Call the United States Attorney. Call the FBI. Have them tell you everything. When Hamilton explained that federal authorities were not in the habit of revealing the details of an ongoing investigation, especially to the likes of a rock magazine, Wenner sputtered, "Well, get somebody good from New York down on it." *Rolling Stone* finally did run a story of sorts, suggesting that the charges were much ado about very little, and that the investigation might just be a Nixonian plot. The federal grand juries in Newark, New York, Philadelphia, and Los Angeles thought otherwise. In July 1975, two years after Davis' firing, they handed down indictments charging nineteen people and six corporations with a variety of crimes, including payola, perjury, fraud, and income tax evasion.

Davis, who by then had become president of Arista Records, was indicted for income tax evasion. When he pleaded guilty and paid a $10,000 fine a year later, the story was consigned to the back pages of the New York *Times*. The emperor was an emperor no more.

The fall of Clive Davis startled Wenner; it did not stagger him. Once, the disappearance of a Clive Davis and all the financial resources he could bring to bear would have devastated *Rolling Stone*. No longer. Now the record companies were "pounding on the door, begging to get in." In its own way, Jann Wenner's magazine had become as powerful as the record companies themselves—able, with its coverage, to all but make or break careers. And no one knew it better than Wenner. He never tired of telling the story of Johnny Winter, who, only a few years before, had been an unknown blues guitarist playing around Austin, Texas. Then a *Rolling Stone* writer heard him and gave him a rave review. The day after the review appeared, a New York club manager invited him East. Before long, the offers from the record companies began pouring in. And one fine morning Johnny Winter signed a contract with Columbia for $350,000—then the highest advance ever paid to a Columbia artist.

Such stories meant power for *Rolling Stone*. No other print medium would match its reach—by 1975, 2,000,000 readers around the world—nor the loyalty of its readers. If they read it in *Rolling Stone,* they believed it. One readership survey in the mid-Seventies found that nearly 80 per cent of the readership was influenced in its record-buying tastes by what they read in Jann Wenner's magazine. And not only did they read—they bought, an average of more than five albums a month, 60 albums a year,

120 million albums altogether. *"Rolling Stone—Gonna see my picture on the cover,"* a hot-selling song by Dr. Hook and the Medicine Show went, *"Rolling Stone—Wanna buy five copies for my mother, Rolling Stone—Wanna see my smilin' face on the cover of the Rolling Stone."* Of course, Dr. Hook wanted his picture on the cover. Any artist would. It could mean millions.

Jann Wenner gave Dr. Hook his cover, and true to promise, Dr. Hook arrived to pick up five copies for his mother. But deciding who was worthy of a cover—or a good review—was not always so easy. In the early days of the magazine, Wenner himself did much of the reviewing, and his critiques were notable more for their enthusiasm than for their aesthetics. Later, after more editors had been added, he continued to rewrite many of the reviews, so that when a writer picked up the magazine, he would sometimes be surprised to find that a record he had reviewed had suddenly taken on wonderful qualities that had altogether escaped him. At that, it was hard to fault Wenner. Many of the so-called "reviews" that appeared in the early *Rolling Stone* came in unsolicited from readers and would-be critics who knew little about music, only that they loved or loathed a particular record. Given the state of the art at the moment, one man's opinion was just as good as another's. The ultimate judge was the marketplace. Musicians who sold were cultural geniuses; those who did not were seldom heard from again.

It all changed with the arrival of Jon Landau. At times, the sheer depth of Landau's knowledge could bog down his prose. "Drummer Charlie Watts lays down an elementary drum pattern, the same one he has been using since 'Route 66,'" he wrote of one performer on the Rolling Stones' "Street-Fighting Man." "He strikes the high-hat with a near-compulsive regularity and hits the snare drum with such a wallop it's hard to believe the sound is coming out of only one drum." But, almost by their very denseness, Landau's reviews demonstrated his expertise, and the seriousness with which he, and *Rolling Stone,* regarded the music. The rock world was unaccustomed to such informed criticism, and Landau's views carried enormous weight. Sometimes, a single review by Landau, positive or negative, could alter a career. His judgment that Eric Clapton's guitar playing was inhibited by the group he was playing with, helped convince Clapton to break out on his own and, once free, to revise his playing style. Virtually single-handedly, Landau doomed "Bosstown," a Boston-based rock sound which, amid great promotional ballyhoo, was launched by MGM Records in the late Sixties. *Time* and *Newsweek* hailed "Bosstown" as a major cultural breakthrough. Landau rendered his verdict in one line: "The Sound of Boston: Kerplop." "Bosstown" disappeared almost as quickly as Bruce Springsteen, whom Landau liked, sky-rocketed. Until Landau bestowed kudos on him, Springsteen had been toiling away in the unlikely milieu of Asbury Park, New Jersey. But after Landau's rave—"I have seen the future of rock and roll," he wrote, "and his name is Bruce Spring-steen"—Springsteen's career exploded. *Time* and *Newsweek* featured him on their covers the same week, and Springsteen went on to become one of the biggest stars in the business.

Sad to say, not all of *Rolling Stone*'s reviewers possessed Landau's taste, and almost none his vision. A survey of *Rolling Stone*'s record review section in 1971, conducted by R. Serge Denishoof, found that of 409 releases reviewed, 71.9 per cent were by established artists. For all their caution, the reviewers made some disastrous mistakes. In 1970, for instance, *Rolling Stone* adjudged Grand Funk Railroad

"one of the most simplistic, talentless, one-dimensional un-
musical groups of the year"—the same year GFR went on to
sell 10 million records and become the most popular rock
group in the world. Janis Joplin, who was savaged by *Rolling Stone* a number of times ("an imperious whore . . . the
Judy Garland of rock"), was especially vehement. "Listen,"
she told one interviewer,

> *Rolling Stone* was always down on us . . . They never
> said a decent word about us . . . They were just always
> negative, always negative, always negative. And when I
> went out on my own, they crucified me, man. I really cried
> behind that, man . . . Shit, man. They're from San Fran-
> cisco, I'm from San Francisco. They came out of the same
> rock culture I came out of. I'm one of their people. We're
> all in the same fight together . . . I expected a little help
> from my friends [but] . . . they shot me down, those
> shits.

Many of *Rolling Stone*'s critical lapses could be traced to
Ben Fong-Torres, a Chinese-Filipino who had been with the
magazine since its earliest days and who, now and again,
held the title of music editor. Fong-Torres had the requisite
enthusiasm, and possessed an almost encyclopedic knowledge of apparently every group that had ever moved across
a stage or into a recording studio. But his insights, like the
proverbial Texas river, were as shallow as they were wide.
Lacking Landau's self-assurance and taste, he was uncrit-
ically "fanzine" in much of his reporting (one exception, a
reference to Elton John's bisexuality, was unintentional;
that did not prevent John from briefly pulling his advertising from *Rolling Stone*) and formulaic in determining
which stories merited coverage, almost to the point of parody. But Fong-Torres was nothing if not prolific, which

seemed to delight *Rolling Stone*'s readers, who, in an early Seventies readership survey, named him their favorite writer on the magazine.

The journalism that won such approval was largely the "cassette" variety: hang out with a rock star, turn the tape recorder on, take everything in, transcribe the tapes, add a few grace notes (Fong-Torres's specialty was houses; Ike and Tina Turner's mansion was rendered thus: "a huge, imperial portrait of Ike and Tina . . . also in the foyer, under the portrait, a small white bust of John F. Kennedy. Next to him, the Bible, opened to Isaiah 42 . . . several fish tanks and over in the family room, splashing, programmed, is a waterfall . . . Next to the waterfall there's a red velvet sofa, designed around a coffee table in the shape of a bass guitar . . . in the blue room, the blue couch, whose back turns into an arm that turns into a tentacle. Above that, on the ceiling, is a large mirror in the shape of a jigsaw puzzle piece, and against one wall is a Zenith color TV, encased in an imitation ivory, whale-shaped cabinet . . . On the wall, over the mantel, a large metallic Zodiac sunburst, with no clock in the middle. Also, a Zodiac ashtray atop the guitar-shaped table . . . Atop the white piano complete with a goose-neck light there's the gold record . . . And next to that, some trophies . . . Now I'm down to the sunlit bookshelf in the corner. A neat junior edition of encyclopedias. A couple of novels—Crichton's *Andromeda Strain;* Cheever's *Bullet Park.* But the main line appears to be how-to's, from Kahlil Gibran and astrology to a series of sharks in suit-pocket hardbounds: *How to Make a Killing in Real Estate, How to Legally Avoid Paying Taxes,* and *How to Scheme Your Way to Fortune.* Atop the pile, a one-volume senior encyclopedia: *The Sex Book*"), run it through the typewriter, and, presto, a story. "I know how to do inter-

views now," Fong-Torres wrote in a collection of *Rolling
Stone* pieces, "having done them with Linda Ronstadt
(over steaks, medium), Michael Jackson (over milk, homogenized), Boz Scaggs (over shakes, milk), Sly Stone
(over coke, his) . . . I know to do research beforehand, to
be friendly during the warm-up ('I heard your new album
just yesterday.' Pause, shaking head slowly. 'Whew.'), to
take notes and keep the recorder going while maintaining
eye contact, and, afterwards, to make no promises." To
make, in fact, very little of anything.

From time to time, Wenner attempted to shore up the
music section by bringing in new critics and editors. It was
a difficult search. One prospect advised him to "teach in
college where you could disseminate your ideas about art
without seriously hurting anyone." Another, who actually
stayed on board for a year, departed, calling the place
"counter-cultural suburbia." By the middle Seventies, the
effort seemed to be a fruitless one. The culture had come
full circle, from not caring about the quality of the music, to
critically revering it, back to unevaluated vibes. "I don't
give a shit about music," *Rolling Stone* music critic David
Marsh told an interviewer. "I wanna rock . . . you know?
Shit, everybody I know got involved in all of this—rock and
roll—to get laid centrally . . . Nobody is in it because the
music is such a killer by itself. It ain't."

As the months went by, *Rolling Stone* increasingly
reflected that attitude. David Hamilton, who briefly took
over the music section in 1973, calculated that fully 70 per
cent of the reviews written for his supervision were positive,
many unreservedly so. At first, Hamilton thought the figure
was a statistical aberration. After a few months on the job,
he concluded it was the norm. Often a review would be
farmed out on no stronger basis than a letter that read:

"I've just listened to the new Gordon Lightfoot album and I love it. Can I review it?" Regular reviewers were suspect because of the economics of the job, typically $25 a piece. To earn additional income, many of them looked to the record companies' calculated largess in the form of promotional albums, press release writing, free trips, and booze. One reviewer boasted to one of Hamilton's colleagues that he had recently traveled on record company junkets to the Caribbean, New York, Los Angeles, Chicago, Denver, and San Francisco—and was on the waiting lists for Tokyo and London. Even on *Rolling Stone*'s own staff, there were questionable relationships. Marsh was living with the chief publicist of Atlantic Records. Fong-Torres was toting a company-given Gucci bag. Gleason himself was working on the side as an executive of a record company. "Look," one reviewer told Hamilton defensively, "no one tells me to write anything. But if a company is going to spend a lot of money in the magazine, the least you can do is give them 1,500 words of copy." Others told Hamilton not to worry. "The record companies and us," advised one writer cheerfully, "we're just all part of one family."

What bothered Hamilton even more was the magazine's tastes. The music was changing, becoming more homogenized. As San Francisco's hold on the culture loosened, it was the South, the Midwest, and New York that were rapidly becoming centers of cultural ferment. But there was no way of convincing Wenner, Fong-Torres, and the rest of the staff. "They were fixated on sixteen people," Hamilton recalled. "They found it easier to do stories on David Mason than Robin Trower. The music conferences lost all spontaneity, except when the discussion turned to people they recognized. I tried to get them to put Patti Smith in the magazine, but they had the suspicion of anything that came from

the East Coast. They always thought that someone was trying to sell them a bill of goods." Finally, Hamilton gave up
and, within a year, quit.

He had been right about Wenner, though. The editor was
losing touch. More and more of the magazine was being
devoted to stories of the struggles of Sixties bands trying to
make it in the Seventies. He wanted big names on the cover,
Wenner instructed his staff, personalities who would sell the
magazine. Olivia Newton-John was one he came up with
personally. The choice sent a small shock wave rippling
through the staff, for Olivia Newton-John was a frankly
commercial artist, not of the rock culture at all. Until then,
Wenner had always joked about her, warning his staff that
"if they didn't behave," he would do something unthinkable,
like putting Olivia Newton-John on the cover. Now, he was
doing it.

There were quiet snickers in the industry about *Rolling
Stone*'s declining tastes. Cornyn, who had been so
impressed by Wenner's bumptious enthusiasm, now smiled
and, choosing his words with great care, observed, "They
have moved, shall we say, from being the boutique of the
music industry to being the supermarket." Bob Dylan was
more direct. At a Norman Mailer-hosted cocktail party in
New York, he accosted Wenner and began berating him
about the magazine. "Your paper is really shitty," he
sneered, going on, in a rising voice, to detail a lengthy indictment. "I might just start my own paper," he finally challenged. "Go ahead, start your own paper," Wenner shouted
back. "I'm a publisher. I'll beat you. I'll beat the shit out of
you."

Wenner carried the day, but there was truth in Dylan's
taunts. *Rolling Stone* was not what it once had been. Nor
was Wenner. He had grown older and, in growing older,

lost some of his enthusiasm for rock. He no longer listened to as many records or attended as many concerts. Now, he had to consult the charts to tell him what was popular; in the Sixties, he knew it instinctively. Much of the new music —disco, reggae, redneck rock—did not please him, and he made no secret of his disdain. "It's not that Jann dislikes the new people," one of his editors tried to explain. "He just doesn't know them." What he did now bored him. Many weeks he ignored even what *Rolling Stone* was saying about music. "I don't even read the fucking record section on a regular basis," he conceded in 1974. Not that his staff needed reminding. "He'd tell you sometimes what a great job you had done on one of your pieces," said one of his editors, "only it was a piece you had done weeks before. And then you would realize that he wasn't even reading the goddam magazine."

It was not that Wenner alone had changed; the whole music culture—that great "source of pro-life propaganda," he had lauded as late as 1971—had been stood on its head. For the moment, the glitter and glamor had gone out of the business. Sales were off dramatically. At the retail level, rack-jobbers were returning 50 per cent of their stock and more. "Two years ago," complained a California record company executive, "twelve-year-olds could afford to buy albums. Now, if they buy at all, they will buy 89-cent singles." The pinch was hitting the artists. There were far fewer contracts being awarded than there were during the Sixties, when it seemed that any group with a modicum of musical talent could sign a record contract. Those who were being signed were taking considerably lower advances. At the same time, the pressure to produce results was greater than ever. Some groups were touring 180 days a year in nearly as many cities, with time off only for recording. The pace took its toll, first on the music—more lifelessly formulaic than ever—ultimately on the performers. One by one, the big stars continued to slip away: Eric Clapton to heroin addiction ("I feel I'm almost continually on trial," he told a reporter before he stopped performing to take the cure. "Everytime I step on stage, I know I am expected to give more than I possibly can"); Gregg Allman to drugs ("Where was your pain?" he was asked at a heroin-smuggling trial. "All over," Allman answered); Jimi Hendrix to suffocation (on his own vomit, after a drug overdose); Jim Morrison to a heart attack at 27 ("OD'd on life," *Rolling Stone* commented); and, most haunting of all, the child-woman Janis Joplin. "To be in the music business," she had told a reporter once, "you give up every constant in the world except music. That's the only thing you got, man. After you boil it all down, the only thing you got left is that music." Finally she gave it all.

When Clive Davis heard that Janis was dead, he went into the office, closed the door, and put on her last tape. And, alone in the center of his empire, Clive Davis began to weep.

It had been different with Jann Wenner. "Did you hear?" his secretary asked him. "Janis is dead." Wenner reflected for a moment. "Cancel her subscription," he ordered. The secretary burst into tears. She didn't get it. It was a joke, you see. The whole thing was a big fucking joke.

10

Rolling Stone Writer

The first day he walked into the office, looking for some back issues of the magazine, they thought he was a cop. "Are you a narc or something?" the receptionist nervously asked. No, the visitor replied, not a narc—just from Cleveland.

Joe Eszterhas couldn't help it. Back home, his short hair, beardless countenance and white car coat were very much the fashion in 1971, the sort of appearance that was expected of an eager young reporter at the *Plain Dealer*. And Joe Eszterhas was very eager indeed—eager to get out. He'd been vacationing in San Francisco when, on impulse, he dropped by the *Rolling Stone* office, anxious to see the place where they turned out the remarkable magazine that arrived in his mailbox every two weeks. He was not what could be called a typical *Rolling Stone* reader. His acquaintance with rock and roll was virtually nil. It was not the music that attracted Joe Eszterhas, it was everything else: the style, the look, the hip brassiness, and, especially, the journalism. He had never read stories like the ones he found in *Rolling*

Stone. Writers like Hunter Thompson were saying things in print which, had Eszterhas turned them in to his editors at the *Plain Dealer,* would have caused cardiac arrest.

As it was, the *Plain Dealer*'s editors were none too happy with their star reporter just then. There was no denying his talent; his reporting was bright, provocative, highly imaginative—sometimes, perhaps, too much so. The *Plain Dealer* was still feeling the repercussions of an Eszterhas episode three years before. He had gone to West Virginia to cover a bridge disaster and had come home with a compelling portrait of the family of one of the victims. His description of the squalor in which they lived—the four-room shack with dirt floors, the children dressed in tattered clothes—read like a chapter from *Tobacco Road.* The picture was so vividly revealing, so true to type, that an editor wondered how Eszterhas had been granted such access. The wonder turned to worry when the family sued for $1 million, charging invasion of privacy and alleging that many of the details Eszterhas had recounted so colorfully existed solely in his imagination. Eventually, the United States Supreme Court agreed and, by an 8 to 1 decision, held against the *Plain Dealer,* one of the rare times in the history of the Warren Court when a newspaper had been deemed libelous.

Joe Eszterhas was like that: brilliant and troublesome. He was an imposing presence—big, burly, tough-talking, a Hungarian version, his friends said, of Ernest Hemingway. He had all his model's mannerisms down pat, all his arrogance, all his volubility, all his sense of being different—better— than everyone else. To understand him, his friends said, you had to know his past, how, as a child, he had fled from the little Hungarian town American bombers had reduced to rubble; how he had shuttled from one refugee camp to the next; how, when the family finally reached America, he had

grown up an only child, living in a tiny flat above his father's printing shop on Cleveland's hardscrabble West Side;
how his schoolmates had poked fun at his awkward English;
how even his teachers had taunted him about his hand-me-
down clothes; how he was always forced to prove himself
with his fists. If you understood all this, they said, then you
would know why, as a friend put it, "Joe grew up with a
chip permanently implanted on his shoulder."

But, oh, how he could write. His friends knew that story,
too: how he had passed his childhood reading adventure
stories, night after night, long after his parents had gone to
bed, tucked under the covers with a flashlight, excitedly
turning the pages until dawn; how he had gone off to college, won a journalism fellowship, been invited to the White
House by Lyndon Johnson himself ("and this, Joe, is a picture of Dolley Madison"); how, finally, he had landed his
first job, an apprenticeship on a Dayton newspaper, then
made his way to the *Plain Dealer,* covering cops, crime, adventure, violence; how he wrote with the savvy and instincts
of a street kid: tough, fierce prose, filled with violent, colorful images. No wonder his stories were a little larger than
life, his friends said. The man was a little larger than life
himself.

At first, his editors had understood that. Eszterhas was
given free rein, and his star rose quickly. By the time he was
twenty-two, he was already the best reporter in town and,
some said, the state. He had a way of taking ordinary events
and giving them a meaning everyone else had missed, an
irony, a pointedness, an almost heroic stature, in a city not
used to heroism of any sort. They couldn't say enough good
things about Joe at the *Plain Dealer,* especially after the
scoop he came up with in 1969. Joe had gotten the My Lai
pictures, the grisly glossies of the women and kids stacked

in piles after Rusty Calley's platoon had gotten finished with them, the pictures that broke Seymour Hersh's story wide open, and just possibly changed the course of the war. Some people called it luck. All Eszterhas had done was take a phone call from an old college chum named Ronald Haeberle, an Army photographer who'd been there that day in My Lai, asking if Joe would like to see the pictures he'd been showing to approving veterans' groups around the state. But a good reporter made his own luck. And what mattered to the *Plain Dealer,* basking in the glory of its My Lai coup, was not *how* Eszterhas had gotten the pictures, but *that* he had.

Eszterhas, in fact, was the only person seriously troubled by the My Lai affair. He thought the paper, and in particular its publisher, Tom Vail, was cynically capitalizing on the atrocity, selling rights to the pictures at exorbitant sums. The more Eszterhas thought about it, the more furious he became. Finally, in 1971, three years after the massacre and shortly after his visit to *Rolling Stone,* Eszterhas poured out his bitterness in a 14,000 word account of "The Selling of the My Lai Massacre" for *Evergreen* magazine. When Vail read the story, Eszterhas was fired on the spot.

Eszterhas wasn't worried. By then, he had convinced *Rolling Stone* that he was not an undercover agent and had begun writing for the magazine. His first piece, a chilling two-part exposé of an undercover narcotics agent, evoked nearly as much response as Thompson's work. But Wenner was beginning to sense the problems the *Plain Dealer* had diagnosed years before. Eszterhas was good, but it was difficult to control him. When he came in with his next story —a 17,000-word opus recounting the life, times and violent end of Charlie Simpson, a young hippie who had killed three people in Harrisonville, Missouri, before taking his own life

—Eszterhas dropped it on his desk with an admonition: "You cut it, I'm gone." Wenner, who had budgeted the piece at 7,000 words, replied: "Maybe you'd better." He thought again, though, after he finished reading. Eszterhas had taken an isolated, seemingly mindless occurrence and given it substance and meaning. The result was not so much a piece of reportage, as a small, beautifully finished novella. Its message was plain: Harrisonville itself had driven Charlie Simpson crazy, its small-town narrow-mindedness, its stultifying smugness, its fear and hatred of young people whose only crime was being different. Charlie Simpson's murders were his rebellion. "It's just something Charles wanted to do," one of Simpson's friends told Eszterhas. "How can I criticize it? It was Charles's thing. Like, it was a far-out thing to do." *Far out*. It was exactly Wenner's reaction. "Charlie Simpson's Apocalypse" ran untouched.

It was the kind of reportorial freedom Eszterhas had always been looking for and, under Wenner's beneficent editing, he blossomed. The lead of one of his stories—"Death in the Wilderness," a retelling of the killing of an innocent young man by federal drug raiders—was a textbook example of magazine writing at its finest.

They were asleep in the cabin, at the edge of a woodline of sequoia and madrone, tucked safely into that vastitude of green darkness. Something woke her. He was staring at the ceiling, eyes large and unblinking. He was trembling.
  "Tell me," she said.
  . . . An execution squad was coming for him. Shotguns in their hands, hair as long as his own, wearing jeans, Army jackets, holstered .38's on their hips. They shouldered the cabin door, ripped it from its hinges, and kicked at the dogs with steel-tipped boots. They saw him and

stopped. He was on the back porch, frozen by panic, and couldn't move. They said nothing. Their faces were blank and waxy. They aimed and fired. He heard the gunshots and saw the glop of his own blood. He was dying . . .

She held him and shushed him, and, together, they sought out the familiar reassurances of their pitchblack nights: Susurrus of coastal wind, the languid whoosh of the redwoods, the thud and patter of their two St. Bernards, the moon's gentle white eye.

She thinks about this dream when she visits him these days. Judy Arnold looks at Dick Dickenson's grave, on the plot of tacky suburban land far from his rugged proud mountains, and she remembers how she calmed him.

"You aren't going to die, babe, it's just a dream, a lousy, rotten, silly dream."

Eszterhas's story was not only good writing, but superb investigative reporting. Within weeks after the article's appearance, one of the raiders was indicted for murder, and the Justice Department announced that special steps were being taken to prevent future deaths in the wilderness. All at once Joe Eszterhas, the once unemployed, perhaps unemployable newspaper reporter, was being talked about as the best magazine writer in the country.

They wouldn't have recognized him back in Cleveland. He had long hair now, and a thick red beard. The white car coat had given way to a fringed leather jacket, part of a uniform that included jeans, work shirts, floppy "drug dealer" hat and heavy boots, inside of which was tucked, in ersatz Hemingway style, a hunting knife. He had become, in short, Joe Eszterhas, *Rolling Stone* writer.

It happened to many of them, the frustrated city room refugees who descended on *Rolling Stone* in the early Seventies, looking for a taste of the hip life that had seemed so alluring back when they were toiling away in places like Des Moines. When they reached San Francisco and the offices of *Rolling Stone,* a strange metamorphosis occurred. As David Felton, who left his job with the Los Angeles *Times* to join *Rolling Stone,* described what happened, "Coming to *Rolling Stone* is the event that changes your life. You're overwhelmed when you get here. There are so many sensual treats: women, drugs, music. And you get into all of them. You leave your wife, try drugs, start listening to music, and forget who you ever were."

The illusion, Felton discovered, died quickly. After a short time on the job, the writers who had responded to Wenner's summons to produce "uh, general interest articles," discovered that working for *Rolling Stone,* aside from certain creature comforts, was as demanding as, if not more so than, laboring for their old bosses ever had been. The hours were longer, the pay, in most instances, lower, the bosses, especially Wenner, more capricious. Visiting writers might be seduced by the seeming looseness of the place, the dogs that wandered through the halls, the secretaries who wore no bras, the pot smoke that occasionally wafted in the air, but *Rolling Stone*'s writers and editors knew better. The less hardy of them quickly crumbled under the magazine's back-breaking regime and, with quiet relief, slunk back to the predictable security of the dull, workaday world from which they had come.

Those who stayed were a tight group. Nearly all of them had come of age in the Sixties. They had been through the same experiences, shared the same attitudes, held the same beliefs, reflected the same vision of life—a special sense of how the world worked, or rather, was supposed to work, and the conviction that *Rolling Stone* saw it exactly the same way they did. Working for Wenner made them even closer. The long hours, the impossible demands, the tension, nervousness and sleepless nights that accompanied every closing created a bond among them, an intimacy of having come through and, against the odds, somehow survived. Many of them lived together, and even of those who didn't, most made it a point to live near one another and spend their off hours in each other's company. Few of them were married, and even fewer had children. *Rolling Stone* was all the family they needed. It was a word they used, over and over again, to describe their feelings for each other: *family,* not in the hip public relations sense of the term, but literally, a father and his children.

Father, of course, was Jann, a figure, like all fathers, both loved and hated. He exulted in the role. He was constantly trying to patch up quarrels in the family, expressing concern when couples broke up, sending elaborate wedding gifts to those who made the ultimate commitment, playing with their children, lending them money, scolding them when they were bad, crying with them over hard times, doing everything possible to ensure that *Rolling Stone* would remain a family. When he was particularly cross with one of his staff, he would walk outside his office, place his hands on his hips, and bellow out the name of the offender— "Dav-id, come heeere!"—like a father summoning a truant child. When he was pleased with something they had done, he would shower praise, award them bonuses, buy them gifts, assure them they were "sweet" and "wonderful," hug them, kiss them, literally pat them on the head.

There was no pleasing him forever, though. Inevitably, something would happen for which there would be no forgiveness. Sometimes, the offense was petty. One female staffer was "fired" (she ignored the dismissal and simply stayed clear of her boss for the next six months) after refus-

ing to fetch him a cup of coffee. By contrast, he could ignore
far more serious incidents. Trusted editors knew that they
could tell Wenner to "go fuck yourself" and that the insult
would slide off. Even employees of the mailroom could, as
one of them did, call Wenner "a fat little Jew," threaten to
kill him, and have their boss laugh at them. The truth was,
Wenner hated firing people, and would go to almost any
length to avoid it. When he had no choice, he tried to force
them out, usually by humiliating them, as he did to Robert
Kingsbury, the magazine's first full-time art director.

Wenner had been unsatisfied with Kingsbury's performance for years, but had been unable to bring himself to get
rid of him. Firing him outright was unthinkable, for in addition to Wenner's loathing of direct unpleasantness, he faced
a ticklish personal problem: Kingsbury was married to
Linda Schindelheim, Jane's sister, and was thus his brother-
in-law. But something had to be done. It was not Kingsbury's work that irritated Wenner so much as his attitude.
Ten years older than the rest of the staff, Kingsbury made
no secret of his contempt for Wenner's inexperience, particularly his ideas of visual design, which, often as not, Kingsbury ignored. Wenner, in turn, proceeded to strip him of his
dignity. One tactic was belittling him in the presence of
other editors. When that failed, he hired someone to do half
of Kingsbury's chores, and let it be known that the new arrival was making a higher salary. When Kingsbury asked
about the reason for the disparity, Wenner bluntly told him:
"Because he's worth more than you are." Eventually
Wenner resolved the Kingsbury dilemma in time-honored
corporate fashion, by consigning him to the bureaucratic
limbo of "special projects."

Grover Lewis was a more difficult case. Three and a half
years before, he had interviewed Wenner while on assign-

ment for the *Village Voice*. The *Voice* had rejected Lewis's
portrait of Wenner as too favorable, but the friendship with
Wenner took. After several weeks of wooing, he signed on
with the magazine as a staff writer, and soon carved out a
special niche with his reportage on books, movies, and the
arts. With Thompson, Eszterhas and Crouse, he was one of
the magazine's shining literary lights. Then he began drinking, and as he drank more heavily, his output fell off. Weeks
passed, sometimes months, with none of his stories in the
magazine. Lewis himself appeared at the office only infrequently, explaining to Wenner that he had decided to de-
vote more attention to his writing skills, and to do so required concentration, which was hard to come by in *Rolling
Stone*'s chaotic atmosphere.

Wenner was initially indulgent. Lewis was a writing
talent of the first order, worth making special allowances
for, and he could not dispute Lewis's assessment of the
mood in the office. The magazine's success had not altered
its high-tension style. Disputes were still resolved by
screaming. In one case, a quarrel between the art director
and the music editor ended with the former throwing a plate
of lasagna at the latter. More than once, disgruntled readers
and musicians had invaded the premises to express their
complaints directly. One musician had shown up in the
office of the associate publisher wielding a shotgun. The
New York editor had been threatened by a band of Hell's
Angels, who, until the police arrived, were planning to hang
him out the window by his ankles. Felton had been accosted
at the office by two of his sources; unhappy with what he
had written about them, they expressed their displeasure by
beating him to the ground and smashing his tape recorder.
Wenner himself had been besieged in his office by a group of
gay activists, promising all manner of sexual retribution.

Hardly had they departed when drummer Buddy Miles arrived, drunken and cursing, demanding to see Wenner about an unfavorable review. On being informed that he was unavailable, Miles vented his frustration on the managing editor by cuffing him about the head and shoulders. After that incident, Wenner ordered an elaborate buzzer security system installed. Even the best security, though, could not stop *Rolling Stone's* internal craziness. Wenner had to admit it; Lewis had a point.

For six months, Wenner temporized, debating how to handle his fallen star. Finally, a mutually agreeable solution was found: Lewis would take a leave of absence, go to Texas and write a book about John Connally, for which Wenner would pay him an advance of $40,000. In due course, a contract was signed, and Lewis made preparations to depart. He bought a car, terminated his lease. It was only then that Wenner, through an intermediary, informed Lewis that there wouldn't be a book after all. He was canceling the contract and Lewis was finished. Lewis sued and eventually collected $13,000 in damages plus costs.

Such experiences were painful for Wenner, for they meant not only losing a valued employee, but casting out a member of "the family." "Don't they understand?" Wenner asked one of his editors, after firing Lewis. "I'm helping them to grow up, to be stronger." He was, in sum, being their father. A father was loyal to the members of his family and, in turn, he expected absolute loyalty from them. He found it incomprehensible that anyone would actually want to leave *Rolling Stone* of his own volition. "No one quits *Rolling Stone*," he told an assistant art director who wanted to resign after four years on the job. "I won't allow it." The employee stayed on, but Wenner's regard for her had changed. They were no longer the friends they had been,

and Wenner stopped speaking to her. Eventually, she did
leave—fired, at Wenner's direction. When another editor
told Wenner he was quitting so he could spend more time
with his family, Wenner snapped, "See you around the day-
care center, asshole."

His obsession with loyalty was total. After the attempted
coup by Burks, he continually worried about plots, real and
imagined, that were being hatched against him in and outside the office. "I know there are some people who would
like to get me," he told a reporter. "They're jealous of my
success. Well, let them be. I know who they are. I'll take
care of them." The staff joked about Wenner's paranoia,
gleefully recalling the time when Wenner, on vacation in
Italy, visited the Sistine Chapel and beheld Michelangelo's
"The Last Supper." After gazing at the work for several
moments, he turned to a companion and asked, "Which one
is Judas Iscariot?" For Wenner, though, loyalty was no
laughing matter. It was the virtue he prized above all others.
If he perceived someone to be slacking off, they were
deemed to be disloyal. "It was," said Felton, "like you had
struck his child." When that happened, the results were fearsome. There was the secretary in the New York office, for
instance, who suffered from a nervous condition that kept
her home more than Wenner thought reasonable. "Fire
her," he instructed Peter McCabe, then the magazine's New
York bureau chief. When McCabe protested, Wenner
glared at him. "Working for *Rolling Stone,*" he said coldly,
"should be a privilege."

Hunter Thompson had another phrase to describe it.
"Mutuality of interests," Thompson called it, writers giving
as good as they got. His workers might, from time to time,
loathe Wenner, fulminate, as Thompson did, that they
would "cut off his arm with a machete and eat it—better yet,

make him eat it." They would threaten, storm, rage about everything they were up against, do almost anything except leave. If *Rolling Stone* was not a pleasure dome, and its proprietor something less than Kubla Khan, Wenner's magazine offered something far more important: a creative freedom that they had never known before and, in all likelihood, never would find anywhere again. Many times Wenner allowed a writer to embark on projects about which he was personally dubious, solely because he trusted him. So long as a writer had Wenner's confidence, everything was available: plane tickets to Africa, unlimited expenses, the space and freedom from capricious editing that allowed him to display his talents. Traits that would have driven other editors to frenzy—alcoholism, drug abuse, profligate spending, missed deadlines—Wenner took in stride, provided there was talent to back them up. Sometimes, he would be burned (one prominent writer, for whom Wenner bought a van so he could explore the Great American Southwest, disappeared into Mexico and used the van for drug smuggling). And, as often as not, the persons who burned him most severely were those he trusted the most. But, invariably, he gave them a second chance, and often a third or a fourth.

Some of *Rolling Stone*'s most celebrated writers were men whose shattered careers Wenner had salvaged. Eszterhas was only one example. Another was Howard Kohn, coauthor of the "Inside Story" on Patty Hearst's captivity and *Rolling Stone*'s most prolific investigative reporter. Immediately before coming to *Rolling Stone,* he had been fired by the Detroit *Free Press* and pleaded "no contest" to a charge of filing a false police report. With such backgrounds, both Eszterhas and Kohn might have found it difficult to find employment elsewhere. At *Rolling Stone,* with Wenner's blessing, they flourished. Even Thompson

was hardly being deluged with offers before Wenner signed
him on. Given his writing style and the space it required,
small wonder. But Wenner gave Thompson the opportunity
that turned a modestly successful, highly eccentric writer
into a journalistic superstar. Thompson, despite his difficulties with Wenner, never forgot that, nor did Crouse or the
others. Years later, his career firmly established and
Wenner no longer speaking to him, Crouse still could say:
"Without Jann, I would be nowhere at all. You can't under-
estimate the galvanizing energy of his personality. And, you
have to remember that we weren't exactly the most em-
ployable people in the world. A lot of us couldn't get into
any other magazine except *Rolling Stone*. No one wanted
me, that's for sure. But Jann gave me the chance. He gave
all of us the chance."

Felton was one of those who required a number of
chances. When he talked of the "sensual treats" that *Rolling
Stone* offered, he spoke from experience. He had tried all of
them, especially drugs. Shy and introspective, Felton had an
otherworldly look about him. After he began dipping into
acid and mescaline, the look intensified, sometimes with hi-
larious results. One Friday afternoon in the spring of 1971,
not long after coming to *Rolling Stone,* Felton cheerfully
devoured two tabs of mescaline, and passed the rest of the
day and early evening, as he later put it, "giggling in awe at
the rubber clouds." By and by, he found himself in front of
a television set, watching Dick Cavett interview four Vietnam veterans. To Felton, television history was being made.
The tales the vets told were woeful and gruesome. When
Cavett closed the show, tears were streaming down his
cheeks. The next day, Felton bounded into the office, informed Wenner of the show, and laid out his plan for "saving the magazine." *Rolling Stone* would get the videotapes

of the show, transcribe them, commercials and all, and run everything in the magazine. It would be, he promised, "very, very heavy." Dubiously, Wenner agreed and, at some expense and trouble, a screening of the show was arranged. After an hour, it was apparent that the show was not quite the historical moment Felton had claimed it was. When it was finally over, three hours later, with not a wet eye (including Cavett's) in the house, they walked out into the parking lot and Wenner pulled Felton aside. "Next time," he smiled, "better give *me* the mescaline."

Wenner allowed Felton such latitude, for when the mood moved him, he could be a writer and editor of astonishing gifts. The trouble was, those moods happened only rarely. Like many members of the staff, Felton was a night person, often not rising until noon, then wandering into the office to sit for hours in a barber chair he had installed as a perch of special contemplation. Hours would pass, and he would remain sitting, lost in some private trance. Sometimes, it was not until midnight that he could bestir himself to work. Even then, he wrote with painful slowness, as if each sentence were a personal agony. As a result, his stories appeared only infrequently, much to Wenner's irritation. He tried various stratagems to prod "the stonecutter," as Felton was known around the office. None worked. First, he "fined" him for his tardiness: $25 for every day over deadline. When the sum of all his fines exceeded his entire paycheck, and he could no longer pay his rent, Felton simply moved into the office, bag, baggage, bicycle, and stereo system. Wenner welcomed his unexpected boarder, figuring that, with Felton in the office, at least he could keep a close watch on him. But the surveillance did no good. In mounting desperation, Wenner locked Felton in his room, cut off his phone, and banned all visitors. Still the deadlines passed.

Finally, Wenner fired him. But Felton ignored his dismissal. So Wenner fired him again, and then a third time, with equally meaningless results. Seven years and several thousand dollars in fines later, Felton was still there, writing no more quickly than he ever had—"Sick," he admitted, "helpless . . . and always broke"—but hanging in. "We're a family," he wrote, "with its own kind of love, and its own kind of respect, a family that's shed its blood . . . And as the world outside grows meaner and more meaningless, who wants to run away from home?"

Holding the family together was never easy. As the magazine grew and the staff enlarged, Wenner, whose own time was increasingly being taken up with planning and financial matters, searched for someone to handle the magazine's day-to-day operations. After the Burks purge, Wenner briefly installed Jon Carroll, a former *Playboy* writer Burks had brought to the magazine as managing editor. He lasted two weeks. Two days after a general staff meeting at which Wenner assured everyone of job security, Carroll was fired. Wenner explained to a friend, "That son of a bitch scares me." Carroll's successor was John Lombardi, a street-smart Philadelphian who had been with the magazine slightly more than a year. An imaginative conceptualizer and text editor, Lombardi got on well with Wenner, if not with his ideas. He did not share Wenner's devotion to rock, and was critical of *Rolling Stone*'s ceaseless celebration of the counterculture. At night, Lombardi had recurring dreams of "drowning in a sea of leisure time activity." After one too many of such nightmares, he departed for *Esquire*. Wenner turned next to Paul Scanlon, an easygoing former reporter for the *Wall Street Journal*. Scanlon had not arrived at the magazine until after the Burks revolt, expressed only marginal interest in politics, and showed no signs of overweening ambition. For Wenner, he was perfect. Likable as Scanlon was, however, some of the staff, especially the lately arrived writing talents, were skeptical of his abilities. *Rolling Stone,* despite its rising journalistic reputation, was still extremely loosely edited. Facts were checked rarely, if at all. What the magazine required, Eszterhas had suggested to Wenner, was a number-two man of demonstrated professional competence. Eszterhas had just such a person in mind: John Walsh, then sports editor of *Newsday.*

Walsh was everything that Eszterhas said he was—a competent, highly respected journalist and, to judge from his position at *Newsday,* a proven manager of people. What Eszterhas did not mention was that Walsh, an albino, was also legally blind, a fact that escaped Wenner's attention until Walsh had been hired, and one which, once known to the *Rolling Stone* staff, became a source of cruel amusement. "Wenner's so insecure," went the line around the office, "that he has to hire a blind man as managing editor." But Walsh's handicap did not prevent him from quickly winning the staff's respect and Wenner's relieved gratitude.

For a time, all went well. Walsh set up a research department—the magazine's first—regularized the copy desk, and gave *Rolling Stone*'s female staff, which until then had been relegated to menial tasks, increasing responsibility. The last was accomplished with some difficulty. *Rolling Stone*'s staff, like its readership, was overwhelmingly male, and a number of the men did not take kindly to "chicks" checking and editing their copy, nor to (worst of all from the male standpoint) deletion of "sexist" language. Out went adjectives like "curvaceous" and "shapely." Forbidden, too, was the former characterization of female musicians as "girl groups."

Walsh's women were sticklers for detail and accuracy.

After the magazine was hit with several major libel suits, the research department began demanding that writers turn in a list of their sources for every story. The sources, some of whom had spoken off the record, would then be checked: asked if they had uttered the quotes the writers claimed they had and whether, if the need arose, they would swear to their accuracy in court. Eszterhas, the most aggressively macho of the writers, was especially incensed. "No broad," he sneered to one of the copy editors, "is going to touch my copy." But it was a losing battle. The groupies of the Sixties, like so much else of the rock culture, were gone, and in their place was a cadre of professional women who, when pushed, pushed back. The final barrier fell when the women, led by copy chief Marianne Partridge, staged a successful sit-in in Wenner's office, ending forever what had been the tradition of all-male editorial conferences.

Wenner watched these developments with detached amusement. Despite the commotion Eszterhas was causing, he was secretly pleased with the arrival of the new order. Fact-checking had relaxed his lawyers. The magazine seemed tighter, better-organized. Stories were beginning to appear in the trade press about *Rolling Stone*'s "new respectability." He had ample reason to be high on Walsh just then, women and all. "He runs this sports department of this huge suburban newspaper, and before that, the op-ed page," Wenner said to the *Columbia Journalism Review*. "On top of which he's a complete rock and roll freak." Wenner fairly glowed with pleasure.

The romance did not last. Walsh, it soon developed, was not the resolute manager his résumé indicated. Responsibility was rarely delegated, and the manuscripts kept piling up. Free-lancers were commissioned to do stories and were given whopping expenses, then failed to deliver. The

production department was being run ragged, after Walsh
decided that it would be better for the book to be laid out
and made up at the site of the printing plant, namely, in St.
Louis. Once, Walsh took the magazine to the brink of deadline without a cover, after a projected free-lance story on
Bill Walton fell through. Eszterhas finally saved them with
a last-minute, slapdash account of the end of the war, just
as the presses were about to roll.

All of it might have been forgiven were it not for Walsh's
style. He was jovial enough; what made his staff cringe
was the utter abandon with which Walsh, the Establishment Easterner, took to the youth culture. He fell into
what he took to be the hip argot, calling things "groovy"
long after "groovy" had fallen out of fashion. Almost every
day, he wore a different rock band's T-shirt to the office,
and once wrote albino guitarist Johnny Winter a fan letter,
signing it, "yours in white power." That, as the staff saw it,
wasn't cool at all.

Within a few months, Eszterhas began lobbying for
Walsh's removal. The new managing editor, he told
Wenner, was hopelessly out of his depth, an embarrassing
square. The staff was on the verge of revolt. Others soon
joined the chorus, but Wenner resisted. Genuinely fond of
Walsh, Wenner had had enough of personnel changes for
the moment. He had larger worries—Thompson, Goodwin,
the "Politics" project, all of which demanded his attention.
"Relax," he told Eszterhas. "It'll work out."

Instead, it got worse. Eszterhas and several other writers
threatened to quit unless Wenner moved immediately. Finally, Wenner faced the inevitable. Fortifying himself beforehand with larger than usual quantities of white wine, he
took Walsh out to dinner and reluctantly broke the news.
Afterward, Wenner appeared at the home of a friend, dazed

and high. "Give me a drink," he muttered. "I had to fire the blind man."

Walsh, whatever his shortcomings, had, by his very presence, enhanced *Rolling Stone*'s reputation as a magazine of serious journalism. By the time of his departure a number of prominent by-lines had begun appearing in the magazine, over articles about topics with not the remotest relationship to music and the youth culture. First and most notable among them was the inventor of the New Journalism himself, Tom Wolfe.

Wenner had been attracted by Wolfe's writing from the start. As Wolfe's notoriety grew, so did Wenner's longing to have him in the magazine. Ironically, much of Wolfe's writing was a scalding critique of the world in which Wenner operated, and of the radical chic culture to which he increasingly aspired. But Wenner was undeterred. What interested him far more than what Tom Wolfe said, or even the way he said it—a kind of adult version of the gonzo style—was that, in saying it so well, and to such a large and influential audience, Tom Wolfe had become a literary celebrity, a name people instantly recognized. "I like talented people," Wenner explained. "You might say, I collect them."

And so the courtship began, slowly and unrequited at first, but with growing ardor. When Wenner wanted someone or something, he could be persistent, "like a lover," as a writer whom he had previously seduced put it. "That's how he makes you feel, as if he only has eyes for you." It was that way with Wolfe—"the *great* Tom Wolfe," as Wenner altered a reference in *Rolling Stone* to read. Wolfe was the best writer in the country, Wenner kept telling him, and *Rolling Stone,* if not the greatest magazine already, would be with the addition of his talents. Moreover, Wenner would pay him well. More, in fact, than any other magazine. In the face of such an assault, Wolfe soon succumbed. The first day he visited the magazine's New York office, Wenner spent two hours personally tidying up the premises in preparation. When, at last, Wolfe walked through the door, Wenner took him by the arm for a guided tour of the office, prefacing each introduction with the line, "I'd like you to meet Tom Wolfe, the *famous* writer."

The topic Wolfe chose to write about—an exhaustive, five-part examination of the astronauts—was not exactly in keeping with *Rolling Stone's* rock format. Wenner couldn't have cared less. With writers such as Wolfe, he meant to change that format, to transform *Rolling Stone* into, as the . promotion ads now put it, "a general interest magazine covering contemporary American culture, politics and arts, *with a special interest in music.*"

After the Wolfe story, Wenner began recruiting in earnest: J. Anthony Lukas, Nicholas von Hoffman, William Burroughs, Charlotte Curtis, Nora Ephron, Carl Bernstein, Gloria Emerson, Yevgeny Yevtushenko, Lillian Hellman, Ken Kesey, Daniel Schorr. Wenner paid them well for their talents. Bernstein, for instance, received $27,500 for a single piece examining the relationship between the press and the CIA. Wenner was also more tolerant than other editors would have been. Provided the by-lines were of sufficient prominence, every liberty was available. Norman Mailer, asked to turn out a tour de force on the CIA, replied that he didn't have the time to do the reporting. No matter, Wenner responded, his editors would do the reporting for him. All Mailer would have to do was whip the story into shape. The offer was difficult to refuse, especially when Wenner was offering $12,500 for Mailer's labors. This time, however, Wenner's generosity backfired. Mailer duly wrote the story, only to publish it in *New York,* when Clay Felker, Wenner's chief rival, offered to double his fee. Mailer was not the only miscue. Truman Capote, assigned to cover the Rolling Stones' 1973 American tour, failed to deliver at all, a disaster Wenner partially salvaged by commissioning Andy Warhol to interview Capote about why he hadn't written the story: One sample:

> *Capote:* Haven't you heard about Dr. Grentreich?
> *Warhol:* No. What does he do?
> *Capote:* He's a dermatologist. He can take your skin and make you look like . . . I don't know . . . Venus de Milo. Overnight . . .
> *Warhol:* Gee . . .

"Star-fucking" they called it back in San Francisco, where Wenner's sequential love affairs with members of the literary establishment were the source first of humor, then irritation, and finally, of dismay. The staff appreciated the cachet that a Tom Wolfe lent the magazine, and there was no arguing that "Astronauts" had been a remarkable piece of journalism. But did it belong in *Rolling Stone?* The mutterings grew louder as other stories came in: Tricia Nixon, Jack Ford, Princess Caroline of Monaco—not *Rolling Stone*'s kind of people at all.

Wenner tried to reassure them. True, he admitted, the fees he paid some writers for single stories were more than most of their yearly salaries. But big names were good for the magazine, and what was good for the magazine would, in the end, be good for all of them. If they doubted him, they had only to read what others were writing about them. "The most exciting magazine to have come along in years," the Boston *Globe* was saying; "one of the latter-day wonders of American journalism," echoed the *Columbia Journalism Review,* even as *Publisher's Weekly* was pronouncing *Rolling Stone* "one of the influential magazines of the day." They *were* influential, Wenner told his staff, and it was because of what he had done. "What are you?" Wenner shot back at one complainer. "Some kind of goddam hippie?"

No one was willing to challenge him. Burks had tried, and he was gone. Thompson had talked union, now he was gone as well. Scanlon, back again as managing editor, was not about to repeat those mistakes. One trip to the New York *Times* dispelled any fantasies he might have had. "Reporters came up to me and said they were reading our stuff and getting ideas from us," he reported excitedly. "Abe Rosenthal came out and shook my hand." The lingering counter-culturists had to face facts. And the central fact was that, by the middle Seventies, most of them had invested their entire careers in *Rolling Stone*. With the economy depressed and magazines seemingly folding every other day, there were few other markets for their talents. Felton stated it starkly: "Most of us are never going to get out of here, and even if we did, we'd just fall apart in the real world; and why fall apart out there when you can do it here and the health plan pays your shrink $15 a visit?" Why, indeed. Wenner, if not overly generous, was at least paying a living wage. "It's his sandbox," Charlie Perry shrugged. "He can do with it what he wants to." But there was more to the staff's caution than that. However much they might disagree with him, even loathe him at times, Wenner was still their corporate father. They knew, only too well, the price of losing Father's affection. One woman who was discharged stayed around the office for a week, imploring Wenner to take her back. Finally, she ended up in a sanitarium. For reasons they could not fully explain, Wenner had an almost mystical hold on them.

Partly, it was the skillful way he played them, beneficent one day, tyrannical the next. "He'd say hideous things that you thought were a joke," Hunter Thompson remembered. "Then he'd turn around the next day and do it. A lot of writers couldn't stand up to it. He broke their confidence."

Wenner himself used to remind Felton, "I can be very mean," in part as a warning, but, in part too, as a kind of boast. Felton could not stand up to the harassment, and he lacked the strength to get out from under it. In time, his talent wilted, and he was eventually reduced to turning out picture captions and the table of contents.

They would not have tolerated the same behavior from those paunchy middle-aged captives of the Establishment from whom they had fled and whom they now so smirkingly ridiculed. Wenner was different, they kept saying. He was one of them, the same age, the same values, the same background. If the fates had spun differently, they could imagine themselves being him, and he them. When that illusion vanished—they, after all, were not the ones who owned two Mercedes and a mansion in Pacific Heights—there was always another excuse to take its place. "Jann is a Capricorn," one of his editors tried to explain. "That tells you a lot of things." It did—not so much about Wenner, but about the people who worked for him. They were the generation that had grown up believing that talent gave license, the *right* to act differently, more brutishly, than those with lesser gifts. And so they suffered his excesses, as they would suffer the excesses of a rock star, giving the god his due.

That he had talent, and in enormous supply, there was no argument. As an editor, he possessed all the requisite tools: wit, intelligence, instinct, taste, boundless and galvanizing

energy. Gloria Emerson, the veteran New York *Times* correspondent who came to work for him in 1977, likened his
insights to "a bright flare that suddenly lights up the sky, il-
luminating everything around it, a flash that comes and goes
in a moment." He extracted the best from people—better, of-
tentimes, than they thought themselves capable of. He had a
knack for cutting through complexity, for seizing the heart
of a story or an idea, picking the quote or headline that
somehow said it all. The passion he brought to his work, the
unshakable conviction that whatever was occupying him at
the moment was, *ipso facto,* the most important concern in
the world, rubbed off on those around him. From the moment he swept through the door at eleven A.M. to the time,
usually well after midnight, when, punchy with fatigue, he
dragged himself home to bed, the office fairly crackled with
energy. When he was away from San Francisco too long, the
magazine showed it. The editing was looser, the ideas less
fresh. It was the inherent flaw of the system he designed. No
one could run the magazine except him. "It's my idea and
I'm still running it," he said in 1974, shortly after he installed Walsh as managing editor. "There's no absolutely
number-two guy." One of his editors said it more succinctly:
"If Jann died in a plane crash, this place would be bankrupt
in six months."

There was no mystery to his prowess. He read voraciously, often obscure publications, from whose pages he
clipped snippets of paragraphs that eventually became
major *Rolling Stone* takeouts. He made it his business to go
to the right parties, talk to the right people, cultivate the
bright, the beautiful, the unabashedly hip. More than anything, though, he simply trusted himself. Time and again,
he was proven right, so right, so often, that his staff, whatever else they might think about him, regarded his instincts

with unreserved awe. "Look at the whole youth thing," one of his editors told a reporter in 1974. "A year ago, Jann started cutting his hair and wearing suits. Now you see stories everywhere about young people cutting their hair and wearing suits. He's ahead of his time. He has vision."

Occasionally, his vision wandered: to Monaco, to Washington, to New York, to anywhere that, Wenner decided, influence and approval led. When, eventually, it came back into focus, as always it did, the results could be spectacular. The spring of 1975 was such a time.

Rolling Stone was lying dead in the water. Walsh had departed. Goodwin had quit. Thompson was in self-imposed exile in Aspen. The music was absolutely nowhere. Wenner, weary of continuing rounds of financial jiggering, had once again turned his attention to the editorial department fulltime. All he needed was a story, a monster hit that would propel *Rolling Stone* to straight respectability once and for all. What he needed most of all was a bit of luck. And then it happened.

Their names were Howard Kohn and David Weir; until then, few people had ever heard of them. Both twenty-nine, they had grown up together in a small town in Michigan and gone on to the same university. After graduation, their paths diverged: the easygoing, voluble Weir went off to the Peace Corps, while the darker, more intense Kohn moved to Detroit and a reporter's job for the Detroit *Free Press*. As Weir toiled away in Afghanistan, Kohn rapidly became one of Detroit's best investigative reporters. His first breakthrough, for which he won a fistful of prizes, including nomination for a Pulitzer, was an investigation of an eighteen-year-old murder-and-bank-robbery case, for which a black man named Lee Del Walker had been sentenced to life in prison. As a result of Kohn's digging, Walker was granted a new trial. He was acquitted this time, and went on to become the chief investigator in the Detroit Public Defender's office, none of which made Howard Kohn popular with the law. Thanks to the Walker stories, however, Kohn developed excellent sources in the black community, and soon embarked on a major investigation of the links between heroin dealers and the Detroit police. For eight months, he quietly kept at it. Eventually, though, word of what he was up to leaked out, and Kohn began receiving death threats. Worried, he started carrying a gun. It proved to be a mistake.

One night, Kohn got a call from one of his informants, a major drug dealer, saying that he needed to meet the reporter, that he had important information to pass on. As Kohn related what happened next, the dealer took away his gun, kidnapped him, and locked him up in an abandoned house. Kohn managed to escape, but on his return to the *Free Press* office he neglected to inform his editors that he had been armed at the time of his abduction. The police, who had been waiting for Kohn to make a slip, pounced. With no proof of his supposed kidnapping other than his own word, and with an important detail consciously omitted, they charged him with filing a false police report, a felony. The *Free Press* thereupon fired him. Kohn later pleaded "no contest" to the criminal charge and was placed on probation. Howard Kohn's career in journalism seemed to be at an end.

He came to California, looking for free-lance work and a chance to start over. He'd not been in San Francisco long when *Rolling Stone* contacted him. Wenner had heard about his troubles in Detroit and wanted to do a story about him. The story was never published, but, in the course of the reporting, Kohn started pitching ideas. Some of them took, and after Kohn turned in a disquieting examination of the death of atomic plant worker Karen Silkwood, Wenner hired him full-time. Weir, meanwhile, had returned from the Peace Corps and, by chance, had also come to San Francisco where he had helped launch *Sundance,* a slickly packaged radical underground. When *Sundance* folded, Weir came to *Rolling Stone* with a proposal for an investigative story on Timothy Leary. Wenner was impressed, and more assignments followed. Three years after leaving Michigan, Kohn and Weir were together again.

Weir wanted to make the most of their partnership. A year before, Patty Hearst had been kidnapped by the Symbionese Liberation Army. Now most of the members of the SLA were dead, and "Tania," née Hearst, had gone into hiding. Weir thought there was an outside chance that they might find out what happened to her. If they did, it would be a newsbeat rivaling Watergate in popular appeal. Kohn needed no urging. Within days, they were on their way.

Kohn and Weir's chief lead was Jack Scott, an author and sports enthusiast who had won a reputation in radical circles with his leftist critiques of the sports establishment. A few months before, Scott had become a major character in the Hearst hunt, after his older brother Walter, a former government computer specialist, had told the FBI that Jack and his wife, Micki, had harbored Patty and the two surviving members of the SLA, William and Emily Harris, the summer before in a farmhouse in eastern Pennsylvania. Scott had denied the allegations, and had refused to cooperate with the FBI. His older brother, he pointed out, had a history of alcoholism and mental instability, and was hardly a credible witness. A grand jury met to consider the charges, then adjourned without either calling or accusing

Scott. After a few weeks in the headlines, Scott dropped from view. As a story in the New York *Times* summed it up: "Scott's role, if any, in the Hearst case remains baffling."

The press's lack of interest in Scott was understandable. It was too hard to imagine him mixed up with a radical group whose credits included assassination, kidnapping and bank robbery. Jack Scott was too mild-mannered, too ardently pacifistic, to be involved in such goings-on. His radicalism, such as it was, was confined to sports, where he had caused a minor stir a few years before by suggesting that big-time athletics exploited athletes and cheapened the meaning of the game. The administration at Oberlin had been sufficiently unsettled by his belief to discharge him, but hardly anyone else was. To all intents and purposes, Jack Scott seemed an eccentric, over-the-hill jock, with no more threatening purpose in mind than writing his memoirs.

Howard Kohn and David Weir knew better. By June 1975, while the rest of the press was pursuing will-o'-the-wisps, they were Scott's confidants, listening in rapt fascination as Scott revealed who he really was. Yes, he had seen Patty Hearst. Yes, he had harbored her. Indeed, almost all of the things his alcoholic, demented brother had told the FBI, the very things he had denied and which no one seemed to believe, were true.

It had all started more than a year before, when Scott, out of work and despondent, was passing his days in a New York apartment, watching television and reading newspapers, and wondering what he would do with the rest of his life. Every paper he opened, there was Patty Hearst, robbing banks, shooting up sporting goods stores, calling her parents pigs, making fools of the FBI. Here, obviously, there was material for a book. But when Scott broached his idea to a publisher, laying out how he wanted to place the

SLA in historical context, the answer was no. No one was interested in theories, the publisher told him. What they wanted was word of Patty: Where was she? Had she really joined the SLA? What had she been doing since her disappearance? More depressed than ever, Scott returned to his apartment, only to witness the televised immolation of the SLA. Two weeks later, he was on a plane heading for San Francisco, his sympathies fully engaged, determined to tell the full story of the SLA.

He tracked down old Movement friends in the Bay Area and they, in turn, steered him to more radical contacts. In time a clandestine rendezvous on a Berkeley street corner was arranged and, within hours, in a ramshackle house stocked with grenades and homemade automatic weapons, Scott had a face-to-face meeting with "Tania," "Teko," and "Yolanda," the last survivors of the infamous SLA.

So began Scott's adventures with the SLA. For the next six months, he stayed with them, shuttling them across country, feeding them, housing them, kidding, joking, and being terrified with them. Patty poured out her entire story to him, all the details of her kidnapping, imprisonment, and eventual conversion. The narrative was rich and detailed, and Scott took it all in. For all his altruism, fondness for Patty, and sympathy for the SLA, he had not given up his hopes of writing a book when his stay with the SLA had ended. When, after a series of bitter disagreements, Patty and the Harrises left him in late September 1974, Scott's chance seemed to have arrived.

But Scott had made a serious blunder. Proud of his revolutionary derring-do, he had gotten drunk one night with his older brother, Walter, and revealed the whole story. From there, it was only a matter of time, alcohol and money changing hands until Walter passed the tale to the FBI.

Scott's notoriety made it impossible for him to write an account of his time with the SLA personally, without exposing himself to legal jeopardy. But if he were insulated, say, by having two investigative reporters with their own connections to the left and an understanding of the Movement, write the story for him, then his legal problems would ease considerably. Enter Howard Kohn and David Weir.

McGraw-Hill, the publisher whom Scott approached, was leery. The company had been highly embarrassed by Clifford Irving's hoax biography of Howard Hughes, and was not anxious to risk ridicule again, however compelling Scott's story. Nor were they as sanguine as Scott about the potential legal complications. Worst of all, though, were Scott's financial demands: he was insisting on an advance of $300,000. When Scott stuck to his figure, the negotiations broke off and, with them, his collaboration with Kohn and Weir.

This left Kohn and Weir in possession of a hot story and, for the moment at least, no place to put it. Wenner quickly resolved that problem. When the reporters told him what they had, Wenner whistled in surprise. "No shit?" Here, dropped in his lap as it were, was the ultimate *Rolling Stone* scoop: a story battalions of straight reporters had pursued fruitlessly for months; a story that not even the undergrounds, with their supposedly excellent connections to the radical community, had surmised; a story *Rolling Stone* was uniquely qualified to handle—"a rock and roll kind of story," Wenner called it, filled with adventure, intrigue, mystery, and mayhem. Was there ever a child who had more completely broken loose, overturned conventions, rejected her background so utterly, than Patricia Campbell Hearst? Wenner had to have it. For an exceedingly modest sum, Kohn and Weir agreed to give it to him.

The only question was when to publish it. Kohn and
Weir wanted to do more reporting. There was still the matter of the "missing year" Patty had spent after leaving Scott,
plus a host of other, juicy details that Scott had not provided. How, for instance, had the Hearsts reacted? What
lengths had they gone to in trying to get Patty back? There
were many questions that needed answering, including the
one that troubled Kohn and Weir the most: what were the
ethics of exposing the underground and, in the process, putting the well-meaning activists who had helped Hearst and
the Harrises in legal jeopardy? Kohn and Weir pondered
the problem, then talked it over with a number of radical
friends and attorneys. Eventually, they concluded that the
SLA was not a true revolutionary group at all, but, as Kohn
put it, "an embarrassment to the left." The only people who
might have legal problems as a result of their story, their
lawyers assured them, would be themselves. With those
worries laid to rest, Kohn and Weir got down to work.

While Kohn and Weir pursued leads, Wenner and a
small but ever-widening circle of *Rolling Stone* editors kept
their secret, fretting that Patty would be killed or captured
before publication date, or, worse, that the competition
would beat them to the story. Already, they knew, another
magazine was closing in on the same information. There
were other concerns. As the months went by, Kohn and
Weir started receiving anonymous threats, unspecified but
ominous warnings that, unless they took "the proper political line," as one caller put it, radical retribution awaited
them. As a security precaution, they arranged appointments
by pay phone, never using the same phone twice, and conducted several interviews in the bug-free environs of California's freeways. Then, in early September, as Kohn was
poring through clips in the Harrisburg library, he got a star-

tling surprise. Looking around the room, he saw a familiar face a few tables away, staring intently back at him. Kohn was sure it was Bill Harris. Before he could do anything, the man nervously got up, walked out of the library and disappeared.

The incident helped convince Kohn that they could afford to wait no longer. Returning to San Francisco, he and Weir sat down to write the first installment of their narrative—some twelve thousand words in all. Security was tight. An armed Wells Fargo guard was posted outside the door, and Wenner, fearful that *he* might be kidnapped, was briefly accompanied by a Pinkerton man. The presumed danger only added to the excitement. Wenner was back in his element, working as he seldom had since the early days of *Rolling Stone,* editing, clearing copy, rewriting, trimming, shaping, interviewing, firing questions, keeping the story on track. Weir had wanted to stress the political aspects of the case, comparing the SLA's terrorist tactics to the pre-Bolshevik Norodniks. Wenner, on the other hand, wanted to emphasize the human dimensions of the story, the anguish Patty had been through, the isolation she felt, the disillusionment with her parents. In the end, Wenner's view prevailed. Kohn and Weir were ultimately glad that it did. At bottom, the story of Patty Hearst was the story of a generation writ large.

In early September, the first draft was finished. Kohn and Weir decided they might be able to chance an additional delay, while they rounded up more details for a projected second installment. Meanwhile, typesetting on the first installment proceeded under tight security. Then, on September 18, just as the typesetting was being finished, Patty was arrested in San Francisco. The initial reaction at *Rolling*

Stone was shock and dismay. Kohn worried that they were too late.

This time he was wrong. Patty was held under tight wraps. Working on a crash, round-the-clock basis, *Rolling Stone* was on the stands in half the normal time. By then, thanks to carefully orchestrated advance publicity, Kohn, Wenner, and *Rolling Stone* were household names from coast to coast. Kohn was stunned. He had always known he was on to a good story, but he never realized, until it was over and his name was in all the newspapers, yes, even on the front page of the Detroit *Free Press,* just how good a story Patty Hearst really was. The night it broke, he and Weir, along with a few of the editors, gathered in Wenner's office to watch the network news. This would be the final test. First, Cronkite, who led with it. Then, Chancellor, who led with it, too. ABC was almost an afterthought, but Reasoner and Smith were headlining it as well. All of them. Three out of three. The last time a press story had received such attention, Scanlon informed them, was when the *Times* broke the Pentagon Papers. "That means we're just as good," Wenner said. "Hell, better." With that, he reached into the office refrigerator, pulled out a bottle of champagne and cracked it open. He paused for a moment, then said quietly, "This is the best. We have never been better than this. Never." As Wenner lifted his glass, the image of his magazine still on the screen in front of him, he could contain himself no longer. Quietly, unashamedly, he began to cry.

11

Citizen Wenner

Jann Wenner was in a mellow, expansive mood. He took a sip from the glass of Ballantine's scotch that rested on the antique oak desk in front of him, savored it a moment, then continued the conversation with the reporter in front of him. This one was from *New York*. There had been others; there would be more. All of them had come to ask the same question: how was it that a man still in his twenties—a virtual adolescent, by publishing standards—could in the space of less than ten years turn a rock sheet started with $7,500 borrowed money into what in this year of 1974 was a $12-million-a-year enterprise? He had already answered the question dozens of times, and always the same way, but somehow they had never gotten the message. It irritated Wenner: not just the question, but the way it was posed, suspiciously, as if he were working some sort of angle, as if, because of his age, he didn't have a right to his success. "They expect you to live their fantasy of you," he grumbled. "Either that, or if they have the idea you've made it, they want to share the secret. And the secret always turns out to be that it's okay to cheat, that it's okay to steal. The great American ethic."

Well, he had to be patient. The publicity, after all, was good for business. Still, he couldn't resist a bit of mischief. Unfolding some white crystalline powder from a paper container, he put a small amount in his hand, held it up to his nose, and snorted. "I hope this stuff doesn't make me begin to yak," he smiled. Now, what was it? Oh yes: Why was *Rolling Stone* so successful? The writer waited indulgently and glanced around the room: color TV, oriental rug, books, posters, all the totems of success, about what he would expect in any senior editor's office at *Time* or *Newsweek*. Finally, the answer: "We have never been an underground publication," Wenner said, launching into the by-now-familiar refrain. "We have always said we wanted to make money."

There was something different about Wenner's words, though, and the way he said them. Making money was no longer a wish. With writers like Thompson and stories like "Fear and Loathing in Las Vegas," not to mention the record industry, God bless them, cash was coming in by the bucketful, and Jann Wenner was being touted by *Money* as "a young American millionaire." No wonder the financial writers lusted after his secret. The story of his success seemed like something ripped from the pages of a dimestore potboiler. *Hippie comes to San Francisco. Listens to rock and roll. Starts magazine. Survives crises. Makes millions. Lives happily ever after.* If that was the story the reporters were looking for, they were destined to be disappointed. The rise of Jann Wenner and *Rolling Stone* to fame and fortune was, when shed of its rock culture trimmings, relentlessly ordinary.

The year was 1969, four months before Woodstock, seven before Altamont. Another reporter, this one from *Time*, all starched and pinstriped, was in Wenner's office, listening to the *Rolling Stone* saga. Wenner was in his denim period, but the clothes could not conceal an ambitious young man who was going somewhere, and in a hurry. The fact that the *Time* man was there was proof enough of that. *Cheetah* and *Eye,* Wenner's far-better-financed competitors, had just folded, and the reporter was asking how it was that Wenner was surviving—indeed, by every appearance, thriving. Wenner used the occasion to wax philosophical. "One of the most exciting things about the rock culture," he began, "is the 'new business' which we're a part of. It's first of all not the destruction of capitalism. Capitalism has given us the opportunity to do this paper in the first place. It's given us the incredible indulgence of rock and roll music. But a rock and roll business means the rearrangement of priorities. We're still a business. We have to make a profit, get out a paper, pay our overhead, pay our employees, pay our printer. But the important thing is not just to make money—but to put the money we make to good use, to make the place where we work pleasant, and to make the people who work here as comfortable as we can." Suddenly, he leaped up. "Look at that Xerox machine," he said excitedly, pointing at the new office photocopier. "Wow! Every time I look at that, then I feel like we've made it. I mean, that's reality." He paced around the office for a few moments, savoring what he had said. The *Time* man was writing it all down. Wenner didn't want him to get the wrong idea. "There's something far more important than making a profit," Wenner said quickly, "and that's having a good time. There's no reason why you can't have a viable business and still have a good time. There's no contradiction. We've just reversed the priorities. We have a good time first and viable business second."

Wenner laughed when he said that, and the *Time* man laughed with him. What Wenner didn't say—indeed, what he was desperately trying to hide—was that he had taken his ·dictum too literally, and that, even as they sat there, *Rolling Stone* was teetering near bankruptcy.

Flushed with *Rolling Stone*'s success, Wenner had over-reached himself. He had abandoned the old rent-free loft above the printing press in favor of two entire floors in a refurbished factory building at a rental of $6,000 per month. Bureaus in New York and Los Angeles were next. Then had come the fiasco at *British Rolling Stone*. And, finally, there was expansion. First, it was "flyers," regional inserts of fresh editorial copy that were supposed to attract advertisers. They didn't, at least not in sufficient numbers; after a year, the idea was dropped at a loss. Next, it was *New York Scenes,* a thin weekly guide to events around town. Wenner had picked up the magazine during a stop-over in New York, liked it, and without much further thought, bought it. The magazine lasted only a matter of months before it, too, folded at a loss. And then came the real crusher: *Earth Times*.

It seemed like a good idea, at first: publishing an ecology magazine. Young people were taken up with environmental concerns. No one could dispute that. Nor could they dispute the happy fact that Wenner had an oversupply of empty desks just then, and the capital in his pocket to fill them. And what with *Rolling Stone* published every other week, the off week could be used to turn out a new magazine. Wenner's logic was impeccable. All he needed was a staff to make the theory work. And it was there that trouble began.

Her name was Stephanie Mills. Dark-haired and deter-mined, ambitious and bright, she had established her com-mitment to the ecological cause the previous spring by announcing in her college valedictory that she would never have children—because the world was not an environmentally fit place in which to live. The text of the speech wound up on the front page of the New York *Times* and it brought her national recognition—along with the attention of Jann Wenner. He summoned her to his office and, after half an hour's conversation, made her a startling proposal: how would she like to edit a new ecology magazine he was founding, a magazine to be called *Earth Times?* Mills gasped her acceptance. On her way out, it dawned on her that Wenner had not even asked whether she had any journalistic experience. She was glad he hadn't. She had none.

With a staff of three, Mills quickly set about turning out a magazine. Amazingly, she did. *Earth Times,* if gloomy in outlook and almost wholly devoid of ads, was attractive to look at, interesting to read, and, given time, might have evolved into a money-making proposition. As it was, the magazine proceeded to lose $40,000 per month, an intolerable drain on Wenner's already depleted resources. When losses passed the $150,000 mark, Wenner killed it and fired the staff.

By then, it was almost too late. The losses and excesses had plunged *Rolling Stone* into a sea of red ink. To add to his troubles, Wenner's personal life was coming apart. Jane, who had left the magazine after their marriage, was preparing to move out and take up temporary residence with a rock guitarist friend of Wenner's. Wenner was depressed and disoriented, given to spending long hours in his office, staring out the window, or sobbing for no apparent reason. Some of his friends worried he was having a breakdown. "It was," he said later, "a real crisis of spirit. I wasn't sure I wanted to continue."

The staff, meanwhile, began to guess that something was

amiss. Memos had issued forth, ordering them to hold phone calls to a minimum, conserve paper, and recycle paper clips. But the true depth of the trouble, like everything else about the magazine's finances, Wenner kept well hidden. It was not until he walked into the office of Alan Rinzler, a New York book editor he had hired to run *Rolling Stone*'s projected book division, Straight Arrow, that the full extent of *Rolling Stone*'s perilous financial condition was revealed. "Alan," Wenner asked, clearing his throat nervously, "do you know what Chapter Eleven means?"

Rinzler was not overly surprised. By now, he had become used to Wenner's financial profligacy, and accustomed to his habit of making dramatic announcements. He had been that way the first day they had met back in 1968, when Jann, bursting with manic energy, and accompanied by two towering longhairs he introduced as "my bodyguards," barreled into Rinzler's office at Holt, Rinehart and Winston, and amidst much arm-flailing, chain-smoking, and extracting scraps of paper from his pocket, made his big proposal. "I ummm, uhh," he stammered, "I want you to start a book company for me . . . The first book, uh, will be a collection of, you know, interviews I've done and then a big history of rock and roll written by me and then a big picture book of the stars. I'll write a running commentary, you know, like *The Family of Man*." Rinzler had laughed at him, but he had also been impressed; the kid thought big. "When I make this company public," Wenner promised him, "we'll all be millionaires." Rinzler, then very much the hot young book editor, with two best sellers to his credit—*Manchild in the Promised Land* and *Bury My Heart at Wounded Knee*— had accepted the offer and moved to California, only to discover that Wenner had made exactly the same offer to another editor, who had also accepted and was already at work. Rinzler grew even more suspicious when, after examining the magazine's books, he found that no funds had been budgeted for the promised book company. Rinzler had shrugged it off. He was having fun at *Rolling Stone,* even if the book company, much less the pledge of millionaire status, had yet to come true. Bankruptcy? Knowing Jann, Rinzler thought it altogether possible.

As they talked, Rinzler discovered just how possible it was. Not only possible, but inevitable, unless they moved soon. Together, they laid out a plan of action. First, a 10 per cent across-the-board salary cut, and all extraneous expenses slashed to the bone. Next, they had to call in all their cards—with the record industry. Then they would find a major source of outside financing. At the moment, though, their chief task was relieving *Rolling Stone* of a ruinously one-sided contract Wenner had negotiated with the magazine's distributor. As they found when they got to New York, it was not easy.

"Jann actually got down on his knees, cajoling, berating, pleading for five cents more a copy, for three cents more a copy, for two cents more a copy in our pockets, not theirs," Rinzler later recounted. "He was sweating and his three-piece suit was too tight around the thighs as he jumped up and leaned halfway across the big cigarette-scarred desk.

" 'Forty per cent is outrageous. You took advantage of me. If I had known what you gave other magazines, I would have never signed that contract. The returns clause is murder. You're going to bankrupt us, you're going to drive us out of business. Is that what you want?'

" 'What do you want, Jann, just tell me?'

" 'We want what's right and what's fair and . . .'

" 'So . . . how much?'

"'Forty-five per cent.'
"'And why should I give you forty-five per cent?'
"'So I'll be happy.'
"'What?'
"'So you'll make me happy.'
"The man chokes in his face. Hahaha. He can't believe it, he turns red with laughter. It looks as if he'll have a stroke on the spot, but he survives and we have to play out the contract."

They had better luck with the record companies and, thanks to receiving advances on future advertising, the crisis passed—but there was a price to pay. For the first and only time in his life, Jann Wenner had a partner. His name was Max Palevsky.

Max Palevsky was no ordinary moneyman. Max Palevsky was no ordinary anything. Everything about him was outsized: his ego, his work, his style of living, and, most of all, his talent for making money. Palevsky had made a lot of it—$90 million or thereabouts, depending on the current market price of Xerox Corporation, of which he was the major stockholder—and had spent a lot of it indulging his fancies of the moment: wives, therapies, movies, publishing, houses, politics. "I've been really running," he said about himself in a reflective moment, ". . . some of it was very healthy, but some of it was running away. Most people who work as hard as I do want to be numbed. I am convinced of that."

The race had begun in the Chicago slum where Palevsky had spent his boyhood. His parents were Eastern European immigrants, barely eking out a living ("We were never hungry," Palevsky said, "just beyond that") on his father's housepainting. Palevsky hated it. "I wanted nothing more than to get away from that house," he said, "to become something different from what my parents were: poor, ignorant people who didn't understand America, didn't understand the world." Palevsky took the usual route for a bright Jewish kid trying to escape his surroundings: academia. At the University of Chicago he studied mathematics, engineering, economics, and philosophy; following graduation and wartime service in the Army Air Corps, he headed for UCLA and doctoral studies. There, he attended a lecture on the infant science of computers. Fascinated by what he heard, he dropped out of school and, at the age of 27—married and with a child on the way—took a $100-a-week job designing computers for Bendix Corporation. His skills soon attracted the attention of Hewlett-Packard Corporation, which lured him and a number of his co-workers away with an offer to run an entire computer-manfacturing group. Eventually, it occurred to Palevsky and a handful of his colleagues that it made no sense lending their brilliance to others—not when there was a market out there for the taking.

The market was small computers. With $80,000 of their own money and a million put up by Wall Street investors, Palevsky and five of his friends set up Scientific Data Systems and built the first working models. Eight years later, Palevsky sold the company to Xerox for $940 million. He divorced his wife, married a UCLA co-ed twenty years his junior (only to divorce her a short time later), entered therapy, bought a hairpiece, put his suits and ties in the closet, and, in a twinkling, became Max Palevsky the man about town, friend of the stars, political plunger, bon vivant and middle-aged pot smoker. It was, to use one of Palevsky's favorite new expressions, "far out."

One of Palevsky's holdover friends from his former life was San Francisco financier Arthur Rock, chairman of

MJB Coffee, *Rolling Stone*'s landlord, and a member of
Wenner's board. When Rock learned of Wenner's financial
straits, he suggested Palevsky as a likely investor. They were,
in many ways, a natural pairing: both self-made men, both
disdainful of their background, both instinctive hustlers.
There were moments when Palevsky even sounded like
Wenner. "Anybody with power—from money, from running
a large corporation, from whatever source in this society—I
think it's corrupting," he said once. "And I have a certain
natural propensity that way. There is a part of me that is
very abrupt and very impatient. But if I'm impatient with
others, I'm certainly impatient with myself." Wenner, predictably, could not resist Max, nor Palevsky him. Soon a
deal was struck. From Palevsky would come cash and business advice; from Wenner, a taste of hip entrepreneurship.
There was one other detail. In return for his infusion of
capital, Palevsky, who would assume the title of Chairman
of the Board, would receive a block of stock—the exact
amount of which would be determined by how well Wenner
improved the balance sheet. The better business got, the less
stock came to Palevsky. It was a formulation destined to
cause trouble.

Ironically, by the time Wenner cashed Palevsky's check,
he no longer needed the money: the record companies had
already come to his rescue. What he still needed, though,
was Palevsky's corporate savvy. Palevsky, who was regularly shuttling between Los Angeles and San Francisco,
quickly discovered why. There were, in the accepted sense
of the word, no business practices whatsoever. "All they
knew," said Palevsky, "was that they periodically ran out of
money and that concerned them. It was an utter mess."
Palevsky drew up a budget, brought in new accountants,
switched distributors, called on advertisers, and everything

else that was required, as he put it, "to end the craziness."

But Wenner was cannier than Palevsky had imagined. While Palevsky installed controls and created systems, Wenner, with the incentive of the stock deal goading him on, went after costs with a meat ax. Profits for the year 1973 were $430,000 compared to $41,000 the year before. As a result, Palevsky wound up with less than 8 per cent of the outstanding stock.

Being outmaneuvered by a twenty-five-year-old irritated Palevsky only slightly. He had not come to *Rolling Stone* to make money; he had more than enough of that. What he wanted was stimulation, and while his relationship with Wenner lasted, Palevsky had all the stimulation he could handle. They'd often spend weekends together at Palevsky's vacation home in Palm Springs—Max, Jann, Thompson, and Rinzler. They'd talk business for a while—Palevsky arguing that *Rolling Stone* should do more to capitalize on its success, perhaps with a television show, a record company or various franchise deals—drink tequila, take snoutfuls of laughing gas, and end up out at the swimming pool, basking in the sun and letting the world go by, convinced that life could not be sweeter. Palevsky was enjoying the role of being a hip capitalist; the more he experienced it, the more he liked it. To keep in closer touch with affairs in San Francisco, he installed an electric telecopier in his Palm Springs digs and, when Thompson expressed wonder at the "mojo wire," provided one for him as well. Some of the editors quietly groused about Palevsky's growing presence. Already, there was a straight business staff, and they had even begun wearing ties. (The order for the business side to improve their sartorial image came, interestingly enough, not from Palevsky, but from Wenner.) Once, when Wenner invited some of the New York staff up to Palevsky's suite in the Sherry-Netherland to meet their corporate benefactor, a secretary muttered, *sotto voce,* "If he's the Establishment, no wonder the country is so fucked up." She was fired within the week. One didn't say such things about Max. Not when he was one of the family.

But there was trouble brewing. Palevsky was used to people taking his advice and following his orders. Wenner didn't. He would listen to Palevsky's complaints—that the magazine was schizoid; that politics and music were fundamentally contradictory; that they had to expand or else wake up one morning to find that young people had suddenly lost interest in rock music, on and on—and he would nod and feign agreement. And then nothing would happen. So long as Wenner controlled the majority of the stock, he retained absolute authority in all matters editorial and financial. Palevsky wanted Wenner to choose one or the other: either be publisher or editor, but not both. He also wanted the opportunity to buy a significant amount of additional stock and, most importantly, for Wenner to place his own stock in a voting trust—in effect, to relinquish operational control of the magazine. Wenner refused. Finally, Palevsky resigned. "I could have fought him," he said later, "but it would have required open warfare, and I didn't need that. I got in to have some fun, not to have problems. Jann just couldn't deal with me. He has a compulsion to always kill his father. Anyone threatening, he doesn't want them around."

It was a pattern with Wenner, one that had occurred before, and would occur again. It had happened with Porter Bibb, who had been the magazine's first publisher. A former publisher of *Newsweek International* and producer of *Gimme Shelter,* Bibb joined *Rolling Stone* in 1971, lured by many of the same promises that had attracted Rinzler. His friends had warned Bibb that Wenner was elusive, and urged him to be sure that all of his promises were committed to paper. Bibb ignored them, trusting in Wenner's assurance that a contract would be drawn up within a matter of weeks. The weeks stretched into months, and in the interval Bibb, after going through the magazine's files, discovered that very little was ever put on paper. At first, he was unconcerned. The contract, he thought, would come in time. Just then he had more important concerns, notably boosting *Rolling Stone*'s advertising. His method was to hire a number of enthusiastic young men with no advertising experience—"hippie guerrilla raiders" he called them—and turn them loose on Madison Avenue. The guerrillas were turned back with heavy losses. Wenner did no better. A friend who accompanied him on one expedition to New York recalled how Wenner's frustration rose as it became apparent that the ad man across the desk from him wasn't buying. "Jann was telling him 'young people read *Rolling Stone,* they believe in it, and they buy things like toothpaste like everybody else.' But all the guy wanted to know about were readership surveys and demographics, all the things Jann didn't know about. Finally, Jann jumped up and started shooting copies of the magazine across his desk, *bang, bang, bang,* like paper airplanes, right into the guy's lap. And then the ad man got up and said, 'Get out of here, kid, until you learn something.'"

The solution, Bibb decided, was to *make* the advertisers take notice: start a radio show, a television show, flood the city with promotion. With a minimum investment, he told Wenner, they could double *Rolling Stone*'s circulation within six months. Then the advertisers would have no choice but to buy. The investment turned out to be ruinously expensive, and circulation fell far short of the tar-

get. Still, they pressed on. If there was a shortage of cash,
there was a positive surfeit of ideas. One of them was
dubbed "Project A," a code name for "shrinkwrapping" the
magazine, and inserting various promotional goodies—
records, for instance—with each copy. That idea came to
naught as well, though not before Wenner had invested still
more money, including sending Kingsbury on a costly excursion to Japan to investigate how the Japanese managed
similar undertakings.

All the while, Bibb was no closer to getting his promised
contract. Finally, he set a deadline and issued an ultimatum. Unless a signed contract was on his desk, he was leaving. The deadline expired, and Bibb resigned. His last day
at the office, he and Wenner went out and, in Bibb's words,
"got drunk together. It was a very emotional moment for
both of us. We even cried. By that time, I had come to think
of him as a brother." Wenner quickly recovered. Within a
week, he posted a notice in the office announcing that Porter Bibb was no longer welcome on the premises.

Where money was involved—or power—the "bad" Jann
Wenner always took over. While he wielded a sharp pencil
with other people's expenses, he indulged himself lavishly.
Meanwhile, secretaries were being fired and editors ordered
to recycle paper clips.

No one could stop him. Palevsky had briefly tried, in-
structing *Rolling Stone*'s business manager that no extraordinary expenses were to be given Wenner without his express approval, but it was a vain attempt. Palevsky's memo
was framed and hung in the business manager's office as a
joke. Rinzler doubted whether Wenner could even stop
himself. Once, he had accompanied Wenner on a visit to a
rack-jobber. As a goodwill gesture, the businessman invited
Wenner to pick out any tapes in the store. Before Rinzler

could halt him, Wenner was running down the aisles, grabbing tapes until his arms were overflowing. "It was as if he couldn't control his appetites," Rinzler said later. "They just overwhelmed him. It was like there was a piece of him missing, as if the control mechanisms were gone."

In truth, Rinzler had few causes for complaint. The book division had finally gotten off the ground, and with a mixed bag of titles that ranged from *The Art of Sensual Massage* to the *Kaballah* it was beginning to turn a tidy profit. The pace was demanding, sometimes killing, but the excitement more than made up for it. "We were exploding sparks of amphetamine energy," he wrote later, "bolts of maniac lightning striking down every obstacle in our path. . . . What a chance to make mistakes, with no grown-ups around, either. It was exhilarating as a roller-coaster ride, a thrill a minute. What freedom, what madness . . . but what fun!" After a few years, however, the fun tapered off. "I found myself constantly in court," Rinzler recalled, "testifying against writers whom in my heart I thought were right. Small claims, depositions, tribunals of arbitration, larger litigations. . . . Working for Jann was like trying to survive in the court of Richard III. It seemed to me more and more that I was on the wrong side."

Bit by bit, Alan Rinzler found he couldn't take it. He and Wenner had been very close at first. Wenner even moved in with him during a few troubled weeks when his marriage was on the rocks. When they quarreled, they made up with affectionate, apologetic notes. It was one of those notes that ultimately brought their friendship to an end. "I can see in your eyes how cold and unfriendly I've been lately," Wenner wrote, "but please understand it is a result of my own personal unhappiness and inherent difficulties in being able to handle human relations and sometimes even love and nothing to do with you as a person or with your work, both of which I secretly highly admire." He closed: "Your friend, harshest critic and greatest admirer."

Their friendship was never the same after that. The next day, when Rinzler greeted Wenner at the office, there was a distinct coolness in Jann's manner. The coolness remained throughout the rest of Rinzler's tenure. "He had opened himself up with that letter," Rinzler explained. "And once he did, it had to change. He knew that I knew that he wasn't the bastard that he wanted everyone to think of him as." Finally, in 1975, Rinzler quit. It seemed an amicable parting. Wenner offered generous severance, promised to stay close. But two weeks after Rinzler's departure, a local weekly quoted Wenner as saying that Rinzler had been fired, dismissed for doing a terrible job. Not long after that, the final installment of Rinzler's severance was withheld. Finally, less than a year later, Wenner, who at one point had been offered a reported $2 million for Straight Arrow, folded the book division, writing it off as a $160,000 tax loss. "Too bad," Rinzler mused. "Guess we expected something that was never there. We had this romantic notion, you see, about the paper and about the music which could set us free. Should have known better."

Executives like Rinzler, Bibb, and Palevsky came and went at *Rolling Stone* with revolving door swiftness. One putative publisher lasted less than two weeks. Another man, hired to be the company's president, was discharged even before he came to work; he collected a healthy settlement. So swift were the departures that, at one point in the early Seventies, Wenner was budgeting $2,000 a month under the heading "executive talent search." The figure later had to be increased. The trouble, invariably, was that the people Wenner hired had different notions of how the magazine ought to be run than he did. There was Larry Durocher, who became *Rolling Stone*'s publisher and president after Bibb's departure. A big, bluff Boston Irishman whose size was exceeded only by his brilliance, Durocher, as had Palevsky before him, counseled Wenner to jettison politics, concentrate on music, and abandon any notions he might have about taking *Rolling Stone* weekly, pushing its circulation to a million, or trying to become another *Time* or *Newsweek*. Durocher, who had made a small fortune during the Sixties with Lear Jet franchises throughout New England, told Wenner that, run right, *Rolling Stone* could make all of them millionaires several times over. And the way to run it right, Durocher insisted, was to increase its circulation, which was then less than 300,000, to no more than half a million. The proof of Durocher's logic was the way the magazine, under his guidance, made money. Profits in 1974 were $660,000 on $7.1 million in revenues, the highest in *Rolling Stone*'s history.

Wenner would hear none of it. Becoming another Luce was a dream that had haunted and driven him on since he had begun publishing *Rolling Stone*. He was forever talking about *Time*—"the demon god," he called it—telling his staff that *Time* was the quintessence of publishing credibility. Luce's magazine had influence, respectability, power, all of which Wenner wanted for himself. If he took Durocher's advice, he would have to content himself with simply making money. The prospect horrified him. Whenever Durocher began talking about his favorite themes—subscription fulfillment, direct mail, advertising density—Wenner wheeled his chair to stare out the window. The day-to-day details of the publishing business bored him. What he wanted from Durocher were ideas on how *Rolling Stone* could be bigger, better known, with its name and his on the lips of the important and the powerful. When Durocher was not forthcoming, and in time became as fed up with Wenner's fantasizing as Wenner was with his, the outcome was inevitable. Slightly more than a year after taking the job, Durocher quit. Profits the next year fell by more than $200,000.

The next inheritor of the publisher's chair was Richard Irvine, former marketing director for Walt Disney Enterprises. To the staff he was "the California golden boy" and, in background and appearance, he seemed just that. Young, blond, not long out of U.S.C., where he had been a friend and classmate of some of the other golden boys who ran the Nixon administration, Irvine was confident that he would succeed where all his predecessors had failed. Shortly after coming to work, he went out to lunch with two of the editors and told them of the "brotherly bond" he had with Wenner, how they had become "almost family." Just then, they bumped into Kingsbury, who proceeded to tell them in highly graphic terms how Wenner was "destroying" him. Kingsbury's recitation was so heated that the editors never had a chance to introduce Irvine. When Kingsbury departed, Irvine gasped, "Who the hell is that?"

His two companions smiled. "That's Jann's brother-in-law."

Irvine lasted an even shorter time than Durocher; he came and went in the space of seven months. It was the usual problem. Irvine saw *Rolling Stone* as a business and attempted to run it like one. But for every new ad Irvine brought in, Wenner increased the editorial space, diluting the profits. Irvine also came up with an idea for publishing a series of one-shot special editions—by his calculations, a no-lose financial proposition. What he failed to count on was Wenner's temporizing. The original schedule called for six to ten one-shots per year; in the end, only three were ever issued. Wenner, meanwhile, was intent on giving the magazine a "more respectable look," as he put it, shifting from *Village Voice*-style tabloid to something resembling the *New York Times Sunday Magazine,* stapled, with a glossy cover. Irvine patiently tried to explain that changing styles would double or triple the printing bill. Wenner ignored him: *Rolling Stone* had to be stapled. Trouble was, there was no such stapler then in existence. Finally, after a year's research and a reported expenditure of nearly $500,-000, Wenner found a company that would build him one.

The two of them continually worked at cross-purposes. Seeking to increase circulation by upping the number of distribution outlets, Irvine persuaded Wenner that the only way *Rolling Stone* was going to make its way to the supermarket checkout stand was for the magazine to appear more dignified, and one requirement was dropping frontal nudity and gratuitous four-letter words. Wenner agreed to a two-year trial period. Then, just as Irvine was beginning to move into the suburban market place, upping distribution outlets from 7,800 to 30,000 (and, in the process, increasing circulation from 350,000 to 450,000 within ten months), "fuck" would appear in bold, black headlines. After one such occurrence, a major drug chain in Chicago pulled the magazine from the stands. Contrite, Wenner promised that it wouldn't happen again. But cleaning up *Rolling Stone*'s act proved to be a struggle. One issue, for instance, included a picture of a rock star with a corncob stuck between his legs and a girl kneeling in front of him. *That* wouldn't do at all. So, even as the presses were running, the picture was altered—several times, in fact. In one edition, the corncob was scratched out, but that made the picture seem even more suspicious. Accordingly, the presses were stopped again, and this time the girl's head was scratched out. Still not good enough. So the presses were halted a third time, and the picture scratched altogether.

After four months on the job, Irvine found that Wenner was sharply reducing his authority. Two more months went by and, finally, Irvine confronted him. "It's just not working out," Wenner told him, shrugging. Irvine agreed. "How long will it take you to get out of here?" Wenner asked. Forty-eight hours, Irvine replied. The California golden boy was true to his word.

His replacement was already waiting in the wings. There was no surprise when Joe Armstrong was named *Rolling Stone*'s publisher and president in 1975. From the moment he walked through the door in 1973 to assume the job of advertising director, Joe Armstrong had the mark of destiny on him. True, he was young, his publishing experience meager (his previous employment had been as assistant *to* the publisher of *Family Weekly,* a job which, in Armstrong's retelling, became *assistant* publisher). But he had reservoirs of toothy charm, a flair for promotion (*"How come he got so smart so fast?"* the house ads read. "14 hours a day and six-and-a-half-day weeks, all at full speed. *Does he ever slow down?* Only when he talks.") Most importantly, he had Wenner's confidence. Jann Wenner wanted to be known, and in a hurry. So, as it happened, did Joe Armstrong.

Born in Abilene, Texas, Armstrong had gotten into the rock business while still a law student at the University of Texas, booking concerts around Austin. After graduation, he went to work for a New York investment firm, became disenchanted, and, after three years, decided to give publishing a try. Some four hundred applicants were after the same job, and most of them had had years of publishing experience. Armstrong, who had had none at all, won out easily. There was something about his manner, so smooth and ingratiating, so eager to please; something about his looks, so clean-cut and smooth-skinned; something behind the earnest gaze and the pearly-white Pepsodent teeth, seemingly always set in a smile, that made him seem to be just what an ad man should be. Everything about him was effortless: the way he moved, the way he talked, even the way he wore his custom-tailored French-cut clothes. It was all so improbably perfect, almost too perfect for belief. "Butter wouldn't have melted in his mouth," they would have said back in Texas. "Slick," his detractors said. They were only half correct. Joe Armstrong was slick, all right, but the beauty of the man, the quality that impressed most of all, was that he was slick without *seeming* slick. It made all the difference in the world, and it made Joe Armstrong a most formidable man.

Armstrong was still at *Family Weekly* when Wenner flew into New York on a business trip, phoned Whitman Hobbs, the promotion director of the *New Yorker,* and invited him to lunch the next day at the Algonquin. Hobbs was well versed in publishing, and Wenner urgently needed some good advice. Everything was going wrong on the business side of the magazine, Wenner confessed. None of his publishing choices had worked out. Worst of all, the magazine still was threatened almost yearly with one financial crisis or another. Wenner said he was tired of the boom or bust cycle. He wanted some tranquillity, a man he could trust to oversee the details he hated, so he could concentrate on *Rolling Stone*'s editorial direction. Did Hobbs have any suggestions? Hobbs wrote down a list of sixteen of them. Number one was hiring Joe Armstrong.

With Armstrong's installation as publisher and president,

Rolling Stone rapidly began to change. The most tangible evidence that something was afoot were the full-page promotion ads that began showing up in the New York *Times*. Until Armstrong, *Rolling Stone*'s publishers were all but invisible. Now the ads said as much about Joe ("Y'all come," he invited advertisers) as the magazine he worked for—and almost nothing at all about Wenner. Back in San Francisco, Armstrong purged the ad staff of Bibb's remaining hippies, and dropped the long-standing ban against cigarette and liquor advertising. A new, fifty-two-year-old circulation director was brought on board and, before long, *Rolling Stone* started showing up in such unlikely places as the checkout rack of the friendly neighborhood Safeway. "We got a bad rap during the Sixties," one of Armstrong's new aides explained. "People thought of us as a druggy, hippie magazine. We're not that at all. And we're going to let people know about it." They began to when Armstrong's ad campaign appeared. It hit the problem head on: "The fiction still persists with many decision makers that *Rolling Stone* readers are a scraggly lot. . . . Well, our brand new Seasonwein Study of *Rolling Stone* readers is just out of the computer and what it tells us is this: he's surprisingly well educated, well traveled, well heeled. He owns his own wheels, his own camera(s), his own stereo system. He buys 61 LP albums a year. He thinks *Rolling Stone* is 'one of the best friends I've got.'"

The pitch worked. Issue after issue, there were more and more strangers: Polaroid, Mobil, General Electric, Eastman Kodak, Sears, Roebuck, AT&T, Colgate-Palmolive, American Airlines—some 90 blue-chip companies in all. By 1976, advertising revenues were $5.5 million, nearly four times what they had been in 1972. Circulation, stalled for years at 250,000, had climbed to 500,000. What made it all the sweeter was that, with the new advertisers Armstrong had brought, *Rolling Stone* was freer of the record companies' dominance than at any time in its history. The change Armstrong had wrought was remarkable: where as late as 1974 the music industry had accounted for 23 out of a single issue's 24 ad pages, now the percentage was down to half for most issues, and promised to drop still further. If there would ever be a moment for Wenner to break completely free, to take *Rolling Stone* out of the rock decade and into the Seventies, to make it, at last, the instrument of his personal power, it was now. But Wenner hesitated.

The future was not as bright as his ads indicated, and he knew it. True, revenues had never been higher. True, there was more money in the bank—some $2 million—than he had ever thought possible. And true, a single issue could bring in as much as $500,000 in advertising revenue. But profits were still the bottom line, and they were sluggish. After taxes, they were slightly more than 2 per cent. A major reason was that Wenner was spending money almost as quickly as it came in, much of it to support an increasingly extravagant life-style. For the last few years, he and Jane had been living in a rambling Victorian-era mansion in Pacific Heights, San Francisco's most exclusive neighborhood. Wenner was very proud of the house, boasting that it was in all the fine-home guides to the city. He was proud of all that was in it: the Warhol prints, the Mies furniture, the $10,000 stereo system, the elaborate sauna, the Advent Video Beam Television System, the antique oriental rugs, even the electronic pinball machine. He was proud of his comparably luxurious co-op in New York (that one, he told visitors, had once been the Gimbel mansion, and Barbra Streisand and Ryan O'Neal had made a movie there), the Chinese servant couple who worked for him, the brace of Mercedes 450 SL's he owned, and the "summer cottage" he rented in the Hamptons for $27,500 (not including Labor Day). All of it was very classy, the mark of just how far he had come. But the possessions, along with Armstrong's penchant for promotion, were draining him, and his stockholders were growing restless. It was hard to blame them. For all of *Rolling Stone*'s success, they had yet to see their first dividend check. "What doesn't go out the window," one of Wenner's publishers commented, "goes up his nose."

Wenner could handle the stockholders, as he had handled Palevsky. There was nothing they could do. With Jane and her family, he controlled the majority of the stock. More worrisome were *Rolling Stone*'s own readers. Palevsky had called them "the ticker" in *Rolling Stone*'s future, the time bomb sitting in the closet, waiting to go off. What would happen, he had asked Wenner, if one day he woke up and discovered that young people had lost their interest in rock and roll? The young were fickle, their tastes continually shifting. Already, there were some disturbing trends. The average age of the readers had increased only slightly during the nearly ten years of the magazine's existence. The conclusion was inescapable: Wenner and his staff might have matured, but his magazine had not. It was, for most of his readers, a phase they went through, the journalistic equivalent of puberty and acne. Once the phase was over and they lost their love of rock and roll, they moved on to something else, a magazine other than *Rolling Stone*. To become another Luce, Wenner had to devise a way to keep them. So far, all his attempts had failed. Changing *Rolling Stone*'s format altogether, abandoning music in favor of the other interests that now involved him and his editors, was to risk the ultimate disaster. Wenner would not chance it.

The dilemma in which Wenner found himself was of his own making. He had had numerous opportunities over the years to make *Rolling Stone* public, list it on the stock market, and, with the millions that would come in, defy the wrath of the record companies. Several times he had flirted with the idea, but each time had drawn back, with vague explanations that "the time is not right." His friends doubted whether it ever would be.

Somehow, though, he had to expand, shake loose of the straitjacket that rock and roll had put him in. He had to prove that Goodwin had been wrong, that he did have the guts to be a "big-time entrepreneur"; he had to demonstrate, if only to himself, that *Rolling Stone*'s success was no fluke, that he—not rock and roll, not kids, not the culture or the times—had been responsible for it, that, having worked a miracle once, he could work it again. He knew what the critics thought of him, that he had stumbled into his success, that *anyone* could make millions from a rock and roll magazine. But anyone hadn't; only he had. That did not stop Gleason from taunting him, though. Sarcastically, Gleason informed him that "the proof that *Rolling Stone* is such a great idea is that it has survived your management." It was meant as a joke and, at times, Wenner even said it about himself. But, in fact, it was not funny. It was precisely what kept him still driving. *Okay, kid, you've done one trick, what's your next one?* The question haunted Wenner, as it would have haunted anyone for whom success came so early. And, after nine years, he was no closer to answering it. He had tried some solutions—*British Rolling Stone, Earth Times, New York Scenes*—and none of them had worked. Now, something had to.

What happened next was like the combination of chance and symbolism that a believer like Wenner found irresistible. The catalyst was a most unusual young man with a most unusual name: William Randolph Hearst III. At twenty-five, "Will" Hearst had become the inheritor of the family journalistic legacy, not to mention a sizable chunk of his grandfather's fortune. Other Hearsts had gone into journalism before, but Willie, so the story went around the San Francisco *Examiner,* where he worked as an editor, was the first to possess the senior Hearst's instincts. Willie even looked like the old man, with the same shock of flowing blond hair atop the same high forehead and, beneath, the same penetrating clear blue eyes—a resemblance so complete, it was almost eerie. In the fall of 1975, Hearst, then editor of the *Examiner*'s "Other Voices" column, wrote Wenner, whom he had never met, asking if he would submit a story. Wenner replied that he never wrote for "competing publications," a small bit of humor that prompted Hearst to call Wenner back and ask him over to dinner.

They started seeing a lot of each other after that. Wenner was fascinated with Hearst. He had studied his grandfather's career, and when his own staff jokingly began referring to him as "Citizen Wenner," an appellation that frequently was repeated in print, Wenner was enormously pleased. William Randolph Hearst had done all the things that Jann Wenner wanted to do. He had had power and fame, and had not been afraid to use them. A word from one of his publications could make or break a career, elect a President, start a war. One day *Rolling Stone* would have that clout, Wenner had told Palevsky. Then "Citizen Wenner" would be no joke, it would be true. Palevsky had believed him—not that it would happen, but that Wenner would not stop trying to make it happen. The Hearstian legend obsessed him. The opportunity to know more about it was one he could not pass up. Besides, he liked Will, especially after he invited him to San Simeon. Wenner tried to contain his awe, but it was not easy. "Wow!" he exclaimed after a tour of the castle, "it's just like in the movie, isn't it?" Willie smiled. "Yes," he agreed, "just like in the movie."

Afterward, they repaired to a comfortable cottage and, over drinks, talked publishing. Wenner asked Hearst if he had any new ideas for magazines. Hearst, an avid outdoorsman, answered that more and more of his friends were hearkening to the call of the wild, backpacking, canoeing, shooting rapids, climbing mountains, "getting in touch with nature," as Hearst put it. There was a market there, Hearst went on, something a new magazine could exploit, not another *Field and Stream,* but a magazine designed specifically for *young* outdoorsmen. Hearst caught himself. "I mean outdoors*people.*" They both laughed, and the conversation turned to other channels.

That was the last Hearst heard of the idea until six months later, when Wenner called him with a business proposition. He was starting a new magazine, he said, the very sort of magazine Hearst had talked about at San Simeon. He was going to call it *Outside* and he wanted Hearst to be the managing editor. Hearst accepted, and a year later *Outside* made its debut. The look of the book was sleek and expensive: glossy, heavy paper, photographs apparently suitable for framing, first-rate writing about outdoor adventures, and ads by the dozens. Every sign was that Wenner had succeeded at last. *Outside* would make it, where all the other attempts had failed. On Madison Avenue, there were predictions that, in time, *Outside* would dwarf even *Rolling Stone*.

Wenner celebrated in the by-now-familiar fashion, a champagne christening party. Many of New York's media and political notables were in attendance, drawn, in part, by

the young man Wenner had installed as *Outside*'s director
of promotion—Jack Ford, the son of the former President.
There were toasts and congratulations all around, but this
time, there were no tears of celebration. *Outside* might be a
commercial and editorial triumph, but it was not the breakthrough Wenner had been looking for. The magazine did
not excite him, any more than the real outside did. "What
do we know about the outdoors?" Jane had asked him.
"The kind of people we are, we ought to publish a magazine called *Indoors*." All Wenner could offer in rebuttal was
computerized market research. But he could not kid himself. At thirty, Jann Wenner was richer, more successful,
better known, more influential and powerful than any
member of his generation. And yet, something unaccountable was missing. Something that kept him running.

12

All Things Must Pass

Across the Bay in Berkeley, Ralph Gleason watched the progress of his protégé with growing unease. The "roly-poly rock and roll kid," so bursting with enthusiasm, that he had met that night nine years before had grown up and, in growing up, had become someone else. Gleason did not like the Seventies version of Jann Wenner, the one who collected cars and mansions and discarded people, including, Gleason sometimes thought, the oldest, dearest friend, the one who had made everything possible: Ralph Gleason himself.

It had never been the smoothest relationship. Over the years, Gleason and Wenner had battled frequently. Months had sometimes gone by with the two men refusing to speak to each other, because of some imagined slight. The friction was just beneath the surface. Gleason was unhappy with the direction *Rolling Stone* was taking, particularly its devotion to the star system, which Gleason believed had undermined the foundations of rock and roll. He continually prodded Wenner, writing long, critical letters on how *Rolling Stone* should have done this or that story better, or had missed another one completely. When the *Columbia Journalism Review* commissioned an article in 1974 on *"Rolling Stone's* Growing Quest for Respectability,"* Gleason made his complaints public, accusing the magazine of "catering to the worst of yellow journalism." "The straight press looks at *Rolling Stone* and says it's doing a great job," Gleason said contemptuously, "but the straight press doesn't know anything about what *Rolling Stone* is covering."

The remarks infuriated Wenner. He was already under pressure from some of his editors to get rid of Gleason and the heat was building. Ralph was a nice guy, they told him, but time had passed him by. He was an old man, writing from the perspective of a teenie-bopper. Wenner knew it was true. As the years had passed, Gleason's columns sounded increasingly like a parody of an aging hipster. "Tune in, turn on, find out," he was still advising. "Music will change the world. . . . More power to the poets, to the artists, to the writers and singers of songs and to the players of music. They are our salvation." No one believed that any longer, not even Wenner, but the fury of Gleason's columns only increased. He wouldn't—or couldn't—let the Sixties go. It was all so embarrassing, Wenner's editors told him, so out of place with *Rolling Stone's* tough cynicism, so hopelessly square. Wenner, they insisted, had to stop it. But Wenner could not bring himself to make the final break, however much Gleason baited him. Instead, he merely ignored him, which infuriated Gleason all the more. He quit once, saying he could "no longer accept responsibility for an editorial and reportorial policy with which I am not in sympathy and over which I have no control." He reconsidered. Then, after another blow-up, he quit again, only to have Wenner ignore his resignation. Gleason was powerless. "It's almost as if I didn't exist," Gleason complained to a friend. "Doesn't he remember? Doesn't he remember anything at all?"

By early 1975, Gleason's patience was at an end. He had decided to sell his 5,000 shares of *Rolling Stone* stock back to Wenner, and leave once and for all. But Wenner was holding him up, offering him a lower price for the stock than Gleason thought was reasonable. In the midst of the wrangling, Gleason bumped into Rinzler one day on a Berkeley street corner and poured out his frustrations. He had gotten Wenner in the door, Gleason said; now Jann was pushing him out. Well, that was fine. He had had it. "Do me a favor," he told Rinzler. "The next time you see him, punch him in the nose for me. It will do him a world of good."

Six months passed while Gleason continued to fume. They had not really made up when, on June 2, 1975, Scanlon walked into Wenner's office and informed him that Gleason had suffered a massive heart attack. To Scanlon's surprise, Wenner broke down and started sobbing uncontrollably. By nightfall, Ralph Gleason was dead.

That evening, Wenner went to Gleason's house in Berkeley to join friends who were comforting his widow. It was Jann, though, who needed solace. For hours he cried, while one of Gleason's friends held him in her arms and tried to reassure him. He did not sleep that night, and rested only fitfully in the days that immediately followed. Most of the time he stayed in his office, reminiscing about Gleason, trying to focus his energies on the memory. As word spread around San Francisco of the tribute Wenner was planning, former staffers drifted into the office and, for a moment, all the old enmities were forgotten. The issue that resulted was emotional and affecting, page after page of accolades from the people Gleason had known and befriended over the

years, from Frank Sinatra to an unnamed junkie Gleason
had taken into his home and helped kick drugs. None,
though, was as pained as the memorial written by Wenner
himself. "Ralph and I were partners," he began.

> Ralph's name was right under mine—consulting editor,
> then senior editor, switching back and forth, up and down,
> through passions and paranoias, disagreements and reeval-
> uations over the years. He was my main man. . . . He
> was number one, boss and the most beautiful. . . . With-
> out Ralph, we wouldn't be here. . . .
> If I was on some kind of trip or another, blithely avoid-
> ing common sense like an infantry kid stepping into a
> minefield, Ralph's words would invariably be, "Janno, this
> is Ralph here." It was a code between us, meaning, "back
> to reality, old pal"—and a lot of other things, but it aches
> to explain it any further, to remember the warmth of those
> words. . . .
> It was our dream that *Rolling Stone* would find a right-
> ful place, as would the music native to America, among
> those ways and means by which we see ourselves and
> learn about our lives—and tonight it eases the frightening,
> childlike fear of the utter, final loss of a part of my body
> and life and years.

It was months before Wenner fully recovered. He tried to
find comfort in work, throwing himself back into editing
with renewed, manic energy. But the torment did not ease.
Late one night, at the breaking point, he tried to push a
pencil through his hand, anything to get the feeling back.
He disappeared for a time after that, driving up the coast
through the gold rush country, doing his best to relax, forget, cool out. And, for a while, it seemed to work. But then
the pain would come again, more intense than ever. His

friends worried about him, especially his increasing drug
use. He had always used drugs—at one point, the staff had
even marked his space in the magazine parking lot with a
small coke spoon in recognition of his tastes, until Wenner,
concerned over its possible effect on advertisers and narcotics agents, ordered it removed—but now he seemed to be
using more of them, especially cocaine. "You'd watch him
putting that stuff into his body," said one of his editors,
shaking his head. "It was like he was putting fuel in a car."
The drugs made the machine run faster, but also more er-
ratically.

Always mercurial, Wenner with a head full of coke was
even more difficult to predict. He would issue orders, con-
tradict them, then threaten and bully anyone who dared to
question him. "I'll put you in jail," he yelled one night at a
group of carpenters who were remodeling the offices according to his specifications, which, he decided on the spur
of the moment, were all wrong. "Jail, do you hear that, you
fuckers? I can do that. You'll all be in jail." By the next
morning, the incident was forgotten, and the work continued as originally planned. In time, some of the staff began to
gauge Wenner's moods, and whether or not to steer clear of
him, by the way he drank his coffee: black usually meant he
was straight; with cream he was on something. And when
Jann Wenner was on something, he was not pleasant to be
around.

One by one, his friends dropped away—as often as not,
were pushed away, consigned by Wenner to the ranks of
"assholes." Marianne Partridge was one of those who had
been a close friend and, like so many of them, was no
longer. She had come far since copy-editing for John Walsh;
now she was functioning as the magazine's managing editor.
If she had stayed with Wenner, she might have risen even

further. But in 1976 Clay Felker made her an offer she found impossible to refuse: managing editorship of the *Village Voice,* a job with considerably more responsibility and better salary than that which she enjoyed at *Rolling Stone.* When she broke the news to Wenner, her old friend went into a paroxysm of rage. "You whore! You fucking slut!" he screamed. "Get out of here. I don't want to see you again." She left, but Wenner was not satisfied. Ordering her office repainted, he moved into it himself, canceled several stories she had been working on, and henceforth referred to her as *"that woman* who works for Felker."

He had strings of epithets for everyone who left him. Burks was "swell-headed," his allies "bad people"; Stephanie Mills "no editor . . . a figurehead"; one former publisher "just a jerk, a complete incompetent"; another "a wild liar," a third "a total asshole." They were "children" or "drunks" or "fruitcakes"—"boobs and nincompoops" all of them—these people who had once worked for him and, in many cases, called him friend. He knew what they said about him in return, the stories that spread about his private life and supposed liaisons, but he pretended it did not bother him. "You've probably heard that I'm a cheat and a liar and a lot of other things," Wenner told a visitor. "Well, the truth is, I'm really not very nice." He almost reveled in the image. "It only adds," he boasted, "to the blackness of my mystique."

Inside, though, it was killing him. He would arrive at a party stoned, make a fool out of himself, then, with tears in his eyes, confide to a friend, "I'm so fucked up, just so fucked up." Other times, he was someone else entirely: the sentimentalist who would read of a tragedy in the newspaper and send off a check to the survivors; the dutiful son who always sent flowers to the grandmother in the nursing

home; the editor who lent his staff money, paid their rent,
sent their kids to school, took care of their hospital bills,
and swore them to secrecy lest his kindness be taken as
some sign of secret weakness. It was this Jann Wenner who,
having banished Marianne Partridge from his life, closed the
door of his office and began to cry; who would stay up all
that night calling friends around the country, making sure,
as a friend put it, "that there were people who still liked
him." "When you saw Jann during these days," one of his
editors said of the period after Gleason's death, "you
couldn't help but remember the scene at the end of *The
Godfather,* when Michael Corleone is sitting there, all
alone, having killed all his enemies, and being able to trust
no one, except family. And now, for Jann, the only family
he ever knew was gone."

As time passed, Wenner gradually pulled himself together
and began to take stock. In his grief and distraction, problems had developed with his magazine, and none more
pressing than the silence of Hunter Thompson. It had been
months since Thompson had done any serious work, and
longer still since he had written on a level comparable to his
work in Las Vegas or on the campaign trail. In part,
Wenner knew, Thompson's absence was purposeful—his
means of expressing displeasure over yet another financial
disagreement between them. But mostly it was Thompson
himself. His celebrity had overtaken him.

Crouse had seen the beginnings of it in 1972, when
Thompson, flushed with the success of his first campaign
pieces, started giving autographs to teenagers. The attention
was heady stuff, especially for a writer who had spent much
of his career in obscurity and, inevitably, it affected Thompson. "He rather liked being treated like a rock star," Crouse

said. "In a way, Hunter thought he deserved it. Candidates and their staffs had to adjust their time to fit his schedule. He was very put out when they didn't." Soon, Thompson was being asked to speak before college audiences. From there, it was only a short step to ultimate pop enshrinement: a place in the funnies as Doonesbury's "Uncle Duke." But, in time, Thompson's mythic reputation began to burden him. He was finding it harder and harder to find something he wanted to write about. The dark moments of the creative soul, when he found himself looking at a blank piece of paper in the typewriter—"down to the deadline again . . . and those thugs in San Francisco will be screaming for Copy. Words! Wisdom! Gibberish! Anything! The presses roll at noon . . . This room reeks of failure once again . . ."—were becoming more and more frequent. Wenner had made story proposals: Coors Beer . . . Cocaine. Nothing worked.

Finally, Thompson tried Zaire. Muhammad Ali was attempting a comeback, fighting George Foreman. The place was dark, mysterious. All the writing heavies would be there. But there was unexplained trouble—"too much voodoo, black magic and witchcraft," he explained later—some fiendish hex had been placed on Gonzo. He came down with malaria. He missed the fight; didn't, in fact, write a word. Instead, he slunk home, depressed and delirious.

Such was the situation Wenner confronted in the winter of 1975. Resolving it would be ticklish, for friendship was involved, Thompson's pride, and, as usual, the old quarrel over money. The last had been Wenner's doing. A few months before, he had flown to Aspen to negotiate a book contract for the upcoming 1976 version of *Fear and Loathing on the Campaign Trail*. He had offered an advance of $75,000 and Thompson had accepted. Then, after he returned to San Francisco, everything had come apart. Wenner had sold the book company. After he told Thompson, it was months before the writer would speak to him again. Then, one night in March, fate intervened. Thompson was at home, watching the evacuation of Da Nang on the evening news, when the phone rang. He picked it up to hear a familiar voice and a rush of words: "How would you like to go to Saigon?" Thompson couldn't resist. The final fiery collapse of the American Empire was a happening tailor-made for his talents. Within days, he was headed out over the Pacific.

The illusion did not last long. Vietnam, it turned out, was not quite what Thompson had expected. He arrived in Saigon hours after Thieu's palace had been bombed and strafed by his own air force. For a man who lived with the conviction that the world was going to end next Monday, it was an especially ominous portent. Thompson was not seen much after that. The story going around the press corps had it that Thompson was bunkered in his room at the Caravelle, preparing for the apocalypse. Already, he was known to have imported an elaborate communications system from Hong Kong, to provide him with up-to-the-moment word of when the helicopters would be making their final ascent from the embassy roof. The tale was a source of much merriment for veteran Saigon hands, who vied with each other swapping anecdotes of Thompson's continuing pratfalls at the hands of assorted bar girls and black marketeers. Thompson, however, was not amused. He was out of his element in Vietnam, confused, and, in not a few instances, terrified. Being in Saigon, he wrote, gave him the "sense of walking into a death camp." The horrors here were all too real. Deep in his gut, he thought he would never get out alive.

Two of Thompson's friends, Nick Profitt of *Newsweek* and Phil Caputo, a former Marine Corps platoon leader who had gone to work for the Chicago *Tribune,* suggested that a tour of the countryside would brighten his mood. Thompson leaped at the chance. At the appointed hour the next day, Caputo and Profitt appeared at his hotel, only to find no sign of Thompson. Just as they were about to leave, the Good Doctor made his appearance, descending the lobby stairs in shorts, tennis shoes, Mexican shirt, mirrored shades, and baseball cap, an ivory cigarette holder clamped between his teeth at a rakish angle. Trailing behind him were two Vietnamese boys lugging a cooler filled with ice and a local brew. When Thompson went to war, he went in style.

The three of them headed off into the sunrise, driving toward Xuan Loc, then the scene of bitter fighting. As the miles went by, Thompson passed the time washing down gaint-size helpings of speed with beer. When they reached a large clearing, to be greeted by the sight of a swarm of ARVN helicopters lifting off, the drugs had their predictable effect. "Freaking Jesus," Thompson exclaimed. "What are those giant locusts doing?" "What are you talking about?" Profitt demanded. "Those aren't locusts; those are helicopters." But Thompson was insistent. "Don't fuck with my mind," he shot back. "Those are locusts."

The car halted and Caputo and Profitt alighted to interview the troops. Thompson, meanwhile, wandered off toward the treeline. The next time Profitt spotted him, he was a quarter of a mile up the road, a hundred yards from where the North Vietnamese were encamped. Thompson seemed oblivious to the danger. He walked on, like a man transfixed, talking all the while into his tape recorder. "He was," said Profitt, "the picture of the innocent abroad."

Another time, well into the evening, hours after curfew had fallen over Saigon, Thompson walked into the streets to test his walkie-talkie, part of the communications gear he had purchased to aid him in the evacuation. Suddenly, the correspondents back at the hotel heard a flurry of shots. Just then, Thompson's voice on the walkie-talkie went dead. His friends were sure he had been killed. Moments later, Thompson burst back into the hotel, raving about the people intent on killing him. For once, he was right.

More trouble lay ahead. Not long after his arrival in Saigon, Thompson discovered that even as he was on his way to Vietnam, Wenner had taken him off retainer—in effect, fired him—and with the retainer went his staff benefits, including health and life insurance. The cable Thompson fired off to San Francisco contained some of his most creative writing in months. "Your most recent emission of lunatic, greed-crazed instructions to me was good for a lot of laughs in Saigon," he began.

> The only round-eyes left to evacuate from Saigon now are several hundred press people who are now trying to arrange for their own evacuation after the U.S. Embassy pulls out with the last of the fixed-wing fleet and leaves the press here on their own. Needless to say, if this scenario develops it will involve a very high personal risk factor and also big green on the barrelhead for anyone who stays; and unless the one-thirties start hitting Saigon before Saturday, that is the outlook.

He closed bitterly: "I want to thank you for all your help." The reply from Wenner was in character:

> My many years of experience in war coverage and running military press corps, involvement in revolutions and gen-

eral talent for blitzkrieg action tells me that you should
make your own decision as to when to leave Saigon for a
safe zone.

Wenner added that no more money would be forthcoming,
and advised Hunter to come home.

Thompson brooded, debating what to do. He wanted
dearly to be on hand for the fall. He had already envisioned
the scene: he and General Giap riding into Saigon on the
lead tank, Hunter drinking a beer and waving to the cheering throngs. But he was worried. For some reason, the NLF
spokesman, whose favor Thompson had sought to curry,
was giving off a lot of bad vibes. At every press briefing, he
warned what would happen to "bogus journalists" once the
revolution came to power; when he used the phrase, he
seemed to stare at Thompson. On the other hand, Thompson would be damned if he'd let the Marines take him out.
How could he live with it? *Saigon fell today and Hunter
Thompson's ass was saved by the United States Marines
. . .* Never. Finally, he made up his mind. He got on a
plane and headed for Laos, hoping to hook up with the con-
querors there. Two days later, Saigon fell. Thompson was
stranded.

The resulting dispatch ran only two pages in *Rolling
Stone*—by Thompson's standards, a virtual note. "The
paper in my notebook is limp," he reported, "and the blue
and white tiles of my floor are so slick with humidity that
not even white canvas, rubber-soled basketball shoes can
provide enough real traction for me to pace back and forth
in the classic, high-speed style of a man caving in to The
Fear." It had finally happened. The mad prince Gonzo had
met Fear and Loathing face-to-face, and it scared the hell
out of him.

His friends had trouble reaching Thompson when he returned home from Saigon. He holed up in Colorado and seldom answered the phone. Rumors drifted back to San Francisco. Cocaine, which Thompson had long scorned as a "drug for fruits," had gotten the best of him, one story went. Another had it that he had embarked on the Big Novel everyone knew was in him, eating at him, raging to get out. But he would be back. Everyone at *Rolling Stone* seemed sure of that. Nothing could hold Hunter Thompson down for long.

But Wenner wondered. Like Thompson, he was a believer in omens, and the drying up of Thompson's talent, temporary or not, was a portentous ending, the final fillip to an extraordinarily bad time. One by one, all the people and things with which he was comfortable and familiar seemed to be disappearing.

One afternoon, he asked David Weir to take a walk with him. There were some things he wanted to discuss, he said, some story ideas he didn't want overheard in the office. Eventually they ended up in a bar and, after several hours of drinking and listless conversation, Wenner finally unburdened himself. "I don't know if I want to do this anymore," he blurted out. "It's just no fun anymore. If this magazine isn't going to be fun for me, I just don't want to do it."

So much had changed for him in the last ten years, so many things were gone. There was no such thing as a San Francisco sound anymore. The ballrooms had closed; most of the bands had broken up or moved away. The Haight had become a ghost town. Berkeley was now peopled by razor-cut over-achievers bustling from class to class, visions of good careers dancing in their heads. The sense of excitement was missing, the time when every day was a trip, more wondrous than the last. Now the mood was grimmer, uglier, more self-hating. Like a giant dynamo run too long at too high a pitch, San Francisco had finally burned out.

How to explain it—money, technology, bad karma, a misalignment of the planets—except to say it was different? Something was missing, a central linchpin, and without it, the culture collapsed as mysteriously as it had been created. It was as if the mystics and the Lovin' Spoonful had been right all along. Everything depended on magic, and magic on childlike belief. Once the belief was gone, the magic, and everything that rested on it, simply vanished.

At Berkeley, they had begun worrying about what their protest meant, where it would finally lead them, whether they were taking the correct political line. And the more they worried, the more they began to doubt. Maybe the Progressive Labor cadres were right when they said that to be revolutionaries they had to read Marx and Lenin, cut their hair, shave their beards, go into the factories and organize. But no one wanted to do that. After a while, no one wanted to do anything. The Sproul Hall protests had been dramatic, but they had not stopped the war, ended exploitation, or brought blacks significantly closer to full equality. What they had done was elect Ronald Reagan. "No appeasement," he was saying. "If it takes a bloodbath to end it, let's get it over with." Who needed it? The war was over—the North Vietnamese had seen to that—the threat was gone. It was time to get a job. Some of them couldn't take it. Savio had dropped out, come back, run for office, been beaten, then dropped out again. No one had seen him for years. The story was that he had had a breakdown. Now he was living in Los Angeles, teaching elementary school and confining his protests to polite requests for more traffic signals to protect children. Nobody cared. Very few people even remembered who Mario Savio was.

Looking back, the organizers felt vaguely foolish. All they had fought for—in some cases, gone to jail for—had gone aglimmering. "It was a big circus," John Sinclair told a reporter. "If I saw anybody doing that sort of thing today, I'd think they were nuts." He laughed at the memory. John Sinclair, the *eminence grise* of the White Panthers, the revolutionary inspiration of the MC 5, the martyred marijuana hero, was now a PR man. "We didn't know anything," he said ruefully. "We were déclassé hippies." He laughed again. "Can you imagine," he asked, "what would have happened if we had turned the country over to Tom Hayden and Jerry Rubin? They weren't ready. They didn't have any programs." Even Jerry had to admit it. He was changed now, as most of the old rads were, "grown up at 37," as his new book put it, into est and primal screaming, trying to be, he said, "as Establishment as I possibly can." As for the past, it was all a bad memory—"insanity," he called it. "We had no time to breathe," he said. "To look at each other and ask who we really were. . . . In a way, we were really revolting against ourselves. . . . I was the screwed-up, middle-class monster that I was railing against." He paused and said wearily: "We were not the new men and women we were talking about."

But, then, no one was; the Haight had proven that. The hippies had left years ago, some to the country, some off riding with the Hell's Angels—like Emmett Grogan, who eventually suffered a fatal heart attack—but most simply to wherever they had come from. Without them, the neighborhood died. It was a spooky, deserted place now, block after block of boarded-up shops and crumbling houses. Only the fading graffiti—"Acid is God"; "Jesus was a runaway"—were left to tell the tale of what had been. Where once throngs had danced and freaked, rats now roamed the shit-stained streets.

It was difficult to catalog the traumas that had descended on the Haight. There had been the tourists, of course, and, right behind them, the sharpies and fast-buck artists. The neighborhood had started changing. A civic association was formed to pressure the city for more services and, when it was not forthcoming, the rip-offs began. "Shoplifters! Remember your Karma!" read a sign posted in one shop window. The injunction had little effect. So mindlessly pervasive did the thievery become that one night even the Diggers' store was looted of goods that were to be given away in the morning. For Bill Graham, the beginning of the end was the day a local greasy spoon put up a sign announcing "Love Burgers." "The sad part of it," he mused to Fong-Torres, "is that deep down, they wanted the same thing those people wanted: money which gives you security, which gives you the right to live your life the way you wanted to. . . . Once they started making money, the majority of them became gluttons. The sandal-maker who had maybe a dozen pairs that were fine, once he started selling them, he had them in all colors and all sizes. Five guys working in the back, punching a clock and grinding out all those fucking sandals and calling them psychedelic."

It was all downhill from there. The hippies started moving out, deserting for the unhassled calm of rural communes. Those who came to take their place were a different breed, tougher and more disturbed. Even their drugs were different. In place of acid, which made concentration, and hence money-making impossible, they mainlined speed, which heightened the senses, made it possible to work long hours at a stretch, and, with prolonged use, brought on irritability, depression, paranoia, violence—and sometimes death. "It's far out, speed," a fifteen-year-old runaway from New York named Randy said excitedly. "The flash takes over your mind. . . . It's like an explosion in your skull, like a monster bomb in there, warm like fire. Your head gets so big you can't imagine how big it is. Then you get into a trance, spaced, makin' plans, buildin' monstrous castles in your head. Like I'll be sitting behind the wheel of my Rolls-Royce on my way to a heroin refining plant with Sixties chicks, running the Mafia, in charge." But then would come the crash, a depression as deep as the high had been great. "Start to come down, my mind collapses," Randy said. "The girders fall apart and I start to feel low and mean and looking for a fight." There was only one cure: another hit. It got to the point where kids in the Haight were shooting, snorting, and popping anything they could get their hands on: Demerol, diet pills, Methedrine, Seconal, Nembutal, Desoxyn, even veterinary anesthetics. With such demand and so little discrimination, "burns" were common. Pushers passed off oregano as marijuana, sold baking soda and called it speed. It was a dangerous trade. One acid dealer who was in the habit of carrying the goods in a satchel handcuffed to his wrist was found murdered in his apartment, his right arm cut off at the elbow.

At first, the high priests of the Haight tried to ignore what was happening. An article in a local underground, detailing the speed-freak gang rape of a fifteen-year-old girl, came in for bitter criticism from the Dead's Jerry Garcia. "Just what we need," Garcia grumbled, "the East Coast mentality pouring into the scene and forming it into easy-to-identify bags. It's reductive." But, before long, all the Haight was bleeding. By the end of 1968 the crime rate had doubled, and the local police precinct was reporting 17 murders, 100 rapes and nearly 300 burglaries—and estimating that twice that number went unreported. So menacing had the Haight become, it was no longer safe to go out alone at night. Meanwhile, the rates of hepatitis (from dirty needles), alcoholism, malnutrition, vaginitis, syphilis, gonorrhea, and suicide soon were among the highest in the nation. By 1969 the Haight was in the midst of a full-scale heroin epidemic. A social scientist who had worked with youth gangs in Chicago and Oakland before coming to the Haight was overwhelmed by what he beheld. "There is a kind of status here more twisted than anything I've seen," he told an *Esquire* writer. "Values are so warped that what we consider a completely negative identity turns out to be a positive one . . . These kids have been told they're hurting themselves, but they either don't believe it, or don't care. . . . Believe me, status here has come to mean being the farthest out, the sickest, the biggest freak around."

Finally, in 1969, the Haight died. There were no television cameras on hand to record the scene this time, no incantations or prayers over a mock corpse, no incense-burning processions through the streets, only a small, neatly lettered sign in the Psychedelic Shop, which had been the symbol of the promise of the Haight and had now gone out of business. "Psychedelic Shop, 1966–1969," it read. "A store that tried to change the world, and succeeded."

By then, the acid gurus had pulled up stakes, gone straight, died, or disappeared. Owsley got out of jail, his nose slightly crooked from being broken in a fight, and took up life as a beekeeper. Allen Ginsberg went home to New York and shaved his beard. Richard Alpert, Leary's right-hand man, changed his name to Baba Ram Dass and became a holy man. Ken Kesey, after two drug trials that ended in hung juries, pleaded no contest to a lesser charge ("knowingly being in a place where marijuana was kept") and got 90 days in the county jail. A few months later, he lost his final appeal on another possession charge, and was sentenced to an additional six months on a county work farm. By the time he was released, the Merry Pranksters had broken up and Neal Cassady was dead, his body found beside a railroad track outside the town of San Miguel Allende in Mexico. Kesey himself was seldom heard from anymore. Returning home to Oregon, he bought a dairy farm and looked after a herd of cows.

At that, he was lucky. He could have ended up like Timothy Leary. Fate had not been kind to the high priest since his salad days in San Francisco. Wherever he went, trouble seemed to dog him. First, the government locked him up for a thirty-year stretch at the Federal Correctional Facility at San Luis Obispo, California, for marijuana possession. Then, six months later, the Weather Underground broke him out, and Tim and his wife Rosemary flew off to Algeria and the hospitality of Eldridge Cleaver and the Black Panthers. For a while, all went well. Rhetorically, at least, Leary seemed to adapt well to his new role as revolutionary, saying all the things that revolutionaries are supposed to say, issuing communiqués urging his followers to "resist actively, sabotage, jam the computer—hijack planes—trash every lethal machine in the land . . . shoot to live . . . blow your mind and blow up all the controlling systems of the genocidal culture." The trouble was, Leary continued to blow his own mind, a behavior which his hosts regarded as most bourgeois. On Cleaver's orders, he was subjected to a "revolutionary bust." "Something is wrong with Dr. Leary's brains," Cleaver explained in his own communiqué. ". . . We want people to gather their wits, sober up and get down to the serious business of destroying the Babylonian empire." And Tim, who was stoned much of the time, did not qualify. "[He] seems to wither away without an audience," Cleaver commented. "He needs people around him who have a worshipful attitude towards him. He has a need to be seen as a high priest, as a god. And in this part of the world such gods don't have a ready audience at hand, so that Leary scrapes around for any audience that he can assemble, whether it's an audience of CIA agents masquerading as hippies and tourists or what have you." So Leary was being kicked out, for his good, and that of the revolution's. "To all those of you who look to Dr. Leary for inspiration or even leadership," Cleaver concluded, "we want to say that your god is dead because his mind has been blown by acid."

Cast out of paradise, Leary turned up next in Switzerland. He bought a Porsche, took a harem of girlfriends and started snorting cocaine and smack. Eventually, Rosemary got fed up and left him for another man. Then the Swiss government kicked him out. In the company of a new girlfriend, Leary flew off to Iran, only to be arrested immediately and shipped back to the United States and the waiting arms of the FBI.

He didn't make much sense at his trial. After all that LSD—five hundred hits of the finest windowpane acid— he'd finally gone crackers. When they asked him his occupation, he said he was a philosopher, but quickly amended that description to add that he was a time traveler from beyond the twentieth century. In his former lives, Leary went on, he had been Socrates and several witches burned at the stake. His lawyer battled valiantly to save him—describing his client as "an eagle beating his wings against the bars"— but his eloquence was not enough to keep the jury from finding Leary guilty and tacking five more years onto his sentence. Added to the time he was already serving, Leary would be seventy-one years old by the time he got out.

In his cell at Folsom Prison, Leary brooded . . . and laid plans. He thought of building a multibillion "sperm ship" that would transport him and five hundred of the most highly developed people on earth to intergalactic space in search of "parental intelligence." When that proved unreasonable, Leary started talking to his jailers. Soon, grand juries began meeting. Before long, one of Leary's former lawyers was busted. Panic quickly ensued. Allen Ginsberg called the betrayal "a hippie Watergate" and chanted an Om for the sake of Leary's soul. Even his own son denounced him. All the while, Timothy Leary remained silent, sheltered by his friends, the Federal Bureau of Investigation. In time, the protests cooled, and Leary, freed by his appreciative captors, took up a new life as a talk show host on Los Angeles television.

It was different with the music: it didn't die, it merely changed, became slicker, safer, more protected. Rock lost its rough edges, the bursting vitality and raw emotionalism that was its birth and power. Some blamed it on technology, the increasingly sophisticated recording techniques that could produce effects no live concert could, even eliminate the necessity for bands to play together at all. With the right twist of a few dials, a band could be given a talent it did not possess. But that did not account for the kind of music they made. Disco and punk were the rage now; musicians with names like Johnny Rotten and Sid Vicious were singing about perversion, violence, death, and despair. "Rock has lost its sense of hope," Landau mourned. "Today's music documents a world in which people are out for themselves instead of for each other, in which people are growing apart instead of coming together."

The San Francisco bands were lost in the new sound.
Country Joe MacDonald and the Fish disbanded and reor-
ganized five separate times between the late Sixties and the
early Seventies. The sixth time they broke up, it was for
good. Without the music to sustain him, MacDonald drifted
into booze and drugs, and wound up thoroughly cynical
about the gestalt he had helped to create. "We were really
playing with fire," he told Fong-Torres. "There were people who just took it too literally. They got strung out on
drugs and killed themselves and other people . . . VD is
rampant because of this great promiscuity riff. 'Free love'
and 'make revolution' really got out of hand. Every band
out of San Francisco was responsible in some way for promoting an image which was really unfair, because the
things that were available to us—money, protection, living
in a kind of insular society—weren't available to the average
working-class young person, and they took some hard
knocks."

The Grateful Dead were still going, but they were a
different band now, making a different kind of sound. When
they moved out of the Haight, the music seemed to change,
lose some of its intensity. "They played like slobs," Landau
wrote after one performance. Steve Miller was not surprised. He had always thought the city's music was over-
rated and, earlier than anyone, he had moved away from it,
out to suburban Marin, light years away from the Haight,
the Fillmores and the music. "It seems to be pretty much
gone," he told Fong-Torres. "It's not like a real energy. It's
like a bunch of people who made their bread in whatever
way they did and held onto what they could, and they're
doing personally what they want to do." He hadn't seen
any of them in years, Miller went on. "The last time I ran
into one of the guys in the Jefferson Airplane, I walked up

to him and said, 'Hi, man, haven't seen you in a while,' and he didn't know who I was. His old lady thought I wanted his autograph."

And so it went. From band to band, promoter to promoter, the details differed; the essential story, however, remained the same: too much, too soon. Too much fun, too much success, and, eventually, all too little music.

Even Bill Graham had gotten fed up. He had talked for years of the vicissitudes of the business—the times his theaters had been torn up, the increasing number of "frontal lobotomies" who were showing up at concerts, the necessity of having to behave more and more like an accountant and less like a showman, the days and weeks spent away from his family on tour—and he had threatened to quit dozens of times. But, of course, he never had—until the day a manager whined to him over the phone, "But Bill, how do you expect my group to work for only $50,000 a week?" That had torn it. He was tired of it all, he said in a press release, announcing his decision to close his ballrooms. Tired of the hassles with managers; tired of unruly, ungrateful kids; tired of the whole business and what it had done to him. "In 1965, when I started the Fillmore, I associated with employed musicians," he wrote. "Now, more often than not, it's with 'officers and stockholders' in large corporations—only they happen to have long hair and play guitars." The only reason to keep the Fillmores open any longer, he concluded, ". . . would be to make money, and though few have chosen to believe me on this point, money has never been my prime motivation; and now that it would become my only motivation to continue, I pass."

Graham would come back, bigger than ever, and there would still be music, more of it than ever before, but an era

had ended, and Wenner knew it. It was painful, realizing
what had happened. Despite everything, he remained deeply
attached to San Francisco and its sad, sentimental charms.
He could reminisce for hours about concerts that had happened ten years before, about taking acid at Cal, about
driving down the Coast Highway on a sunny day, top down,
stereo radio belting out the rhythms of the Airplane. There
were moments when he would stare out his window at a
rainbow over the Bay Bridge and become emotional about
the sheer beauty of the city. "God," he'd murmur to anyone
within earshot. "Have you ever seen anything like this? Is
there any other place like this on earth?" But the time had
come to face the facts. The spirit of the Summer of Love
was gone, and nothing, not even the continual protestations
of his own magazine that the culture was healthier than
ever, was going to bring it back. What had been once could
be memorialized, as *Rolling Stone* did in February 1976,
and the memoirs could be fulsome in their praise. What the
writers said was true. It *had* been a "charged, glowing,
enormously important time," as a woman from Santa Mon-
ica put it. They *had* all "grown there," and looking back on
it, as a mother from San Rafael wrote, was "like remembering an extravagant love affair that ended savagely." But the
words were all past tense. San Francisco was over.

Armstrong had been telling him that for months. By now,
virtually all the magazine's business and advertising operations had been shifted East. Wenner himself was spending
nearly half his time in New York, and Armstrong, always a
New Yorker at heart, had taken up a semipermanent residence in the city. There was nothing left in San Francisco
anymore, Armstrong argued: no music, no vibes, and very
few good stories. To pretend otherwise, he insisted, was
only costing the magazine needless expense. The long-dis-

tance phone bill alone was running to $150,000 a month. Armstrong kept hammering away. Get out, he told Wenner. Get out for the business. Get out for the magazine. Get out for yourself. San Francisco doesn't appreciate you; New York is your kind of town.

Slowly, Wenner began to listen. Joe was right. Staying in San Francisco was an extravagance he could no longer afford. And Joe was right about something else, as well: It wasn't his kind of town. The city had never appreciated the full extent of his talents, never given him what Wenner thought was his proper due. *Rolling Stone* had been in San Francisco nearly ten years now, almost a decade in which Wenner had helped put the town on the map. And what had been his reward? The rare times the newspapers mentioned him, it was to take potshots at his achievements, to belittle him, as columnist Herb Caen continually did, poking fun at his trip to a Mexican fat farm, exulting when yet another staffer left him. Twice, in fact, the *Chronicle* had run a picture of someone else and identified the person as Wenner, as if to prove they didn't care. San Francisco took him for granted. When he walked into the Washington Square Bar and Grill, no one prepared the way, no one even looked up. San Francisco was like that, his friends consoled him; it was part of the city's charm. *No one* got noticed, whatever their fame—not Coppola, not Hinckle, not Ellsberg, none of the city's stars. In San Francisco, everyone was supposed to be alike. No one asked what they had done, or were planning to do—in fact, it was most unseemly to be overly involved in planning anything—only what was happening now. Were they feeling mellow, did they give off good vibes? That was all that mattered to people who lived in San Francisco. That is *why* they lived there.

New York was so much different. Up early in the morning, pulse racing, speedy, eager, gotta have one big deal before lunch, snap, crackle, pow. New York reverenced talent. They didn't ignore him here. When he walked into Elaine's, everyone looked up, there was a table waiting. The papers fawned over him, the smart set wined and dined him. They appreciated him the way San Francisco never could. He was so much like them: on the way up, running to get there, smart, nifty, finger-popping. New York was his kind of town—"the place," he said, smiling, "where people with ambition live."

A year after Gleason's death, Wenner made up his mind. In June 1976, he summoned his key editors and executives to a conference in Hilton Head, South Carolina, to begin planning the move. For many people in attendance, it was their first chance to meet their colleagues from the other coast, a demonstration of how schizophrenic the magazine had become. All of that was going to change now, Wenner promised. Soon the magazine would be in one place, and that place would be New York. First, though, there were details to be nailed down: office space to be let, promotion ads to be placed, parties to be planned. Someone suggested a cross-country train, filled with staff, belongings, dogs, cats, lovers, maybe even a rock band or two. The press at every stop would be enormous. The notion was intriguing, worthy of P. T. Barnum himself. But Wenner wanted something slightly more practical: a massive blowout at one of New York's chic in-spots. Everyone would be there, he promised, all the important people. No one doubted him. By now, all the important, beautiful people were Jann Wenner's friends. Nodding their assent, they adjourned for a round of golf.

When the staff in San Francisco got the news a few months later, there were, surprisingly, few complaints. Most of them had seen the move coming long before the formal announcement. It was the way Wenner burbled when he returned home from New York, the new names he dropped, the non-San Francisco kinds of stories that were turning up more and more in the pages of the magazine. At first, they had joked that Jann was "going through his New York period." But as the stories continued and Wenner stayed away from San Francisco for increasing lengths of time, it became obvious that New York was more than just a passing fancy. Wenner's newfound love for the "sophistication," as he put it, of New York, had all the markings of a permanent affair. Now, he was merely confirming it.

Some of the die-hard San Franciscans, like Fong-Torres and Charlie Perry, doubted they would be able to pull up roots so deeply set. Wenner promised to make provision for them. He would make provision for everyone, in fact. It had all been arranged: the rental agencies, the movers, the clothing allowances and cost-of-living adjustments, even the membership in a Manhattan tennis club. Nothing would change, he insisted. They would remain a family, just as they always had been. Only later, and privately, did some of them get the news: they wouldn't be coming along; their services would no longer be needed; the severance, however, would be very generous. "Jann is always very good about that," said one woman who had been with the magazine for six years, and was being let go. "He's really very generous." She paused for a moment, as if struggling for words. "You know," she said, "this has been my life." And she burst into tears.

They went to Big Sur for what turned out to be their last time together. It was supposed to be an editorial conference, but it quickly became a party—three days of sun and drugs and soaking in the mineral baths. Having them all together, talking about the old days, touched Wenner and, at a fare-well meeting, he told them how much he loved them, how much they had done for him, that he would never forget any of them. He wanted to show his appreciation: the weekend was on him. They cheered and applauded, and Wenner sat down, wiping the tears from his eyes.

Afterward, they went out to an especially pretty spot, stripped off their clothes, and put their arms around one another, naked and innocent, for a group picture. Annie Liebovitz said "smile" and they all did. They had to hurry, though. The sun was going down.

13

A City
of Ambition

It was a fine place they moved to: four handsome floors in a Fifth Avenue skyscraper, just across the street from the General Motors building. Jann had told them that it would be a classy place, something befitting *Rolling Stone,* and classy it was: clean, color-coordinated, icily sleek, worth every bit of the $5 million the fifteen-year lease had cost. "Doesn't it look like the *Daily Planet?*" Wenner asked a visitor, craning his neck up at the twinkling lights of his office. He held out his hands and traced an invisible rectangle in childlike wonder. "I should put a sign up there," he said: "DAILY PLANET."

The staff settled in easily. The San Franciscans had worried about coming to a new town, the cold weather, the bustle, the cost of living, the utter strangeness of the place. But they were coping, enjoying themselves, as pleased as Wenner was with their new surroundings. "There's just more talent here," one of them explained, a small note of defensiveness in her voice. "San Francisco had sort of played itself out as a center of cultural change." Of course, some

things were different. The offices were quieter and cleaner
—Jann had let it be known that he didn't want "all those
glunky psychedelic posters" cluttering up the walls—and
now, when one of the researchers had a question, she
had to make her way through a maze of lookalike
cubbyholes or wrestle with the computerized phone, in contrast to the old days, when she had simply shouted down the
hall. But, in New York, such was the way things were done.
"In San Francisco, you score points for being funky," one
of the editors mused. "You score points in New York,
well . . ." It was different, but then, so were they. They had
gotten older, changed, grown up. "Now, everybody here's
cut their hair and everybody's cleaned up and wearing skirts
and suits and things," one of the associate editors told a
guest. She paused for a moment and glanced out her window
at the towers of Manhattan. The view was awesome. "But so
has everybody out there," she said at last. "It's really the
difference between the Sixties and the Seventies."

Some of them had not been able to make the transition. In
the end, Charlie Perry could not bring himself to leave
and, with a few of the secretaries, he remained behind,
still crazy after all these years. Joe Eszterhas was missing, too, gone to Hollywood to write screenplays. At first,
it was supposed to be just a leave of absence, a chance
for Eszterhas to try his talents at fiction. But the studios had
liked what he had written, and one of them had given him a
big advance—$800,000, it was said, a record. With a new
career set, Eszterhas wouldn't be coming back. Neither
would Tim Crouse. Marianne Partridge had lured him away
to the *Village Voice*. Wenner had taken Crouse's departure
well at first, and the two of them had promised to remain
friends. But then had come a fight, a quarrel over the edit-

ing of Crouse's final piece, and the inevitable words—harsh, bitter, mocking. But this time, Crouse would not take it. Looking back, he was sorry he ever had. David Weir was a special case. He had not left and had not really been fired; he simply did not fit in. Shortly before Christmas, Wenner had talked with him about the stories he wanted to do for the magazine. Weir mentioned a number of ideas. The look on Wenner's face told him all he needed to know. Jann was apologetic. Patty Hearst had been an important story for the magazine, he said, and he knew David's wife had a baby on the way, but now, with the move to New York, he had to reevaluate where the magazine was heading. All the stories Weir wanted to do were great investigative ideas, Wenner said, but he had the record industry to deal with and, well, they just didn't mesh. He was sorry, he went on, and he hoped Weir would understand, but that was life, that was reality.

It was different with Joe Armstrong, the publisher who had made it all possible. He went quite on his own. Few people were surprised when Armstrong departed, and fewer still when, several months later, he was named publisher and editor-in-chief of *New York* and *New West* magazines. There was always a market for a man of Joe Armstrong's talents. They were considerable, perhaps too considerable to remain in tandem with Wenner's for long. His friends said that an article in *More* magazine the previous December had marked the beginning of the end. The piece was highly flattering, saying, among other accolades, that "No longer is *Rolling Stone* just Jann Wenner, it's Jann Wenner and Joe Armstrong." "You can begin counting the days," one of Armstrong's associates said at the time. "A rival is one thing Jann will not tolerate." It wound up taking slightly more than four months. When his resignation was announced,

Armstrong maintained a discreet silence about the reasons for his departure. All *Rolling Stone* would say was that Joe had done all that he could, that he had left to find other worlds to conquer. Within weeks, though, other stories began to circulate. Armstrong was not that good, this version went; he really didn't know the magazine business; in fact, if it had not been for Wenner's steady, guiding hand, Armstrong's recklessness might have led *Rolling Stone* into financial chaos. Such were the stories that Jann Wenner told. "Jann," smirked one of his former writers, "has killed off the old Bolsheviks. He had to. They remembered."

Jon Landau, the last of them, hadn't waited for the move. He had gone long before. As he put it: "Sooner or later the obsession had to wear off." Leaving had been difficult for Landau. More than once, he had quit and come back. But there was no denying what he knew. As a critic, he was getting stale, falling into predictable patterns, losing touch with the music he loved so much. The problem was the nature of the job. He explained in a long essay:

> The first time a critic writes a piece of criticism, he does it as an act of love. . . . As his assignments increase, he finds himself organizing more, planning more, thinking more about the act of criticizing itself. . . . A year later the critic is still using the words, but the inspiration and the enthusiasm that made them mean something the first time is gone. . . . Two years later he has learned to sound like a critic without actually criticizing, without doing the thinking that a critic ought to do. . . . Years pass and he learns to cope with this situation. . . . He no longer even pretends he is a critic; he is now a reviewer, a guide, a consumer reporter.

For Landau, there was only one solution: to quit journalism altogether. It had been several years now since he had made the break, and there were no regrets. He had a new career now—producer of records of artists like Jackson Browne, Livingston Taylor, and Bruce Springsteen, and he was blooming as never before.

If only that had been true of Hunter. But something unaccountable had happened to the Gonzo Prince. He had, it seemed, stopped working altogether. It had been almost two years since his work had been in print, in *Rolling Stone* or anywhere else. And, from the reports coming back from Aspen, there was no telling when, if ever, he would be writing again. He seldom left Aspen these days, except to fulfill college speaking dates. Those did not go well. At Harvard, he appeared to be drunk and/or stoned, and finally had to be hauled off the stage by Dick Goodwin. A few months later, he showed up two hours late for an appearance at the University of California at Santa Barbara, and enraged the several hundred students who had paid five dollars to listen to him, by informing them that coming there had really been a waste of his time, and that, in fact, he really didn't like young people very much. The audience hissed and booed, and many of them walked out.

Since then, he had been in Aspen almost exclusively, surrounded by his guns, his pet peacocks, and his single Doberman, which, rather than being trained to kill, usually licked a visitor's hands. Rumor said he was laying a variety of plans. One story had it that a movie deal was in the works; another that there would be a movie about Thompson himself. Hunter was enigmatic. At one point, he told a visitor that he was at work on that big novel everyone thought was churning within him. "It'll be about Texas and gun-running and the American dream," he promised. "That's what I've always been interested in: Whatever happened to the American Dream?" But a few months later, he was telling an altogether different story. He was giving up writing for good, he announced, to concentrate on gun-running—"only with the heaviest, foreign revolutionary-type operators"—full-time.

He might have been telling the truth. With Thompson, one never knew. All that was certain is that something in him had changed. About Wenner, he had only bitterness now. "Jann could have had the whole world—he was that close—if he could have just reached out and been decent for a minute or two. Instead, he reached out for nickels and dimes." Wenner could sue him for saying that, Thompson went on; he wasn't worried. "He'll have to come here," Thompson said. "I'll tie him up for years. When his lawyer leaves the courtroom, I'll have him arrested for speeding, no matter how fast he is going. When he goes back to his hotel room at night, I'll have him busted for weed. I won't give up. It will go on and on. Five years it will go on and then I'll settle with him for six dollars." There were other plots, equally nefarious. But the passion had drained out of him. He could not even muster the energy for a good insult. To call Wenner a "rotten little dwarf," his favorite epithet, would have required too much caring. Now Wenner was "Iago," the treacherous friend who had betrayed the black prince.

"When a jackrabbit gets addicted to road-running," Hunter Thompson had written years before, "sooner or later, it gets smashed." The words sounded disquietingly prophetic now. His days of road-running were over. A quote kept flashing through his head. It was Herbert Matthews writing about the Spanish Civil War. "In those years we lived our best," it went, "and what has come after and what there is to come can never carry us to those heights again." "You like that quote?" he asked a visitor. "It's my favorite." Time went by, and the visitor asked him,

"What about the American Dream?" "To hell with the American Dream," Hunter Thompson said. "Let's call it a suicide."

In New York, all of this went unnoticed. Jann Wenner was very busy now. Since coming to the city he had been in non-stop motion, now lunching with Malcolm Forbes (a young man of "genius" and "vision," the editor of *Forbes* pronounced him in an editorial), now helping to save Central Park, now being pictured in private tête-à-tête with Jackie O. ("She's fascinating," he insisted. "People don't understand her. . . . She's one of the most dedicated, hard-working people in this city"), now planning this reception or that. There was so much to be done, so little time to do it. The BBC was flying in to do an hour-long documentary, and CBS was setting aside two hours of prime time to celebrate the magazine's tenth anniversary. And, what with two up-coming special issues, one on New York, the other on the magazine's first decade of life, *Rolling Stone* itself demanded his attention. Then, as if he did not have enough to busy him, *Outside* was not proving the success he had hoped. Indeed, he would have to sell it. When everything was put together, it scarcely left him time to breathe.

Just at that moment, he was desperately trying to line up talent for the CBS special. All the San Francisco groups were boycotting him. They were miffed at the published remark of one of his editors that San Francisco was "a dull cultural backwater." The show turned out to be a shambles ("A true fiasco fabuloso," a reviewer for the Washington *Post* would later call it, "a ghastly mess . . . fatuous and gratuitous moral cant . . . this Hallelujah Chorus for the world's ex-hippies"), and costs were escalating hideously. One four-minute film segment alone had cost $110,000.

But it was two hours of prime time, it had gotten Donny Osmond, the squeaky-clean Mormon, to play his part, and, whatever the critics might say, what other magazine had been given such a send-off? None. So let the *Chronicle* snipe at him, as they were still doing, printing a picture of him arm in arm with Caroline Kennedy, with the caption "unidentified man." That was the price he paid for being who he was. "A lot of people are jealous of my success," he told a visiting reporter. "It's not new. I can't help it. I don't think about it. I don't let it worry me. I find it fun, actually. It's really lucky to be happy."

And he *was* happy, happier than he had been in a long time. All the things he had worked for so hard, for so long, were coming true. He had status now. His name was on the "A lists" of the best parties in town. Everyone knew him. He was an item. So, of course, they were jealous. And, of course, the rivals like Felker would say things like, "Where is it written that Jann Wenner should inherit the earth?" He wouldn't let it bother him. In fact, he rather liked the Felker quote—so much so that he had it reproduced, framed, and hung in his office. There was no doubt about it anymore. One look out the double-length windows of his office into the bowels of New York confirmed it. He had arrived.

Jann had been planning the official announcement for months: a special issue of *Rolling Stone* celebrating New York. As the publication date neared, the lights in his office burned late at night. He wanted the issue to be just right, truly memorable in its impact, and, to ensure that all would go well, he had taken personal command. Already, he had commissioned Andy Warhol to do a multiple-image portrait of Bella Abzug for the cover. Bella was running for mayor—a sure bet, all the experts were saying—and in New York even more than San Francisco, it was important for *Rolling*

Stone to be positioned on the side of the winners. Even now, the companion pieces were being readied: an interview with Elaine, the proprietor of the city's premier literary saloon; a history of New York's most exclusive clubs; a look at the ghetto; a housing project; a gay activist—a whole magazine full of glittering prizes.

The editors were pleased with what they had wrought. "Better than that Vreeland shit," one of them murmured, referring to a piece that had appeared a few months before on the Grande Dame of international fashion. They had gotten a lot of nasty mail over that article—and considering the opinions Ms. Vreeland had delivered up, it was not surprising. "Why don't you," she had asked, "put all your dogs in bright yellow collars and leads like all the dogs in Paris . . . sweep into the drawing room on your first big night with an enormous red-fox stole of many skins . . . rinse your blonde child's hair in dead champagne to keep it gold, as they do in France? . . . serve individual Pfirisch Bowle, which is a peeled peach in a chilled glass with ice-cold Moselle or Rhine wine poured in? Marvelous at tea time!" "Tea time!" one of the editors had exclaimed. "What the fuck . . . ?" But this issue would be different; this would be *real* New York. And then, just as they were readying the magazine for the press, the unthinkable happened. In Memphis, Elvis Presley dropped dead of a heart attack at forty-two.

It was like an omen, an announcement, as if more were needed, that an era had come to an end. Even the way he died—fifty pounds fat, stoked full of downers, alone in the bathroom of Graceland, his garish mansion—only the most determined of the myth-makers could miss the symbolism. Elvis was the King, the father and progenitor, the last link with rock's beginnings, the star who lived to see it all—and now the King was dead.

To imagine him gone was to think of history suddenly slipped away. His was the career that had lasted longer than any other—twenty-three years, six Presidents, a war, assassinations, riots, changes without number. And always he endured. He never claimed that he had a message to deliver, or that his music would change the world. He sang simply because he wanted to sing. Music, he told one of his biographers, was "a way to escape from problems . . . my way of release."

There was always that innocence about him, even at his most greasy and vulgar. The success that came to him puzzled him almost as much as it did everyone else. "I don't know what it is," he said once. "I just fell into it really . . . It just caught us up." As it caught America up. He burst on the country like a bomb, shattering, explosive, unexpected, an energy suddenly let loose. They tried to ban him at first: "nigger music," they said in the South; "too country," they said in the North; too much for anywhere. The Sullivan Show camera-censored him; Arthur Godfrey's talent scouts rejected him outright; even the Grand Ole Opry advised him to go back to truck-driving. But his power was irresistible. In the space of twenty-seven months, there were fourteen gold records in a row, and the young had been taken by storm.

He was the perfect hero for the country: the poor boy made good, the nice young man who always remembered "please" and "thank you" and "sir" and "ma'am" and that Jesus was still the Lord. What better representation of America could there be than someone who counted his wealth in Eldorados? That was America and that was Elvis. And they remained so, one and inseparable, for two decades, neither able to shake the wonder of the other. "When I was a boy," he said, "I was the hero in the comic books and movies. I grew up believing in that dream. Now I've lived it out. That's all a man can ask for."

But rock demanded more, in time, than even Elvis could give. His body began to give way. Several times he checked into the hospital for treatment of a variety of disorders: high blood pressure, stomach inflammation, enlarged colon, liver dysfunction, even arthritis. The stays, usually two weeks at a time, were kept well hidden. Finally, though, it became apparent that something was going disastrously wrong. His superb physique, kept in top condition by a mania for physical fitness, ballooned grotesquely. As his weight increased, he started wearing a girdle. Then, one night on stage, he split his pants up the rear. After that, appearances were mysteriously canceled at the last moment with no explanation. The few times he appeared in public, usually in Las Vegas, before ballrooms packed with blue-haired grandmothers and double-knit salesmen out on the town, he seemed an overstuffed caricature of his former self. The voice—*that voice,* so leeringly suggestive—still had its trademark huskiness, and none of the flash and glitter had left his performance, and now and again he even swooped and swiveled, as he had done in the old days, years before, when "Elvis the Pelvis" was a moral affront, a challenge to everything sacred and decent. But the power was gone. He laughed now when he shook his hips, and the audience laughed with him. All that was left was memory, and the memory was a joke.

It was said later that he had been depressed during the last few weeks of his life, worried over the upcoming publication of a book written by three of his ex-bodyguards, a lurid little volume that would strip the King bare, reveal the darker side of the legend, expose him, finally, for the lonely man he was.

They found him stretched out on his bathroom floor, still in his pajamas, unconscious and beginning to turn blue. "Breathe, Presley, breathe," his doctor kept imploring him on the way to the hospital. But it was too late. "Elvis had the arteries of an eighty-year-old man," a hospital employee said. "His body was just worn out."

Greil Marcus was vacationing in Hawaii when the call came in from *Rolling Stone*. The magazine had scrapped the New York issue and was planning a tribute to Elvis in its place. From Marcus, who had written more passionately about him than anyone else, they wanted an obituary. Marcus didn't understand at first. He thought perhaps it was some sick kind of joke. But the voice on the end of the line was serious. "He died today. A heart attack, apparently." Marcus went down to the hotel bar and ordered a drink, a shot of Tennessee whiskey and, over the booze, collected his thoughts.

> I didn't accept it all, not in any way but at the same time I knew it was true. . . . For some reason, I still could not make the event real—every time I focused on it consciously, the idea of Elvis dead, *not here,* seemed to imply that he had never been here, that his presence over 23 years had been some kind of hallucination, a trick . . . I wanted to cut loose from it all, but I was still too angry, and confused, not at anyone or anything: not at Elvis, or myself or "them," or the fans, or the media, or "rock," or "success." It was simply rage. I was devastated.

The issue was what *Rolling Stone* did best: a memorial for what had been. "He was as big as the whole country it-

self," Bruce Springsteen wrote in tribute, "as big as the
whole dream. He just embodied the essence of it and he was
in mortal combat with the thing. It was horrible and, at the
same time, it was fantastic." And so it went, page after
mournful page, the whole story in all its grisly, glorious details. "It is not simply a man's death that makes no sense,"
Marcus eulogized; " . . . when history is personified, and
the person behind that history dies, history itself is no
longer real." The feeling was genuine and affecting—this
was the finest issue *Rolling Stone* had published in months.
But it was the brief sidebar on the inner pages, a few awk-
wardly written paragraphs on the mourners at Graceland,
that attracted the most attention, not for what it said, for
that was unremarkable, but for who had said it. The by-line
read: "By Caroline Kennedy." "Caroline is a nice little
girl," Wenner said of the newest member of the *Rolling
Stone* family. "I would have published the piece no matter
who wrote it."

When the New York issue hit the stands two weeks later
much of the impact Wenner had been hoping for was missing. In the interval, Bella had lost the election. So there she
was, smiling out from the New York *Times* back page
Wenner had bought to herald the magazine's arrival. "We're
new in town," the headline read. And so they were.

Gradually, the novelty of New York wore off, as reality
slowly began to sink in. No longer was *Rolling Stone* the
only journalistic game in town, as it had been in San Francisco. Now, it was one of many publications competing for
readers and writers. That it would survive and grow even
more prosperous, despite the rumors of its impending sale,
even despite Wenner's brief flirtation with running a
doomed revival of *Look* a few years later, there was little
question. The record companies would see to that. But it

would be a different magazine. "Like a tree in Central Park," one of the editors said wistfully, "in need of help, but still standing. Finally, we won't know it's there."

A reporter heard the remark and jotted it down. One thing had not changed: adults were still trying to unlock Jann Wenner's secret. Wenner was patient with her. If she wanted a story, he would give it to her, not in his office, but in a more relaxed setting—a quiet, after-hours drink at a little place around the corner, the lounge of the Sherry-Netherland, New York's best hotel.

The waiters smiled and nodded when Jann Wenner and his guest walked through the door. They were used to him by now. They knew who he was and what he did and where he wanted to sit: a table with a good view of the door, so he could keep tabs on who moved in and who moved out, who was up and who was down. He sat down, ordered a drink, drained it, and, as the questioning commenced, began twisting in his seat. He extracted the swizzle stick from the glass in front of him, chewed on it a moment, then put it aside. His eyes flicked back and forth: up, down, around the room, to the door, and, finally, to the person asking the questions. She was staring at him. Wenner was apologetic. "I've got every nervous tic known to man," he kidded, and started fidgeting anew. The questioning resumed, about his enemies, the people who had left him, the stories they were telling. Wenner brushed it all off. It didn't bother him, he said; that was the price people in his position always had to pay. Besides, they were wrong. Rock and roll hadn't sold out, he insisted. "Any steps rock and roll has made toward the Establishment, the Establishment made toward rock and roll." A pause, and then he was running again, proving his point. "Vietnam was America's first rock and roll war. Star Wars was a rock and roll movie. Mick Jagger is more important than Dustin Hoffman, and, yes, *The Graduate* is a rock and roll movie. I'm a rock and roller. I love rock and roll. That's what *Rolling Stone* is all about. Rock and roll is here to stay. Do you see any signs of its death?" There was no time to answer the question. The conversation had shifted, to New York and *Rolling Stone* and Wenner himself. "Am I a genius?" he mused. "I don't have the objectivity to answer that question. I mean, that's for you to decide." It was true, he admitted, the magazine could be better—"if we could just stop fucking around, it could be really good"—But, all the same, he was having a good time doing what he was doing. It was fun being in New York, he said; that's why he had come—to have fun, just as he always had. "For ten years I've been in a position of doing nothing I didn't want to do," he said proudly. "Am I happy? Very. I'm extremely lucky. I got my own magazine. I got to do what I wanted to do."

It was midnight now and time to go. The Sherry-Netherland was clearing out. Across the way, the lights in the *Rolling Stone* office still burned brightly. Another issue was in the works. "Leave a big tip," Jann Wenner ordered the reporter. "This is my hangout."

"You know what I think of Charlie Kane?" Joseph Cotten says in the movie. "Well, I suppose he had some private sort of greatness. But he kept it to himself. He never gave away anything. He just left you a tip. He had a generous mind. I don't suppose anyone ever had so many opinions. That was because he had the power to express them, and Charlie lived on power and the excitement of using it."

It was funny about that movie. It was the impression that Jann Wenner liked to leave on people, that he truly was Citizen Wenner. And yet he could never watch the film without becoming upset. Maybe it was the ending, or the loneliness that overtook Charles Foster Kane. Maybe the whole thing was all too true.

If he ever had any regrets about the way it all turned out, he never expressed them. "I'm in a hurry," he said once, as if it explained it all—and, in a way, it did. He never had time to stop or look back; he was always rolling on. Too fast for most people to know him. If some despised him—and many did—it was never completely. They would always have that ambivalence about him that Hunter Thompson felt, knowing that he could do hateful, horrendous things, and beautiful, wonderful things. He was like Kane in that way, and in the way he gathered power—sometimes, it seemed, for its own sake. He did not always use it well or wisely, and often he employed it selfishly and capriciously. But he used it for good, for talent—for "pro-life propaganda," as he called it—more often than not. It was there that he diverged from the Hearstian legend. Hearst had used his press to start a war. *Rolling Stone* had tried to stop one.

What he created, in the end, was a work of personal genius, a showcase for a generation's excellence, a forum as troubled, brilliant, and contradictory as his own life, indeed, as so many lives that passed through that special moment called the Sixties. He was a child of that decade, full of enthusiasm and hope, convinced that the time of his youth was unique in all history, that he was growing up, as he wrote in *Rolling Stone*'s 200th issue, in the midst of "the greatest mass alteration of personal consciousness since the country began."

Now everything is different. Music has lost its mythic power. The people who play it are no longer gods. And *Rolling Stone,* like the generation that reads it, has grown up, and in growing up, has become something else. "Middle age, what a drag," Jann Wenner said once. But there was nothing he could do to prevent it from overtaking him. Jann Wenner didn't sell out—he simply moved. Not to another city, but to a different time.

The Sixties did not end when the decade turned. They were a time of feeling, and they endured as long as the feeling remained. It was there at Kent State in 1970, and at Mayday a year later, and in George McGovern's campaign for the Presidency a year after that. And it was there one night in New York in 1975 in a darkened hall filled with people who had once believed, and wanted to believe once more. On the stage, dressed in black, a man was singing. As the sound swelled up, a cheer arose, as it always did when he sang this song. They surged toward him. This was his final number, their last chance to touch. They reached out, and he kept on singing, louder now, angrier . . .

> *You said you'd never compromise*
> *With the mystery tramp, but now you realize*
> *He's not selling any alibis*
> *As you stare into the vacuum of his eyes*
> *And ask him do you want to*
> *Make a deal?*

All over the hall now, people were crying, yelling, holding on to each other, rocking back and forth. And still the music came.

> *When you got nothing, you got nothing to lose*
> *You're invisible now, you got no secrets*
> *to conceal*

Someone held up a lighted match. Then another appeared, and another and another, until there were thousands of tiny flames, flickering in the dark. And lost in that sea of lights, Jann Wenner was there, remembering.

> *How does it feel*
> *To be without a home*
> *A complete unknown*
> *Like a rolling stone?*

The music rose in final crescendo, and then, nothing. "More, more," they chanted. "More, more, more." But they could not bring him back. He was gone and the music had ended. They knew, then, that it was over.

Robert Sam Anson was a reporter for *Time* in 1966 while still an undergraduate at Notre Dame. He remained with *Time* and, while on assignment in Cambodia, was taken as a prisoner of war. More recently, he was host of his own contemporary affairs program for WNET-TV in New York and was also a Senior Writer for *New Times*. His feature articles have appeared in *The Atlantic* and *Harper's*. Mr. Anson is the author of two previous books and a novel-in-progress.

INDEX